The person
sponsible f

Comparative Economic Systems

Recent Economic Thought

Series Editor:
Warren J. Samuels
Michigan State University

Previously published:
Feiwel, George R.; Samuelson and Neoclassical Economics

Wade, L. L.: Political Economy: Recent Views

This series is devoted to works that present divergent views on the development, prospects, and tensions within some important research areas of international economic thought. Among the fields covered are macro-monetary policy, public finance, labor, and political economy. The emphasis of the series is on providing a critical, constructive view of each of these fields, as well as a forum through which leading scholars of international reputation may voice their perspectives on important related issues. Each volume in the series will be self-contained; together, these volumes will provide dramatic evidence of the variety of economic thought within the scholarly community.

Comparative Economic Systems:

An Assessment of Knowledge, Theory and Method

edited by
Andrew Zimbalist
Smith College

Kluwer-Nijhoff Publishing
A member of the Kluwer Academic Publishers Group
Boston   The Hague   Dordrecht   Lancaster

Distributors for North America:
Kluwer Academic Publishers
190 Old Derby Street
Hingham, MA 02043, U.S.A.

Distributors Outside North America:
Kluwer Academic Publishers Group
Distribution Centre
P. O. Box 322
3300AH Dordrecht, The Netherlands

Library of Congress Cataloging in Publication Data

Zimbalist, Andrew S.
  Comparative economic systems.
  (Recent economic thought)
  Bibliography: p.
  1. Comparative economics. I. Title. II. Series.
HB90.Z55 1984   330   83-9442
ISBN 0-89838-087-1

In Memory of
my sister

Michelle Zimbalist Rosaldo

(1944–1981)

Acknowledgments

The assignment of collecting essays to review such a wide field as comparative economic systems is rather intimidating. I benefitted from the thoughtful suggestions of several colleagues in organizing this volume: Debbie Milenkovitch, Joe Berliner, Bob Averitt, Sinan Koont, Mike Montias, Michael Ellman, David Conn, Heinz Kohler and Alec Nove. The burden of my assignment was eased considerably by generous support from the Jean and Harvey Picker Fellowship and excellent research and clerical assistance from Darcy Naumowicz and Beki Mahieu. Above all, my gratitude and love go to Lydia, Jeffrey and Michael for putting up with their distracted husband and father, particularly during the final stages of manuscript preparation.

Contents

Comparative Economic Systems

1 INTRODUCTION: REFLECTIONS ON THE STATE OF THE ART OF COMPARATIVE ECONOMICS

Andrew Zimbalist

According to Morris Bornstein, ". . . comparative economic studies make a unique contribution to economics as a whole, by providing the perspective to overcome the parochialism inherent in economic thinking — on both theoretical and policy questions — based on the experience of a single economic system." [1] The scope of comparative economic systems as a field singularly offers the potential, inter alia: (a) to explore and challenge the assumptions and methods of traditional economic analysis; (b) to reinterpret conventional wisdom; (c) to understand the interplay of economic and noneconomic forces in different institutional contexts; and (d) to evaluate the desirability of alternative economic policies and structures.

This open property of the field has its costs as well as its benefits. In their book, scion to the original 1938 text in comparative economic systems, Loucks and Whitney warn: "Some people regard the study of economic systems as an opportunity for nationalistic propaganda and for instilling 'right' viewpoints in the minds of supposedly impressionable students." [2] Whether or not such biases creep subtly into our research or teaching as comparative economists is a matter for each of us to contemplate individually.[1]

It is, however, a common problem that we must use source materials which are clearly afflicted by propagandistic motives or manipulative political goals.

1

Thus, what are sinologists to make of new official government data sets which portray several Maoist policies as utter failures? In a closed society such as China's, do we have sufficient access to corroborative material to evaluate the reliability of the "new evidence"? Or, closer to home, can one resist a rush of cynicism when confronted with the CIA's estimates of Soviet military spending using satellite photos, unspecified evidence and US factor prices? Can one, moreover, restrain questions about the CIA's sudden discovery in December 1982 [3] that the Soviet economic growth rates since 1950 have been higher than previously thought? A discovery which fortuitously comes during a major Congressional debate over the rate of increase of the US defense budget.

Another cost of the field's openness, especially from the perspective of an editor of a volume like this, is that it does not lend itself easily either to self-definition or comprehensive review. It is no coincidence that none of us has stepped forward to do a review of the field for the *Journal of Economic Literature*. Indeed, since its inception the *JEL* has only published two very short and very specific articles related to socialist planning. [4]

The last major effort to assess the state of the field emerged from a 1969 conference at the University of Michigan organized by Morris Bornstein and Alexander Eckstein. The conference papers were edited by Alexander Eckstein and published as a volume by the University of California Press in 1971. [5] In the introduction to this volume, Eckstein wrote: "Comparative economic systems might be characterized as a field in search of a self-definition. This volume represents an attempt to contribute to this search. . . ." [6] The Eckstein volume, albeit serious, stimulating and valuable, did little to resolve the field's identity crisis. Twelve years later a coherent self-definition still eludes the field. To be sure, Gus Papanek, the 1982 president of the Association for Comparative Economic Studies, has suggested that an abiding schizophrenia inhabits the field, seeming to embrace development economics along with the study of advanced socialist and capitalist economies. In this volume, we shall be content to leave any forthcoming clarification of these issues to interdisciplinary-oriented psychologists.

Properly self-identified or not, comparative economic systems is bigger and stronger in 1983 than it was in 1971. The *ACES Bulletin* is entering its twenty-fifth year and, by most assessments, is steadily improving as a scholarly publication. In addition, the *Journal of Comparative Economics* was born in 1977 and has greatly enhanced scholarly communication in the discipline. In particular, the literatures on the economics of labor–management and on incentives in planned economies have experienced marked quantitative growth. While it is clear that our understanding of certain economic processes has grown, there is also a sharper awareness of the deficiencies of our knowledge, methods and theory. I turn now to some of my own reflections on this score.

Some Reflections

My first proposition is that if we are interested in analyzing the performance and dynamic properties of the world's economies, it is only at significant peril that comparative economists can overlook noneconomic or "political" factors. This is not to say that it is illegitimate to abstract from non-economic factors for particular purposes; rather, such abstraction should occur only with cognizance of the influences being suppressed.

I have argued elsewhere that the analytical compromise in suppressing noneconomic variables is greater for the study of planned than for market economies. [7] Borrowing from Polanyi [8], it is claimed that in market systems the economic sphere is disembedded from (separate and not subordinate to) the political, social and cultural spheres, while in planned systems the economic sphere is embedded in the noneconomic spheres. To be sure, market economies are strongly affected by political and cultural factors, but planned economies have and often exercise the potential to let political goals dominate in making production, allocational, or distributional choices. Indeed, it is difficult in practice to separate out what are political and what are economic decisions in planned systems.

In terms of procedures, the internal functioning of a capitalist enterprise or a university is a useful metaphor for a planned economy. Within such institutions, most decisions are made administratively rather than through market signals. Thus, the effectiveness of the organization depends largely upon informational and motivational systems (x–efficiency) which are fundamentally interpersonal in nature as distinct from impersonal and market-oriented.

In the impersonal market environment, decentralized and self-interested decisions are congruent with the successful operation of the system. In the absence of a market mechanism, either surrogate market signals or interpersonal processes or both must be used to transmit information and motivate agents. There is abundant evidence that in today's planned economies surrogate market signals (e.g., bonus schemes to elicit effort or accurate information) are unavoidably riddled with loopholes and, hence, to one degree or another inadequate (see the essay by Koont and Zimbalist in this book). Therefore, performance in planned economies can be enhanced where there are effective interpersonal processes (or social relations).

The question then becomes: what are effective interpersonal processes?

Although it is neither the most elegant nor the most robust research methodology, I believe part of the answer can be found through introspection. Why do professors try to give interesting courses and why do they publish in professional journals? Certainly, to some significant extent, junior faculty are concerned about promotion and tenure. Senior faculty scholars, however, perform so assiduously due not to monetary rewards but, I would assert, to their internalization of the norms and goals of their university and their profession. That is, they believe in critical thinking, the pursuit of knowledge, etc. and they enjoy conceptualizing and playing with ideas. Moreover, the fact that professors generally have appreciable participatory rights in deciding upon the circumstances and output of their work (e.g., who their colleagues will be, what faculty committees they will serve on, what courses they will teach, how the courses will be taught, what hours they will be taught, what they will research, and so on) fosters their identification with their university and profession. Having assimilated these values, they are largely self-motivated. They are, to an appreciable extent, *homo universitaticus*.

By extension, it is plausible to contend that an important ingredient to effective social relations in any organization is the extent of agent participation or what Nove in this volume calls producer preferences (e.g., management participation in plan formation, worker participation in the same as well as the conditions of work, etc.). There is now an extensive and growing literature which confirms this relationship at the level of the enterprise. [9]

However, agent participation in moulding processes and formulating goals by itself is unlikely to be a lasting sufficient condition for effective social relations in an organization. If, for instance, the organization is a firm and the agent lacks job security, there is reason to anticipate agent reluctance in suggesting innovations which would raise productivity (and possibly obviate the agent's job). Furthermore, due to the operation of the well-known ratchet effect, the use of piece rates for production workers cannot be counted on to elicit greater effort or creativity. [10] Both reasons point to the importance of job security and a reward system which reflects the longer term success of the enterprise. Certainly, central factors underlying the apparent success of Japanese quality circles are the presence of job security (lifetime employment) and seniority wages for a large part of the work force in Japan's large firms.

In addition to participation and job security, the agent's perception of equity in the outcomes or rewards is a component of effective social relations. In a firm, should the worker come forth with a productivity and profit raising idea and should the worker be recompensed a pittance or nothing, it would hardly be surprising were this outcome to violate the worker's norm of equity.[2] [11] Nor would it be surprising were the worker to withhold such ideas in the future. In this view, we have a further explanation for the success of Japanese quality circles. That is, in Japanese firms, (a) increases in productivity raise profits which, in turn, increase workers sizeable bi-annual bonuses and (b) salaries of top executives tend to be well below those in the United States and elsewhere (in the cases of Toyota and G.M., some $200 an hour below). Each of these factors may contribute to a sense of greater equity in the distribution of benefits in Japanese large firms. The role played by culture and enterprise familism in Japan contributes to and is reinforced by the aforementioned circumstances. [12]

This mode of analysis can be generalized, *mutatis mutandis,* to any set of agent–principal relationships at the micro or macro level. Moreover, the political economic approach is in no sense incompatible with the study of economic behavior assuming *homo economicus.* The social relations/political economic perspective does, however, take seriously Berliner's observation [13] that both *homo economicus* (self-interested agent) and *homo sovieticus* (altruistic agent) are extremes — reality lies somewhere in between.[3] [14] In this view, then, it is distressing that virtually all attempts to analyze (to model) agent behavior in the burgeoning incentive literature only consider one extreme. [15] Conversely, it is encouraging when Milenkovitch (in this volume) suggests the desirability of making worker participation or x–efficiency an argument in the production function.[4]

One notable effort to analyze the "in between," more complex reality is the work of expatriate Polish economist Wlodzimierz Brus. Brus claims that worker participation is an essential feature of any effective effort at a reform of central planning: [It will] "release the initiative of those directly engaged in the production process and . . . [create] a feeling of responsibility for the success of the enterprise as a whole which, in turn, cannot be expected unless employees have a real influence in the running of the enterprise." [16] Brus also avers that worker participation will result in widening the enterprise's time horizon and, thereby, diminish the traditional resistance to technological change and new products which follow from the unidimensional focus by "one-man managers" on meeting the enterprise's quarterly or annual production target. He writes: "An enterprise must be able to work for its long-term interests and the best way of ensuring this is to develop collective decision-making, collective interests and collective responsibility." [17] These intriguing propositions have both intuitive plausibility and some empirical support [18] and merit further investigation.[5]

Further, apart from the instrumental reasons for introducing worker participation as seen from the perspective of managers and planners, it must be recognized that industrial democracy has been a central demand of all workers' movements for democratic reform in Eastern Europe. Spontaneous worker councils were present and prominent in the Soviet Union in 1917–1918, in

Czechoslovakia in 1948 and 1968, in Hungary in 1956, and in Poland in 1956 and again in 1981. [19] Of course, the only East European country (possibly excepting Albania) which has managed a clear-cut break from the Soviet model is Yugoslavia where worker councils and worker self-management are basic pillars of their industrial system. This brings me to my next point.

Political economic approaches aid not only in understanding economic performance, but also in interpreting the historical evolution and dynamic path of an economic system. Although other influences are surely at play, there appears to be a correlation between the degree of decentralization, participation and relative openness in socialist economies and the degree to which the socialist revolution in a particular country was home-grown. The expression "home grown" is shorthand to refer to socialist revolutions preceded by the establishment of an indigenous, longstanding and successful socialist movement within a country. The stronger and more mobilized such movements, and the more popular domestic forces participated in making the revolution, the more decentralization has tended to characterize the country's post-revolutionary economic system. Here, Yugoslavia stands out as the only East European country having made its transition to socialism with principally indigenous forces. I have elaborated on the Yugoslav experience elsewhere. [19a]

Although the Red Army "liberated" Hungary after World War Two, it is significant that domestic actors previously had brought the socialist government of Bela Kun temporarily to power in Hungary in 1919 and that the Communist Party together with the other socialist parties received a majority of the popular votes in the two post–World War Two elections. A Soviet puppet, like Rakosi, was unlikely to survive in this environment. The Hungarian Party chief since 1956, Janos Kadar, realized immediately that important concessions had to be made to the restive workers and peasants if political stability was to be restored. Through initial reforms, particularly in agriculture, and repression of the left and right extremes within the Party, Kadar was able to fashion a strong political unity. This unity, in turn, served as the basis for preparing for the 1968 economic reforms. Specifically, unlike the Party disunity and impatience in Poland, beginning in 1965 Kadar was able to methodically build greater slack and balance into Hungary's economy — both necessary pre-conditions for a meaningful market-oriented reform. Once initiated, the reform created political and economic pressures which threatened to undermine it. Here again, the Party unity and growing political legitimacy enabled Kadar to prevent serious backsliding in the early seventies and to rebuild a consensus to push forward with the reforms at the end of the decade.

As an aside, many analysts of the Hungarian reform [20], in my view, have confused the presence of forces resisting reform with the actual direction of the reform. Although we owe much to Kornai's formulations regarding sellers' markets and the economics of shortage [21], Kornai too has recently understated the uniqueness and strength of the Hungarian model by applying these concepts too rigidly. [22] There is now clear evidence in Hungary that: (a) budget constraints on enterprises are being tightened; (b) subsidies are being curtailed; (c) job rights constraints are being attenuated and (d) other decentralizing features of structural reform are proceeding forward.

China and Cuba are two other socialist economies with home-grown revolutions. China, of course, on the basis of a very different historical process and revolutionary ideology than in Russia found the imported Stalinist model to be incompatible with the processes and goals of their revolution. [23] In 1957–1958, they began the Great Leap Forward, characterized by administrative decentralization, the formation of communes and the introduction of small scale industry in agriculture, along with other policies. In 1961, they began four years of experimentation with market-type decentralization. This period was followed by a decade of "Maoist economics," combining administrative decentralization, greater regional and local control, less specialization, deemphasis on consumption and material rewards, etc. Since 1976, as is well known, they have reverted to a market-oriented decentralization which emulates several features of the Hungarian model and includes special trade zones in the South which emulate Hong Kong more than Beijing. Without a meaningful price reform and with soft enterprise/ministerial budget constraints, however, their current reform is experiencing serious setbacks. Nonetheless, the fact remains that China has alternated between models of market-oriented and administrative decentralization since eschewing the Soviet model.

I have written about the Cuban case elsewhere. [24] Suffice it here to assert that Cuban economic management has been relatively decentralized since 1959 and increasingly participatory since 1970. And this despite Cuba's small size which, other things being equal, might facilitate centralization. Even in the 1970s, as many institutions of Cuban planning assumed the same form as those in the Soviet Union, the content or operation of these institutions varied considerably from Soviet practice.

The Soviet Union, of course, also experienced a home-grown revolution. However, the circumstances of the Bolshevik revolution, familiar to most readers, were quite special. First, the Bolsheviks, Mensheviks, Socialist Revolutionaries, etc. had to operate in any extremely repressive political environment. The top leadership of the Bolsheviks were in exile for most of the fifteen or so years preceding the 1917 revolution. Even the secondary leadership experienced periodic incarceration or internal exile to Siberia.

Second, and partly due to the first condition, Lenin believed in an elite, conspiratorial party that would lead the economistically-minded urban work-ing class. Since less than fifteen percent of the labor force at that time worked in industry, Lenin's view was hardly congruent with the conception of the dictatorship of the proletariat being a dictatorship of the majority over the minority (bourgeoisie).

Third, the Bolsheviks had a small, weak base relative to the other parties even in this diminutive urban proletariat. It was not until the late summer months of the failing Provisional Government in 1917 that the Bolsheviks approached a majority of support in the Petrograd Soviet. The Bolshevik base in the peasantry was smaller and more ephemeral. It grew temporarily with Lenin's tactically adept land decree of November 1917, providing a crucial source of support during the civil war.

Fourth, whatever base of support the Bolsheviks had when taking power in late October 1917 was greatly eroded by two and a half years of civil war. By the time of Lenin's death in January 1924, the Bolsheviks were an ex-tremely isolated party with little legitimate connection to the mass base they purported to represent. Only grasping this severe isolation can we understand what followed.

Fifth, Stalin carried this process to an extreme by isolating the Party even from itself. Seweryn Bialer helps make this point: [25]

> It is not enough to dwell on the insecurity and constant fear of a false step. . . . Stalin followed a set of principles and used a number of devices which kept the elite off balance and made the formation of an alliance within its ranks, a challenge against him, hard to conceive. The regular secret police maintained dossiers and surveil-lance of high officials through a separate branch, the Special Department.

This was the atmosphere, then, among the Party leaders and top economic bureaucrats. The prevalent insecurity and distrust infected the entire planning hierarchy and contributed to the excessive centralization and tautness of Soviet planning. Although the severity of these conditions perhaps has diminished some over time, they are still strong enough to have undermined efforts at substantive economic reform.

The details of the revolutionary experience, Party practice and ideology, material conditions, etc. in Cuba, China and Yugoslavia do not directly con-cern us here. Suffice it to note that in each of these cases the popular support base was much broader and more seasoned (and in two of the three cases, more mobilized), and the Party's practices and ideology much less elitist than in the USSR. These historical circumstances help to account for the more decentral-ized character, relative to the USSR, of the economic systems in these coun-tries.

I have sketched arguments and given illustrations of how integrating noneconomic factors can enrich our understanding of the behavior and performance of socialist economies. Of course, most comparative systems economists concede this point and many have even committed themselves in print. [26] Morris Bornstein, for instance, has written: "Perhaps more than other branches of economics, the comparison of economic systems requires a multidisciplinary or — better still — interdisciplinary approach." [27]

Exhortations are one thing, actions are quite another. Little has been accomplished in terms of integrating an interdisciplinary approach into the comparative economics field. On the contrary, studies in the field seem to have progressively stripped themselves of troublesome institutional details. As comparative economic analysis has drawn closer to mainstream theory, it has drawn mainstream theorists into comparative economics. Bornsteins's claim (cited above) that comparative economic studies provide "the perspective to overcome the parochialism inherent in economic thinking" is, in my view, premature. Nontheless, the potential remains.

Obviously, not every study needs to be political economic in scope, but every study should be informed by an appreciation of the institutional context and noneconomic factors from which it abstracts. This is not the case today. The only reliable road to rectification is to incorporate the political economic approach into the training of prospective comparative systems economists in our graduate schools. In England and Western Europe, they are well on the way. In the United States, we have scarcely begun.

Hopefully, this book will contribute to the rectification. There is room for both optimization and political economic analysis in the comparative systems field — and each can be enriched by the other.

Volume Overview

When originally asked by Warren Samuels to edit this collection, my thought was to touch all bases and provide a comprehensive review of the comparative economic field. After an hour or so of reflection, I realized that the field was too broad and intractable for such a treatment in a single book, especially given the publisher's stipulated length constraint. My alternative strategy has been to select authors who could provide either interpretive surveys of the literature in particular subfields or who could reflect on general questions of theory, method and knowledge in the field as a whole.

Furthermore, I endeavored to strike a balance of perspectives and possibly to promote an exchange on certain methodological and theoretical issues confronting researchers in the field. As we should well know, plans and outcomes do not always coincide. The bottlenecked sector, in this case, is easy to identify. I enlisted Alec Nove to provide a critique of formal theoretical and optimization analysis and David Conn to provide a review, explanation and defense of math modelling and formalism. *A priori* these were excellent choices. However, following an objective function assigning a strong weight to his own intellectual integrity, Conn switched his product mix in midstream. By way of explanation after delivering his first draft, Conn confided that he didn't believe math modellers had a clear sense of what they were doing.

As a reward for his fidelity, I lead off with Conn's essay. Conn's piece lays out a very careful, rudimentary methodology for system evaluation. He begins by identifying four central component parts of any economic system and defining the core characteristics of centralized and decentralized economies. He then models and meticulously explores the problems of inter-system comparisons. Conn's conclusions are at once cautious ("any claim that one system is definitely better than another should be greeted with utmost suspicion") and optimistic ("the field of comparative economic systems offers increasing returns to further research").

The second essay by Alec Nove lives up to its billing. In his discussion of various econometric and theoretical models Nove characteristically engages in sweeping iconoclasm. He also gives a useful survey of the many pitfalls of interpreting comparative quantitative evidence. The piece is loaded with insightful nuggets and wit.

The third essay by Deborah Milenkovitch is a thoughtful and thorough evaluative survey of the literature on market socialism. She identifies two strands in this literature — Langean market socialism and worker–managed socialism. For the latter, Milenkovitch reviews and appraises the various assumptions and the micro and macro-economic conclusions of the original work by Ward, Domar and Vanek as well as the more recent extensions. She then summarizes the key empirical work (primarily on Yugoslavia) done to test these theories. Tying together the two strands in the literature with the experiences of Hungary and Yugoslavia, Milenkovitch concludes with an excellent discussion of incentives, risk-bearing and uncertainty under market socialism. Finally, she sets forth an agenda for future research.

In the fourth essay, Ruud Knaack contends that existing theoretical models of economic systems are "undercomplex." After discussing these models, he analyzes at some length the failures of Soviet central planning and its associated adaptations. On this basis, Knaack purports to elucidate a framework for a dynamic approach to comparative economic systems.

In his essay, David Granick employs set theory to conceptually separate out the sources of economic problems in Soviet-type systems. Granick argues that some of these problems are caused by central planning per se; others are engendered by the malfunctions of the incentive system; and, yet others are attributable to the nature of Soviet-type job rights. Granick has emphasized the importance of job rights in earlier writings. For instance, in his analysis of the Hungarian economic reforms, Granick identified the major impediment to effective change as workers' rights to a specific job, which, in turn, he perceived to be at the root of the soft budget constraint. [28] In the present essay, Soviet job rights are seen to provide an important part of the explanation for (a) excessive vertical integration within an organization and insufficient product mix adaptation and (b) inefficiency in capital allocation due to a reluctance on the part of enterprises to undertake substantial labor–saving investments. Granick, then, offers statistical support for the second proposition.

Granick's formulations are ingenious and he has performed a useful function in focusing greater attention on the issue of job rights. His analysis, however, leaves me with a few doubts. For one, it is not clear what production processes Granick has in mind when he argues that job rights thwart flexibility in enterprise product mix. There are a large number of technologies where the worker can perform, in essence, the same job and produce a different product. Where this is not the case, what is there about Soviet-type work incentives which would lead the worker to resist retraining?

Another problem is that Granick's empirical evidence is weak. Since high turnover and attrition are counter tendencies to the immobility resulting from job rights, data on these phenomena would have strengthened his case. What Granick considers to be his strongest evidence (the comparative growth rate of the capital–labor ratio in the USSR and the United States) does not adjust for two crucial facts: (1) over the period considered, 1959–1970, the average industrial work week in the Soviet Union falls by over seven hours [29]; while it remains practically constant in the United States and (2) the United States data includes all private business, while the Soviet data applies only to industry. These empirical shortcomings aside, Granick's insights are valuable and his theoretical formulations will provoke further empirical research. [6]

One theme common to each of the above essays is the centrality of incentives. This topic has also commanded increasing attention in the field since the mid-seventies. The final piece by Koont and Zimbalist proffers a short critical review and some extensions (hopefully favoring reality) on this literature.

Finally, a note of omission. The necessity to delimit the scope of this volume led to the exclusion of comparisons of economic institutions and·economic management among the advanced capitalist nations. The subjects of supply management, indicative planning, labor market policies, among others, are of vital policy-making concern. Do the private sectors in the advanced capitalist nations have sufficient vision, coordination, resources and risk-bearing ability to conduct their affairs in an optimal manner? If not, what, if anything, can be done by the public sector to improve performance? Although simple transplants from one economy to another are highly problematic, properly performed comparative study can inform the choice to adapt certain policies and/or institutions to a particular economy.

Is the divergence between the social and private costs of unemployment great enough to warrant the massive intervention in labor markets practiced by the government of Sweden? These and related questions have been relatively neglected by comparative systems economists and in our journals. For instance, the sole empirical piece in the *Journal of Comparative Economics* on indicative planning, in my view, misidentifies some of the agencies of economic planning in the countries studied and many of its goals. [30] Since most of us acknowledge that there are strengths and weaknesses in both planned and market systems, it would appear sensible and efficient to reallocate some of our time away from the study of the polar prototypes and toward the examination of those economies which have gone furthest in combining features of markets and planning. This too is a matter for our apprenticeship programs.

Notes

1. Although I, on occasion, address practitioners in this essay, the entirety of this book, with the possible exception of a few pages, should be accessible to advanced undergraduates.

2. This problem plagued the "Scanlon Plan" in United States firms and was compounded by the difficulty of identifying the source of an idea as distinct from the messenger of an idea.

3. Comparing the motivation of industrial and enterprise managers in Lange's model of market socialism, Abram Bergson offered a variation on this theme: ". . . as he ascends a bureaucratic structure an executive tends to identify more with those at the highest levels".

4. Milenkovitch refers to the positive production effects (more effort, more creativity, less monitoring, etc.) resulting from worker participation. It must not be overlooked, however, that worker management in a Yugoslav type context might at times have deleterious effects on production. Workers' utility functions might lead them to opt for more leisure (e.g., lackadaisical work, shorter hours) and less income once the workers are in control. Such a response could be quite rational in the presence of either high incomes or goods shortages. The latter has pervaded the Yugoslav economy in recent years. A September 1982 interview I conducted with the manager of Mercedes in Yugoslavia indicated that workers nowadays are often opting for more leisure.

5. To avoid possible confusion, it is perhaps useful to point out that worker participation in management without property rights (advocated by Brus) is rather distinct from worker management with usufruct rights (as in Yugoslavia). Hence, the formal labor management literature with the presumed objective function of maximizing income per worker is not directly pertinent to the case of worker participation espoused by Brus and others.

6. One likely candidate is Japan where lifetime employment guarantees benefit some 25 percent of the labor force. They have to date managed quite well with their labor saving investments. In part this is due to hidden sources of flexibility which one wonders about also possibly being present in the Soviet case.

References

1. Bornstein M., "An Integration," in A. Eckstein (ed.), *Comparison of Economic Systems*. Berkeley: University of California Press, 1971, p. 355.
2. Loucks W. and W. Whitney, *Comparative Economic Systems*. New York: Harper & Row, 1973, p. 16.
3. Central Intelligence Agency, *USSR: Measures of Economic Growth and Development, 1950–80*. Prepared for the use of the Joint Economic Committee, US Congress. Washington: United States Government Printing Office, 1982.
4. Bajt, A., "Investment Cycles in European Socialist Economies: A Review Article," *Journal of Economic Literature*, Vol. 9, No. 1 (March 1971): 53–63; George Feiwel, "M. Kalecki's Introduction to theory of growth in a Socialist economy," *JEI*, Vol. 9, No. 3 (September 1971): 814–818.
5. Eckstein, *op. cit.*
6. *Ibid.*, p. 1.
7. Zimbalist A., "On the Role of Management in Socialist Development," *World Development*, Vol. 9, Nos. 9/10 (1981).
8. Karl Polanyi, *The Great Transformation*. New York: Holt, Rinehart & Winston, 1944.
9. Espinosa, J. and A. Zimbalist, *Economic Democracy: Workers' Participation in Chilean Industry, 1970–1973*. New York: Academic Press, 1978. Carnoy, M. and D. Shearer, *Economic Democracy: The Challenge of the 1980s*. White Plains: M. E. Sharpe, 1980. Bernstein, P., *Workplace Democratization: Its Internal Dynamics*. New Brunswick: Transaction Books, 1980. Frieden, K., *Workplace Democracy and Productivity*. Washington, DC: National Center for Economic Alternatives, 1980.
10. For evidence on the U.S. see: Whyte, W. F., *Money and Motivation*. New York: Harper & Row, 1955; R. Opsahl and M. Dunnette, "The Role of Financial Compensation in Industrial Motivation," in V. Vroom and Deci (eds.), *Management and Motivation*. Baltimore: Penguin Books, 1973. For evidence on the USSR, see Leonard Kirsch, *Soviet Wages: Changes in Structure and Administration since 1956*. Cambridge: MIT Press, 1972, especially chapter 2.
11. Cf. Whyte, W. F., *op. cit.*, pp. 173–180 and Frederick Lesieur, *The Scanlon Plan*. Cambridge: MIT Press, 1958.
12. There is, of course, a substantial literature on Japanese labor relations. An interpretive synthesis can be found in "Japan: Business and Government Coordination," chapter two in Zimbalist A. and H. Sherman, *Comparative Economic System: A Political Economic Approach*. New York: Academic Press, 1984.
13. Berliner, J., *The Innovation Decision in Soviet Industry*. Cambridge: MIT Press, 1976, p. 401.
14. Bergson, A., "Market Socialism Revisited," *Journal of Political Economy*, October 1967, p. 658.
15. One recent, provocative exception is Vladimir Kontorovich, "What Do Managers in the Centrally Planned Economy Do?" xerox, 1982. This paper is adapted from

his PhD dissertation under H. Levine and borrows from the author's experience in the USSR economic bureaucracy.

16. Brus, W., *The Economics and Politics of Socialism.* London: Routledge and Kegan Paul, 1973, p. 41.

17. *Ibid.*

18. Espinosa, J. and A. Zimbalist, *op. cit.,* especially pp. 148–157.

19. For an interesting discussion of the emergence of the demand for workplace democracy in Poland's Solidarity, see Howard Wachtel, "Self-Management Proposals in Poland, 1981," paper delivered at the Third International Conference of the International Association for the Economics of Self-Management, Mexico City, August 1982.

19a. See "Yugoslavia: Self-Management and the Market," chapter 16 in Zimbalist and Sherman, *Comparative Economic Systems: A Political Economic Approach.* New York: Academic Press, 1984, forthcoming.

20. See, for example, David Granick, *Enterprise Guidance in Eastern Europe.* Princeton: Princeton University Press, 1975, Part III, "Hungary"; and, Edward Hewett, "The Hungarian Economy: Lessons of the 1970s and Prospects for the 1980s," in JEC, *East European Economic Assessment,* Part I. Washington, DC: United States Government Printing Office, 1981.

21. See his most recent theoretical treatment, Kornai, J., *Economics of Shortage.* Amsterdam: North-Holland, 1980.

22. Kornai, J., "Comments on the Present State and the Prospects of the Hungarian Economic Reform," *Journal of Comparative Economics,* Vol. 7, No. 3 (September 1983).

23. Two excellent, detailed sources on the process of breaking away from Soviet-style management practices are: Schurmann, F., *Ideology and Organization in Communist China.* Berkeley: University of California Press, 1968, ch. 4; and, Andors, S., *China's Industrial Revolution.* New York: Pantheon, 1977, ch. 3.

24. H. Sherman and A. Zimbalist, *op. cit.,* ch. 13, "Cuba: Socialism Next Door," A. Zimbalist, *op. cit.,* 1981; Zimbalist, A., "Soviet Aid, U.S. Blockade and the Cuban Economy," *ACES Bulletin,* Vol. 24, No. 4 (Winter 1982); Zimbalist, A., "Worker Participation in Cuba," *Challenge,* Nov.–Dec. 1975.

25. Bialer, S., *Stalin's Successors.* Cambridge: Cambridge University Press, 1980, p. 34.

26. Bornstein, M., *op. cit.;* Koopmans and Montias, "On the Description and Comparison of Economic Systems," in Eckstein, *op. cit.;* and, Ward B., "Organization and Comparative Economics: Some Approaches," in *Ibid.*

27. Bornstein M., *op. cit.,* p. 353.

28. Granick D., *op. cit.,* 1975.

29. Nove A., *The Soviet Economic System.* London: George Allen and Unwin, 1982, p. 227.

30. Peter Murrell, "Planning and Coordination of Economic Policy in Market Economies," *Journal of Comparative Economics,* Vol. 3, No. 2 (June 1979).

2 THE EVALUATION OF CENTRALLY PLANNED ECONOMIC SYSTEMS:
Methodological Precepts
David Conn

Introduction

Every thinking person comes at some time to question both the way in which man-made constructs function and how such structures can be altered so as to improve their performances. Among the constructs resulting from human endeavor, none is so important as our social systems, which determine how people relate to one another in pursuit of both common and individual interests. It is thus natural that economic systems, which to a great extent determine how people both compete and cooperate with one another on a day to day basis to produce and distribute goods and services, have a rich history of both descriptive and normative appraisal. This history begins (at least) with Plato and runs through the writings of early modern Utopians and scholastics, the Physiocrats, the classical liberals, nineteenth-century Marxists and anarchists, and continues to present day socialists, capitalists, Maoists, liberals, and conservatives.

A repeatedly posed question in these writings is the relative superiority of

I wish to thank Andrew Zimbalist for helpful comments on an earlier draft of this paper.

centralized versus decentralized forms of economic systems. Obtaining an
answer to this question is perhaps the most common objective of students who
enroll in courses on comparative economic systems.

In fact, whether the question is couched in terms of Capitalism vs. Socialism
or Planning vs. Markets, it is difficult to find a person who has no interest in
the comparison of centralized and decentralized economic systems. However,
one curious fact must be recognized at the beginning; while most economists
(in the United States, at least) believe in the superiority of decentralized
systems over centralized ones, it is very hard to find specialists in comparative
economics (the present author included) who are willing to commit themselves
on this issue. Some comparative economists do venture personal opinions, but
these are almost always hedged by either confessions of prejudice or lengthy
lists of qualifications and disclaimers.

My opinion is that this situation is in no way anomolous. Rather, the fact
is that it is presently impossible to make legitimate, definitive, comparative
evaluations of economic systems. This is primarily due to three factors. The
first is a lack of adequate knowledge about the natures and performances of
different systems. Fortunately, this problem is constantly mitigated by advances in empirical research.[1] The second factor is a lack of consensus as to
the criteria that should be used for evaluation. Finally, even with full knowledge and clear criteria at a given point in time, any evaluation is necessarily
historically relative.

Thus, in evaluating centrally planned economies (CPEs) I begin with several premises: that evaluating CPEs is definitely a worthwhile endeavor; that
it is better to do the evaluation correctly than to achieve a quick, but false,
certainty; and that no evaluation can ever attain the status of a universal truth.
Because of this, the focus of the present essay is on how economic systems
should be evaluated generally, with emphasis on the particular problem of
evaluating CPEs, which are somewhat alien to Western economists.[2]

Two points should be emphasized at the outset. One is that the problems
of evaluation are not unique to the study of economic systems. Consider, for
example, the evaluation of scientific theories. For the past several centuries
philosophers of science have attempted to formulate methods for definitive
evaluations of theories. All of these have proved inadequate, and the current
consensus is that theory evaluation is necessarily comparative, incomplete, and
tentative (Cf. [4] for a discussion that is highly pertinent to economists).
Alternatively, consider the problem of evaluating specific economic policies,
such as energy policies. Again, such evaluations must be comparative, based
on incomplete information, and liable to revision as circumstances change. As
a topic, comparative economics lies somewhere between the ethereal philosophy of science and the concrete problem of economic policy, and so evaluation

in comparative economics should not be assumed to be different from evaluation in these other areas.

Second, even if evaluation can not be done perfectly, it should be attempted. In either the philosophy of science or energy policy it proves profitable to evaluate alternatives and to act on these evaluations. The costs of not doing so are simply too great. Thus, the following is not offered as a criticism of previous attempts to evaluate CPEs. Rather, it is a request for modesty — the acknowledgement of potential limitations — in interpreting these evaluations. In my opinion the choice among economic systems is far more important than the choices among either scientific theories or energy policies, which means that mistakes have more serious consequences.

The organization of the paper is as follows. In the next section the theoretical framework for analysing economic systems is briefly reviewed. The following two sections provide a careful definition of CPEs and an outline of two rudimentary methodology of systemic evaluation. This background material is then used to discuss the evaluation of CPEs in particular, and a few summary comments end the chapter. Given that Professor Nove deals with empirical evaluations of CPEs elsewhere in this volume, I do not consider these in the present paper.

Economic Systems: A General Framework

In this section we outline a framework for the comparative study of economic systems. The purpose of such a framework is to provide a system-free method for analyzing various economic systems. Only in this way is it possible to approach any particular type of system, such as a CPE, free of prejudice. At the outset it is necessary to ask the reader to suspend the habit of formulating all economic questions in reference to a particular type of economic system, such as the competitive price system.

An economic system must be defined relative to the underlying economy in which it is situated. The system then consists of the set of institutions through which the economy works to make the traditional decisions of what, how, and for whom to produce. This view of the nature and role of economic systems is briefly outlined in the present section (cf. [5], [6], [11], [12], or [13] for more complete treatments of this topic.)

The underlying economy for a system is the environment in which it operates. This environment contains all relevant variables that are thoroughly exogenous (i.e., not subject to change or choice). If the analysis is to span a period of time, then the environment consists of all initial conditions (and prior history) as well as autonomously occurring changes. In the limiting case of purely static analysis, the environment collapses into the set of initial conditions.

Precise specification of the relevant set of environmental variables depends on the type of analysis to be done. For a national economy, this set likely includes: the economy's members (the population), including the members' skills, aptitudes, preferences, and knowledge; the resources and technology available to the economy; other aspects of the physical environment, such as climate; and the external world surrounding the economy.

The environment, or the underlying economy of a system, provides all of the raw materials or basic inputs that can be used. As such the environment determines all *a priori* limits and possibilities for actions and outcomes. Yet the environment is a dormant mass that needs to be activated. This is accomplished by the economic system, which is thus said to operate on the environment to produce actions.

Actions refer to all events that are subject to endogenous control or influence. The set of actions includes both physical events (putting nuts on bolts, transfers of commodities over space or among agents, etc.), and informational events (issuing orders, making bids, keeping records, etc.). Actions may or may not be of direct interest themselves, but yield outcomes which are defined to be intrinsically significant. The definition of significance is relative to the analysis at hand, but refers to such things as the types, quantities, and qualities of goods produced, resource utilization, income distribution, macroeconomic phenomena, and so on.

This formulation, that an economic system operates on an environment to produce actions which result in outcomes, provides a context for the positive analysis of economic systems. For purposes of evaluation, two further steps are required. The first is to formulate performance criteria, such as per capita consumption, efficiency, equity, stability, etc. Such criteria are broad based measures of a system's performance. The final step in evaluation is to aggregate all performance criteria into a single measure of performance. This is done by means of a norm function, which may, but need not, be a standard Bergson–Samuelson Social Welfare Function.

The usefulness of a norm function, as is argued below, arises primarily from the lack of congruence of various performance criteria. Sometimes criteria are largely unrelated (such as the percentage of the population attending college and the export of wheat) in which case they might move in opposite directions. Other pairs of criteria stand in direct conflict (e.g., greater income stability might require lower average growth rates). Thus, when the list of performance criteria is moderately long, evaluation requires some form of weighted aggregation, via a norm function, in order to achieve definiteness.

This broad outline provides a context in which economic systems can be studied. What remains is to elaborate the nature of economic systems themselves. In reality, economic systems are incredibly complex and varied. As always, analysis requires that some detail must be sacrificed, so we here focus on four aspects, or components, of economic systems. The justification for this is a belief (which is presently only partially confirmed by empirical study) that these four components capture the essential or crucial features of economic systems, considered either singly or comparatively. The four component parts of an economic system are called the information, decision-making, incentive, and coordination structures.

The Information Structure

The questions of who knows what (or can know what) are dealt with by the information structure. Information can be obtained either by observation or by message transmission, which are discussed in turn. First, it is helpful to have a basic working definition of what information amounts to. For present purposes, it suffices to simply define information as any knowledge that might be of relevance in the making of decisions by a system's members. Thus, knowledge concerning the environment (technology, resource availability, preferences, etc.) obviously qualifies as relevant information. So does knowledge concerning the behavior of other individuals, the criteria and norm function of the system (when these exist), as well as the system itself. These factors have significance in terms of what is feasible, the overall desirability of various courses of action, the capacity of an individual to affect an action, and the consequences (to oneself and others) of various actions.

The prospects for obtaining information via observation are necessarily limited for two reasons. First, some information is inherently private. For example, the preference ordering of a given individual can only be directly observed by that individual. Second, any one individual has a limited capacity for observation (in terms of time and location, at minimum). Thus, direct observation is of necessity a dispersed activity for any reasonably complex system. Further, some items of relevance defy observation by anyone. Examples here include the total reserves of petroleum in the earth and all future realizations of random events, such as weather or inventions.

The limitations of observation can be partially overcome by communication. Person A might not be able to observe B's preferences, but B might be able to tell A what these are. Or, while no one individual can directly observe the stocks of rice available in China, segments of this information can be sent to a central information agency from various sources, and then added together to obtain complete information.

In addition, raw data can be processed into more useful and efficient forms, either before or after messages are sent. Information can also be stored and retrieved in various ways. The processes of storage, retrieval, and computation are all of potentially great importance in rendering information useful and getting it to where it is needed.

The information structure of a system is simply a specification of the open and closed channels of observation and communication for an economy, which determines effectively who knows, or can know, what. Two essential limitations of any information structure must be stressed. First, errors of observation, transmission, and computation can never be completely avoided. Second, the processes of observation, transmission, and computation are usually under human control, in which case self-interested manipulation or distortion of information is a pervasive possibility. At first blush, these might seem to be minor or technical problems, but they are truly fundamental.

The Decision-making Structure

While the information structure effectively determines who knows what, the decision-making structure determines who has the power within a system. Economists normally conceive of a natural allocation of authority within a system, e.g. consumers control their own incomes and firms control their own production. This is a very system-bound perception, however, and is not really true in any extant economic system. In fact, the distribution of authority varies considerably among systems and over time. While there might be logical or practical limits on the actual allocation (or reallocation, if reform is the question) of authority, it is best to take pains to avoid being overly restrictive in defining what is possible here.

For a given environment and information structure, there is a (very large) set of alternative actions available to the members of a system. The decision-making structure is a specification of the allocation of authority, among an economy's members, to actually and effectively decide on the actions to be taken. This approach is broad enough to include: one agent having complete or partial control over the actions of another agent; processes for resolving conflicting decisions; and the possibility of either individual or group decision-making.

The terms decision and action are left intentionally vague above. The reason for this is that these include not only real actions, such as putting nuts on bolts, but also all informational acts as well as the payment of rewards (incentive acts). Thus, in a sense, the decision-making structure is the most fundamental aspect of an economic system. The separation of the four structures is maintained, however, for analytical purposes.

The Incentive Structure

The incentive structure effectively determines who gets what. People receive payoffs for their actions. These payoffs always depend (in all but Robinson Cruso economies) on both the actions of others and the information possessed by others (e.g., the IRS, one's boss, or trading partners). Further, the distribution of payoffs is obviously constrained by the total amount available for distribution within the system.

The incentive structure is a specification of the procedures or rules by which the various members of a system are rewarded or penalized. Rewards and penalties, it should be noted, can refer to either money, actual goods and services, or nonmaterial items.

The Coordination Structure

The last basic aspect of an economic system is the process by which the activities and decisions of various individuals are resolved into a group action or decision. This process is called the coordination structure. Examples of coordination structures include bureaucracy, markets, central planning, bargaining, arbitration, unanimous consent, majority voting, anarchy, and various combinations of these. The purposes served by coordination structures are to (1) ensure feasibility of individuals' decisions; (2) facilitate cooperation; and (3) resolve conflicts.

Needless to say, the coordination structure overlaps considerably with the other three structures. It is given a separate identity solely for expositional clarity. One thing that must be kept in mind at all times is that the set of feasible coordination structures is constrained by the information and decision-making structures in use. More generally, feasibility is a joint property of the four component structures.

An economic system is identified by a specification of the information, decision-making, incentive, and coordination structures. The implicit argument is that all of the relevant characteristics of the arrangements by which an economy is run can be captured by these four structures. Then the complete schema is that: (1) there are given initial conditions, called the environment; (2) the system operates on the environment to produce actions, which in turn yield outcomes; and (3) these outcomes are judged by means of criteria or norms.

It should be obvious that the four component structures of an economic system are highly interdependent, and that the connections between the environment, the system, and the behavior of system members are all closely related. To be specific, what ever an individual chooses to do depends on his authority, the information available, preferences, the behavior of others, and the payoff received.

Not only are all of these factors tightly related, but they can conceivably exist in potentially infinite combinations. Some of these combinations might in fact turn out to be infeasible, while others will be feasible but obviously not sensible. Still, the number of potentially reasonable combinations is likely very large. This is precisely what makes the study of comparative economic systems so rich and worthwhile.

Centrally Planned Economies

The ultimate purpose of this paper is to outline, on theoretical principles, a basis for evaluating CPEs. This task necessarily comprises two distinct stages: an objective analysis of exactly what CPEs are and how they operate, and a specification of the criteria or norms to be used in passing judgement on CPEs. The latter aspect of evaluation is necessarily subjective, meaning that reasonable people can agree to disagree about it, and is treated at length in the following two sections.

Ideally, the objective part of the analysis has (at least) potential claim to universal assent. Unfortunately, no such consensus exists at present for CPEs. Simply put, there is nothing like a universally agreed upon definition of a CPE, and, as a result of this, there are significant differences of opinion as to how CPEs actually function and perform. In part this phenomenon results from the fact that definitions of the essence of a CPE frequently result from implicit normative criteria which it is presumed that a CPE should satisfy. In other words, CPEs are frequently designed with objectives in mind. Since these objectives are often different, the ideal types frequently diverge.

Nonetheless, it is necessary to begin with a description of the nature and operation of CPEs. Since the empirical appraisal of CPEs is the subject of another essay in this volume, I shall here focus on primarily theoretical issues.

The first true national CPE came into existence in the early twentieth century with the creation of the USSR. Since that time numerous other countries (including Eastern Europe, China, and Cuba) have become CPEs either by choice or as a result of Soviet action. Throughout history, as well as contemporarily, many other organizations (some private companies, churches, government operations) have existed which could be considered as subnational (now, transnational?) CPEs. All told, an astounding amount of both empirical and theoretical research on CPEs has been conducted. Thus, there is presently a fairly rich storehouse of information available on the functioning and performance of CPEs. Yet this information does not constitute a basis on which economists can claim to have a true understanding of the nature and practice of CPEs. The reason for this is that the world's CPEs differ significantly one from another (and the disparity is presently growing, not shrinking), which has meant that the voluminous studies of CPEs amount to a wide range of case studies. This is true of both theoretical and empirical research.

The diversity of CPEs among countries and over time has made it impossible to develop a reasonably unified theory of CPEs. As a result, any general discussion of CPEs has to concern itself with a class of systems rather than a single model or case. This contrasts quite sharply with the study of DMEs (decentralized market economies). While DMEs do differ significantly (consider three examples: the United States, Sweden, and Brazil), there is a nearly universal textbook model (*viz.,* perfect competition) which, while never taken to be descriptively inviolate, is thought to be an ideal representation that bears a useful resemblance to all actual DMEs. To date, no such comparable model of CPEs exists. The significance of this lack of parallelism becomes clear below.

What is meant then by a centrally planned economy? The term itself suggests that planning occurs and is done centrally. Does planning require only forecasts or projections? Or does it suffice to announce intentions? Or is it necessary to announce intentions and attempt to (or actually) implement them? All of these practices have been called planning. It seems, however, that what is normally meant by planning is to decide on what is to occur and to exert control in order to realize those decisions.

French indicative planning, amounting as it does to forecasts more than decisions as to what is to happen, and attempting to persuade rather than to actively control, is not really a form of planning, although it is in an informational sense very centralized. From this example it is clear that centralization is not a sufficient condition for planning, but it might well be necessary.

It is necessary to define centralization more carefully. It seems that the essence of centralization involves two items — the concentration of authority within a system, into one or a few hands, and the hierarchical exercise of that authority over the whole system. Concentration without centralization would entail competing centers of power which did not operate cooperatively. An example would be the judiciary without channels for appeals. But authority over what?

In general, authority is a nebulous concept, but for present purposes (i.e., planning) it can be defined with reasonable clarity. Authority is the capacity to control, either directly or indirectly, the objectives, nature, and implementation of the plan. Implementation, of course, can be done either directly or through agents. If done through agents, then authority can be exercised via persuasion, manipulation, or use of force. It seems best, however, to restrict the notion of authority to those instances where explicit sanctions (rewards or penalties) can be used to control agents' implementation of the plan, thereby excluding any compliance which is completely voluntary. No doubt voluntary compliance or cooperation is sometimes quite significant, but it is often ephemeral and dependent on psychological factors which make it analytically intractable.

Authority as the right to control might be based on moral or legal grounds, but is best thought of as being primarily effective and secondarily legal. In French indicative planning the planning commission has no legal or effective rights to control implementation. The federal government does have some legal rights of control, but these have been used less often than not. Thus no effective control exists at all, which again argues for not categorizing France as a CPE.

One thing that should be noticed is that central planning does stand in contradiction to the practice of liberal (unfettered) property rights. Control by the center does imply lack of (complete) control by the periphery.[3] In other words, to the extent that authority rests with the center, so do property rights. There seem to be only two alternatives consistent with this: either property rights are possessed personally by a small number of individuals who by virtue of their possessions become the center, or else property rights are possessed by no individuals, but reside with the office of the center, and are exercised by individuals who occupy the office at a given time.

It is worth mentioning here that moral (i.e., "all things considered") arguments for the existence of private property rights can be used to justify only partial rights. That is, there is no compelling argument for either giving unlimited reign to liberal private property rights or for banning them completely (cf. [2]). Thus, it would perhaps follow that there is no moral basis for requiring or proscribing full central planning.

There are necessarily at least two stages of economic planning, namely plan construction and plan implementation. These are obviously related, but procedures used in these two stages can differ markedly. Plan construction is primarily informational. Presuming centralization, the center constructs plans by collecting information by either (1) making observations directly; (2) soliciting information from peripheral agents; or (3) introspection. This last procedure might seem bizarre, but must be included for completeness.

This information generally concerns various aspects of the environment, such as technology, resource availability, behavioral relations, or members' preferences. On the basis of this raw data, the center makes estimates of (or decisions on) the feasible courses of actions for the economy and the rankings of these actions. The finished plan is then a selection of that feasible course of action which is best according to the given ranking.

The range of possibilities for the process of plan construction includes the following extremes: (1) the center plays a passive role of simply asking the peripheral members what it is they plan to do, then amalgamating these into a national plan (perhaps making some adjustments in order to assure consistency); (2) the center unilaterally announces, on the basis of its a priori beliefs, what it deems best according to its own preferences (the introspection process); or (3) the center elicits information from the peripheral members of what is feasible and what they prefer, and then constructs a plan that is feasible and optimal[4] for the periphery. Although (1) would hardly seem to count as central planning, it is often used in combination with (2) or (3). Most CPEs use combinations of (2) and (3) in plan construction, with Stalinist planning in the USSR bordering on (2) while the Maoist ideal for the PRC was close to (3).

From this it is clear that the process of constructing a plan in a CPE need not (but may) be authoritarian in any sense. On the other hand, if plans are not enforced (implemented) with some authority, then it could be argued that there is no real planning. Of course, the extent to which authority is exercised in plan implementation can (and does) vary significantly. At one extreme, plans can be legally binding, with deviations from the plan subject to criminal prosecution and varying sanctions applied. (In the military, which is very centralized, disobeying orders is sometimes punishable by immediate execution.) Alternatively, the center might exercise authority solely through monetary rewards and penalties for compliance or disobedience. Either coercion or manipulation can be used to ensure plan implementation (within feasible limits) and so both are tools for the exercise of authority. (Persuasion might be equally effective, but if not backed by sanctions, it is probably best not thought of as a tool for exercising authority.)

The net result of this, quite significantly, is a considerable indeterminacy with regard to how central planning is done. At one extreme is the totalitarian possibility of the central planner making unilateral decisions which are then imposed by brute force. At the opposite pole is a central planner who acts as a facilitator in constructing a plan that is in the public interest, which can thus be viewed as a legitimate social contract, then using its authority noncoercively to enforce this social contract.

While neither of these extremes is actually practiced by CPEs, those who wish to extol or condemn CPEs normally use either one or the other as their textbook model of how CPEs function. In reality, CPEs vary considerably, one from another and over time, so that the entire class of CPEs cannot be judged commonly. The argument I would make is that CPEs need to be evaluated individually because of their diversity. But what of the legitimate desire to compare CPEs, as a class, with DMEs? If economies are treated singly, it is unlikely that all intergroup pairwise comparisons would yield the same results.

This then requires the use of some ancillary procedures for comparison, which is necessarily arbitrary. Does one compare the best or worst case from each class? The median or mean (defined how) of each class? There is no compelling reason for any of these methods, but there are compelling arguments for forbidding some practices, such as comparing the worst case DME to the best case CPE.

It is necessary to return to the question of identifying the class of CPEs. The above considerations give rise to the following definition: an economy is centrally planned if there is a central agency which has the capacity to: (a) collect information from other members of the economy; (b) define the preferences of the economy as a whole; (c) determine the course of action that is to be pursued by the economy; (d) implement this plan; and (e) the central agency actually exercises its authority.

Any definition of a CPE less general than this would probably be too restrictive and would not be able to encompass all those systems which are obviously centrally planned. Any more general definition would probably allow essentially market economies to sneak in as CPEs. Neither possibility would be desirable, so we shall stick to the above definition.

In terms of the four structures of section two, a CPE (1) requires the possibility of a centralized information structure (wherein all information is at least supposed to flow to the center); (2) definitely does require a centralized decision making structure in which a large proportion of authority ultimately resides with the center; (3) requires a centralized incentive structure (significantly, it seems this term has never been used before), meaning that the center has the capacity to parcel out rewards and penalties in order to ensure compliance with the plan; and (4) the coordination structure must obviously be planning. Specifically, (3) implies (1) (to some extent) because information regarding compliance must be available if sanctions are to be made. Further, (3) is necessary in order for (2) to have force, unless one is willing to assume an omnipotent center.

Two remaining issues should be addressed presently. First, which actual economies fit this definition of a CPE? Consider the set normally defined as CPEs, including the USSR, the PRC, North Korea, Viet Nam, Cuba, East Europe and Yugoslavia. Of these Yugoslavia is excluded by our definition via criteria (c), (d) and (e). The USSR is, and always has been, a CPE by our definition. Of the East European countries, these were obviously CPEs during the 1950s. (Except even here the scope of planning did not always include, e.g., all of agriculture.) Have these countries ceased being CPEs because of their various reforms? The most likely candidate here is Hungary, which adopted extensive use of markets in its 1968 New Economic Mechanism (NEM).

The Hungarian government voluntarily gave up some of its power with respect to items (b) through (e), but has retained its right to take these powers back. In fact, there has been some pressure for recentralization in Hungary, and the center does still exercise a considerable amount of authority. This does tend to be more manipulative (via price setting, for example) than administrative, as was the prior situation. At minimum, the Hungarian reform has resulted in less detailed planning than in the USSR, and the planning is also done differently, but it is still done centrally and with some vigor. Hence, Hungary might be a borderline case, but it is still a CPE. The other East European economies have verged at times on becoming decentralized, but remain CPEs, as is the case with the PRC, and the other state-socialist countries mentioned above.

Are there other CPEs in the world today? While some Western industrialized economies engage in planning, either this is of very limited scope (e.g., Sweden) or the plans are not enforced with any authority (e.g., France), so that none of these would qualify as CPEs. My knowledge of third-world countries is extremely limited, but it seems that some (Afghanistan, Tanzania) might be deemed centrally planned, but several "socialist" countries such as India obviously are not, at least by criterion (e). Japan and some OPEC countries (Saudi Arabia, Kuwait) come to mind as capitalist countries where property is centered in private hands to the extent that the resulting practice in these countries might be called central planning. The problem here is that what occurs in these countries is an extreme form of cooperation between business and the government (which are hard to distinguish), but the latter has limited or no authority to control the former. Thus the center in these cases would be extra-governmental and would simply work through the government.

It is worth noting that when one leaves the realm of national economies, the class of CPEs increases dramatically. Most governments are CPEs for their internal operations, as are most unified-form corporations and some multidivisional firms, even when these operate within market systems. Most organizations, in fact, meet all criteria for being CPEs, with only the qualification that they are limited primarily to manipulation in order to implement their plans.

It should also be noted that centralized authority itself is not sufficient for an economy to be a CPE. There are obviously countries where the government is despotic and coercive but does not engage in planning. Alternatively, consider a bureaucracy. Such an organization is dominated by rules which must be followed, and deviations from which are met by negative sanctions. Bureaucracies also have a central agency which is in charge, but here the center actually has very limited authority. In fact, for a true bureaucracy authority resides not with any individuals or even offices, but with the rule book, which might be imposed by external sources, or merely history. Thus, bureaucracies are not necessarily CPEs, and can often be shown not to be CPEs. Still, bureaucratic institutions can be, and are, used in CPEs. The line of demarcation is simply whether the bureaucracy is a malleable policy tool or takes on a purpose of its own which cannot be controlled by the planners.

The second item that needs to be considered is the nature of planning. Plans, as documents, can vary greatly in their scope and specificity. A plan might be restricted to the commanding heights of an economy, or it can cover all industry, or it can encompass all economic activity. Plans can also differ in detail. For example, a manager of a firm could be instructed as to total output to be produced, or be given a precise assortment plan. Or the manager could be instructed to produce exact amounts, or be told what the acceptable range is. Again, this potential diversity is reason to not lump all CPEs together.

In fact, by now it should be clear that the variety of CPEs actually calls for a study of CPEs that can compare them to one another, identify differences, and, one would hope, lead to explanations of their different performances. This is far from becoming a reality, however.

For purposes of evaluation, the diversity of CPEs is very significant. Basically, the distinctions among CPEs make it impossible to come up with a single evaluation. While this is a regrettable situation, it is unavoidable.

Evaluating Economic Systems: General Aspects

Evaluation of economic systems is undeniably both important and difficult. The importance of systemic evaluation stems from the facts that there are considerable differences among economic systems and that these differences are significant both in and of themselves and in terms of the resulting quality of life. The difficulties of evaluating economic systems are numerous. Most obvious are the empirical problems of discovering and interpreting factual evidence. In addition, the process of evaluation is necessarily subjective, comparative, and, if it is to be complete, moral, meaning that the perspective has to be one of all things considered.

These topics are dealt with in the present and the following sections. The present section presents universal criteria for evaluation, while the next deals with those aspects of comparative evaluation particularly relevant to the appraisal of CPEs.

Applying Criteria

The present section first considers the requirements for comparative evaluation given the acceptance of either a single norm function or a class of such functions. Next, the problem of selecting criteria and norm functions is discussed. This sequencing is employed in order to avoid bias by the prior selection of ethical criteria.

The process of evaluation is ultimately normative or subjective regardless of the item to be evaluated. This does not mean, however, that the process of evaluation is completely arbitrary. Rather, there are a few rules of evaluation that can be applied in order to obtain clarity as to what the conclusions are and how they are arrived at. The subjectiveness of evaluation arises from the fact that any appraisal can be rejected by dismissing the normative criteria on which it is based. The only hope for universal agreement lies in the possibility of accepting the underlying evaluative analysis contingent on the validity of the ethical precepts employed.

In addition to being subjective, the process of evaluation is necessarily comparative. Any evaluative statement that an item (an economic system, a scientific theory, etc.) is superior, good, satisfactory, poor, or unacceptable can only be made in juxtaposition to some reference point. The only two possible referents for comparative evaluation are an ideal standard or some fixed alternative. Thus, for evaluation of economic systems, the two approaches would be either to establish criteria or to select a particular system as the benchmark for comparison. In fact, both of these methods are commonly used. For example, claims that unemployment in the United States is too high are always based on some definition of full employment, the prevailing unemployment rate in Western Europe, or past US unemployment rates. Without the use of such a referent, the concept of too high an unemployment rate is operationally meaningless. The real problem then, is one of selecting a suitable benchmark for evaluation.

In order to establish the relative rankings of various economic systems, recall the framework outlined above. There it was stated that an economic system operates on an environment to produce actions which yield outcomes to be evaluated by a norm function. These relationships can be expressed in a very simple schema. To begin with, there is an admissable class of environments, $\mathscr{E}$, with elements E_j. Further, there is a class of systems, $\mathscr{S}$, with elements S_i, to be investigated. Then system S_i operating on environment E_j produces outcomes θ_{ij}. Note that actions, being thoroughly determined and intermediate, can for present purposes be ignored. Note further that the outcome θ_{ij} is actually a vector, $\theta_{ij} = (\theta_{ij}^l, \ldots, \theta_{ij}^n)$, the n components of which are specifications of the values of all criteria that might be deemed important, including both performance criteria and system characteristics.

In terms of outcomes, all relevant features can be expressed by the relationship

$$\theta_{ij} = S_i(E_j). \tag{2.1}$$

Next consider the evaluation of these outcomes by means of a norm function. For simplicity, assume that the set of reasonable norm functions, denoted $\mathscr{N}$, can be agreed upon. Then, for a given norm function N_k in $\mathcal{N}$, an evaluation is assigned to θ_{ij} by the function $N_k(\theta_{ij})$. Implicitly, $N_k(\theta_{ij}) = N_k(S_i(E_j))$, which indicates how the evaluation depends on the norm, the system, and the environment.

It should be recognized that what has been described here is a full information situation, where the system, environment, outcomes, and norms are all completely known. This assumption is dropped below, but is temporarily maintained for expository purposes. Specifically, let us attempt to compare two systems, S_1 and S_2, operating respectively in environments E_1 and E_2. This yields the relevant outcomes θ_{11} and θ_{22}. Assume that for some given norm function, N_1, the result is that $N_1(\theta_{11}) > N_1(\theta_{22})$. This is a complete description of the way things are, and leads to the conclusion that S_1 is better than S_2. Unfortunately, this conclusion is invalid because of the (hidden) effects of the environment. It might be the case that $N_1(\theta_{11}) > N_1(\theta_{22})$ because E_1 is more bountiful than is E_2.

This is a truly fundamental difficulty in that it is almost impossible to find two systems operating in identical environments. In order to claim that S_1 is better than S_2 in our example, what would be required? Either it would be necessary to show that E_1 and E_2 are equivalent, or essentially so, or to prove that $N_1(\theta_{11}) > N_1(\theta_{21})$ and that $N_1(\theta_{12}) > N_1(\theta_{22})$, meaning that S_1 would out-perform S_2 for either environment. The first possibility is implausible in practice as stated before.

The problem with the second option is that S_1 is observed operating only in E_1 and S_2 only in E_2. Thus to claim the superiority of S_1 regardless of the environment is necessarily counterfactual. Stated another way, in practice no amount of empirical evidence is ever sufficient, by itself, for the evaluation of economic systems.

This does not mean that evaluation is impossible or that it is independent of empirical evidence. Rather, the counterfactual nature of evaluation means that evaluation must be primarily a theoretical endeavor. What is needed is a full-fledged theory of how different systems perform in various environments. Of course, such a theory should be based as much as possible on whatever empirical evidence is available.

Were full theoretical knowledge to exist, there would remain several significant conceptual issues in evaluation by comparison. Assume first that the given norm function, N_1, is retained and that the comparison is between only two systems, S_1 and S_2. Consider, however, that the set of potential environments, $\mathscr{E}$, really contains an infinite number of elements. Then the prospect that S_1 outperforms S_2 for all possible environments is not very plausible. The best one could hope for is to prove that S_1 outperforms S_2 for some definite subset of environments, while S_2 outperforms S_1 for others. Thus, any claim for the superiority of one system would necessarily be contingent on the environment being of the right sort.

Further, the norm function employed obviously has a bearing on the evaluation. Even if it could be established that $N_1(\theta_{1j}) > N_1(\theta_{2j})$ for all E_j in $\mathscr{E}$, it would be necessary to contemplate other reasonable norm functions. To see this, consider the simple class of linear norm functions, and recall that the outcome variable is a vector, $\theta_{ij} = (\theta_{ij}^1, \ldots, \theta_{ij}^n)$, so that a linear norm function can be viewed as a vector of n paramaters, each of which is the weight assigned to the corresponding component of the outcome vector. For simplicity we need only two such vectors: $\alpha = (\alpha_1, \ldots, \alpha_n)$, and $\beta = (\beta_1, \ldots, \beta_n)$.

For specificity, assume that $\alpha = (1, 0, \ldots, 0)$ and $\beta = (0, 1, \ldots, 1)$. Further, assume that $\theta_{2j}^1 > \theta_{1j}^1$ for all j, but that $\theta_{1j}^h > \theta_{2j}^h$ for all j and for all $h = 2, \ldots, n$. This extreme situation gives rise to the conclusion that S_1 is superior to S_2 when the β weights are used, but that S_2 is superior when the α weights are chosen.

For this example, it might seem reasonable to conclude that in fact S_1 is better than S_2 since S_1 gives rise to better performance in all categories but one. The point is, however, that the evaluation should in some sense depend on how important the various outcomes are. For instance, θ^1 might refer to average life span, while θ^2 through θ^n refer to per capita consumptions of various goods. Then if $\theta_{2j}^1 = 70$ and $\theta_{1j}^1 = 10$ for all j, it might well be reasonable to conclude that S_2 is superior to S_1.

The above example is designed to be an extreme case. The result, however, is in no way anomolous. Even for the class of linear norm functions, unless one system's outcomes are always better than another's, component-by-component, there are always two sets of weights that would yield either system as being the superior one. Obviously, this problem is heightened by moving to a more general class of norm functions.

In sum, any claim that one system is definitely better than another should be greeted with utmost suspicion. To be valid, such a claim would have to either (1) be based on a (fallible) theoretical proof that one system outperformed the other in terms of all potentially relevant outcomes for all conceivable environments; or (2) be hedged by specifications of the classes of environments and norm functions for which the evaluation holds. Option (1) seems implausible for any interesting pair of systems, which leaves (2) as the desirable format for evaluative statements.

The above comments on evaluation by comparison apply with full generality to all environments, systems, and norms. In the next section greater specificity is attained for the evaluation of CPEs. In the remainder of the present section a few more detailed comments are offered on the potential types of norms that can be used. The two questions to be dealt with are (1) what types of outcomes should be deemed relevant in the evaluation of economic systems, and (2) the amalgamation of these outcomes into an overall evaluation via a norm function, which often amounts to deciding whose norms to use.

Selecting Criteria

The problem of selecting criteria for evaluation is one of determining which outcomes are potentially of interest. The first thing to note is that in principle all outcomes could conceivably be of interest to someone. At a theoretical level, then, it would be best to evaluate all outcomes. Practically, however, it is not possible to be so comprehensive, which necessitates the selection of some subset of outcomes for evaluation. Of course, any such selection of criteria is itself subjective or normative, but it seems possible to maintain an open mind at this stage of the process.

The second reason for beginning with the selection of criteria, rather than jumping immediately to the adoption of a norm function, is simply that it is much easier to achieve agreement as to what is or might be significant than it is to arrive at consensus as to exactly how important various outcomes are. For example, income distribution is universally acknowledged as being of interest, but great divergence exists even as to what constitutes a desirable distribution of income. Because of this it is most likely that objective analysis and evaluation can be pursued by investigating specific criteria prior to attempting an all things considered evaluation. Of course, any analysis of a specific subset of outcomes is necessarily partial and cannot by itself lead to truly general conclusions.

The intent of defining a class of relevant outcomes is to develop universally applicable evaluative criteria, in the sense that it would be legitimate, although not necessary, to use these in passing judgment on any economic system. To repeat, it is impossible to present an exhaustive list of such criteria. Therefore I shall mention only a few that are widely held to be significant.

Evaluative criteria can be variously categorized. The most useful category consists of those "purely economic" criteria that seem to be common to all developed, and most developing, economic systems. These include (1) high levels of per capita income or consumption; (2) growth of per capita consumption; (3) equity (not necessarily equality) of the income distribution; and (4) stability of income, employment, and prices. From these follows a fifth economic criterion, efficiency, that is commonly accepted among disparate systems. Efficiency, however, is best construed in its most general sense, meaning that no desirable criterion can be improved upon costlessly, rather than in the technical sense normally employed in economics. As such, efficiency cannot be discussed until all other criteria are specified.

In addition to these common criteria are other economic criteria that are emphasized in only some societies. These include the provision of public goods, insulating individuals from economic risk (or encouraging risk taking by individuals), and equality of income distribution. Another category can be described as economic freedoms, including freedom of choice in consumption and work, as well as freedom to participate in determining workplace procedures, plan formulation, and so on.

In terms of economic objectives, stated as broad, aggregated goals, these are probably the major ones. There are, however, many other effects of economic systems that are of interest but which are not considered to be economic. These include both aspects of performance and traits of the system itself. While economists can of course choose to ignore these noneconomic outcomes, no argument can be made that these should be ignored (in fact any definitive evaluation must deal with the noneconomic aspects of economic systems).

While noneconomic criteria of system evaluation are quite varied, it is probably safe to refer to them generically as political factors. Given the recurrent theme above that system evaluation is inherently subjective or normative, it is not surprising that political criteria play a legitimate role in evaluation. Due to a lack of sufficient expertise, I can only briefly mention potentially relevant political criteria.

Consider first the political appraisal of the performance of economic systems. Surprisingly, and importantly, there is little to be said on this topic. Emphasis is given above to the fact that evaluation — the selection of criteria and norms — depends on preferences. Fundamentally, there is no natural demarcation between political and economic preferences over outcomes. Although common usage might, for example, hold that the efficiency of outcomes is an economic criterion, while the fairness of outcomes is political, it is clear that this distinction is purely polemic and serves no analytic purpose. In fact, attempting to maintain such distinctions probably serves only to encourage economists to exclude political criteria from their analyses.

The distinction between political and economic appraisals of economic systems themselves, however, is quite important. The reason for this is that traditionally economists have adopted a strict means-ends dichotomy where preferences are defined only on outcomes obtained, and not on the processes by which they are attained. To maintain consistency, economists do grant that the choice among means is important to the extent that they might entail different costs (resources used for nonproductive purposes), but that this automatically shows up in the differences among final outputs. The tradition in political science, however, has been to devote considerable attention to the processes of collective decision-making. While these different traditions might be arbitrary (i.e., without analytical foundations), the result is that a purely (traditional) economic approach to system evaluation misses much of relevance.

As an example, take the attribute of procedural fairness (as distinct from outcome fairness). For simplicity, consider a given outcome of two individuals with different jobs and incomes. Let Mr. A be an accountant with an income of $20,000, while Ms. B is a secretary with an income of $10,000. Any evaluation of this situation should depend on how it was arrived at. Two possibilities are that (1) by law or social custom only men are allowed to be accountants, and (2) assignments to occupations are determined solely by proficiency exams. Note that in neither case are the preferences of Mr. A or Ms. B considered. Yet these two methods of assignment will not be viewed as equivalent by most observers in spite of the identity of both the initial conditions and the final outcomes. The point of such an example is to show that process (the system) matters in and of itself, not merely by virtue of the outcomes it yields.

What, then, are the systemic attributes that are of potential relevance to evaluation? Procedural fairness is an obvious candidate, as the above example shows. Economists (e.g., Hurwicz [9],[10]) have also suggested that privacy and efficiency of the information structure are significant, as are decentralization of the decision-making structure and the equity of the incentive structure. Sociologists (e.g., Tannenbaum [15]) have focused on the total amount of control exercised within an organization, as well as the senses of perceived control and participation. Of course, central control is viewed as a desideratum by some (Stalinists), an odiosum by others (anarchists), and as an instrument of true democracy by still others (Maoists).

In the next section greater attention is paid to a few political attributes of economic systems with particular relevance to the evaluation of CPEs. For now it suffices to recognize the legitimacy of political factors in system evaluation. Perhaps the most difficult problem of appraisal is that of combining various criteria so as to achieve an all things considered evaluation. Essentially, this is a problem of determining whose preferences are to guide the evaluation.

The most fundamental observation on this issue follows from Arrow's analysis of social choice [1]: if there are at least three distinct alternatives and three evaluators who do not necessarily agree in their preference orderings, then there is no method of aggregating preferences that (1) is truly responsive to each individual's preferences; (2) yields well-defined and consistent social preferences; and (3) satisfies other, seemingly innocuous, technical conditions. This means that, where differences of opinion exist, unanimity of evaluation is not to be expected, and that there is no obviously satisfactory method for overcoming this lack of unanimity.

In terms of the evaluation of economic systems, then, comprehensiveness requires that a choice has to be made as to whose values are to prevail. While making such a choice is never perfectly defensible morally, it is a practical necessity which should be scrutinized for its reasonableness.

One obvious candidate for whose preferences are to prevail in the evaluation of a given system is to use the preferences of that system's members. This does not actually get one very far, however, because Arrow's results apply to any society that is not extremely homogeneous. (In fact, the greatest diversity consistent with a truly representative social ordering would be a two-class society with strictly identical interests within each class.) However, it might be possible to identify well-defined preferences for some group within a system which are of potential relevance. For example, self-selection might render uniform preferences for the leadership of a system. This is potentially of extreme significance in that the leadership, the group in control, have the capacity to change the system and can be expected to do so according to their own preferences. Thus, it is possible, by this method, to develop a normative analysis of economic reform that has positive merit as well. Alternatively, it is conceivable that the preferences of the median member of a system (or some subsector, such as the masses) could be identified and used to guide evaluation.

These possibilities cannot be ruled out on logical grounds, but it must be admitted that they are, practically, very implausible. The most likely situation is that an economist attempting to evaluate a given system would be able to extract only very rough guides from the system's members. Further, what information that can be identified regarding members' preferences should be treated with some suspicion. For any system that exists over an extended period of time, its members' preferences eventually become somewhat endogenous. This endogeneity of preferences can manifest itself in evaluation in the following ways: (1) a given system, through discrimination, indoctrination, or self-selection, might lead naturally to the survival of certain preference types at the expense of the extinction of others; (2) the system itself might encourage its members to focus on either the successes or the failures of the system, which would obviously render internal evaluation more positive or negative, respectively, regardless of "objective reality".

In sum, an evaluator cannot really find any natural bases for the norm function to be used in the evaluation. Rather, it is necessary to make difficult choices as to the criteria to be used, and how these are to be amalgamated. It is possible to seek guidance from other reasonable people, but evaluation necessarily remains a subjective process. Eventually, the evaluator must personally take responsibility for the norms he or she employs, and acknowledge the fallibility of the evaluation that follows.

Evaluating Centrally Planned Economies

In the previous section general principles were outlined for the evaluation or comparison of any economic systems. Clearly, these methods are fully applicable to the evaluation of CPEs. The question remains, however, as to exactly how to put the above-mentioned principles into practice. This task is undertaken in the present section. The analysis comprises three parts: first, the problem of evaluating CPEs is formulated for general criteria, including those which enjoy near-universal assent; second, those criteria emphasized by neoclassical economists are considered separately; finally, criteria pertaining directly to systemic traits are briefly mentioned.

Formulating the Problem

As argued above, it is possible, in principle at least, to identify the class of CPEs. For present purposes attention is restricted to actual CPEs, and this class is denoted $\mathscr{S}^{CA}$. By convention, the class of existing systems which are not centralized is called decentralized and labeled $\mathscr{S}^{DA}$. (In fact, it may be useful to utilize a third class, $\mathscr{S}^{NA}$, which are neither centralized nor decentralized. However, this would here serve no practical purpose.)

From the population of national economies, $\mathscr{S}^{CA}$ would contain roughly a score of members and $\mathscr{S}^{DA}$ somewhat over one hundred members. For each existing system in each class there is a corresponding environment and a resulting outcome vector. Because each actual system is in practice associated with a specific environment, we can add the same subscript to both, giving the following simple notation $\theta_i = S_i(E_i)$. Thus the sets of relevant observations can be identified as $T^{CA} = \{(\theta_i, S_i, E_i) | S_i \epsilon \mathscr{S}^{CA}\}$ and $T^{DA} = \{(\theta_i, S_i, E_i) | S_i \epsilon \mathscr{S}^{DA}\}$, respectively. Note that this formulation allows for, but does not require, the recognition of idiosyncrasies among members of $\mathscr{S}^{CA}$ and $\mathscr{S}^{DA}$. If, in fact, the intention is to draw grand conclusions regarding the relative performances of CPEs and DMEs, then these idiosyncrasies should be repressed. This would result in comparing outcomes among CPEs and DMEs, with due allowance being made for differences in the underlying environments.

In order to conduct an evaluation of CPEs vis-a-vis DMEs at this level, it is necessary to account for the differences in the underlying environments. As should be clear from discussions above, environments are truly multifaceted, and thus require multidimensional representations. In order to actually conduct a comparative evaluation, however, it would be necessary to heroically assume that the influence of environment on performance could be reduced to a very small number of variables. For simplicity, assume that environments can be ranked by a single measure, called propitiousness. Properly done, this would assign a number $p_i = p(E_i)$ to each environment. At best the numbers p_i could be given an ordinal interpretation — even heroic confidence would not allow us to state that one environment was twice as good as another.

Even an ordinal ranking of environments, however, greatly facilitates systemic evaluation. First, this ordinal ranking allows for some unambiguous pair-wise comparisons. This occurs whenever the situation arises where $p(E_i) > p(E_j)$ yet θ_j dominates θ_i in each component, meaning that system S_j performs better than S_i in spite of the fact that it is handicapped by a less propitious environment. In such a case, the only possible explanation for the superior performance is the system.

Additionally, a rank-ordering of environments allows the sample-set to be adjusted to correct for outliers. In absence of a complete theoretical understanding of how environments affect performance, this is necessary in order to avoid biases that might be exclusively the result of unknown environmental effects. Recall, for example, that CPEs account for at most one-sixth of all national economies. In this situation it is quite likely that the range of CPE environments is considerably smaller than for DMEs. Any general comparison based on full samples would then be obscured by outlying DME environments on both ends of the sample. Further, the direction of the resulting bias is unknown.

Two responses to this situation are sensible. One is to start with the CPE population and to select a subset of DMEs with environments as similar as possible. The other is to restrict the DME population by throwing out all outliers. Either procedure has the virtue of yielding environmentally comparable samples of systems on which the comparative evaluation can be made. Of course, the resulting conclusions would only hold for the retricted sets of observations.

This process of ranking environments and restricting the observation sets creates greater opportunities for comparisons both within and between T^{CA} and T^{DA}. For example, if within the restricted subsets it were observed that all outcome vectors associated with DMEs dominated those corresponding to CPEs (or vice versa) then a legitimate claim for superiority could be made. Further, a weaker claim of superiority could be made if, for example, for each CPE with environment E_i there could be found a DME with environment E_j such that $p(E_j) > p(E_i)$ *and* θ_j is dominated by θ_i. This would be an indication that the superiority of θ_i over θ_j could not be explained away by the environment, hence it must be systemic in origin.

Such systemic comparisons could also be made within a class of economic systems. For example, CPEs are not homogeneous, and some would claim that those CPEs which rely on free markets to allocate produce, say, are superior to those that do not. By the methods described here, such statements can be tested. Similarly, the above-described methods of comparative evaluation can be applied to restricted subsets of environments to answer such questions as: is the relative efficacy of CPEs, as compared with DMEs, affected by how bountiful the environment is?

Still, it must be recognized that ranking environments merely mitigates, but does not obviate, the problem of comparison *via* outcomes. Even for relatively similar environments it is unlikely that one system's outcomes will clearly dominate those of another system. Thus, definitive comparative evaluations still require, in all likelihood, resort to a norm function.

Invalid Comparisons

So far in this section the process of comparative evaluation has been fairly open-ended in that care has been taken to isolate potential environmental impacts on outcomes, but without restricting attention to particular outcomes or weighting outcomes in specific ways. Before proceeding to the construction of norm functions it is worthwhile to consider potential methods of comparative evaluation that must be rejected as invalid.

Invidious Comparisons.   An invidious comparison is one designed to cast a bad light on a particular type of system. Thus, one could guarantee a specific ranking of CPEs and DMEs by selecting only outcomes for which relative performance is a foregone conclusion.

It is clear from the above, for example, that CPEs entail, as a matter of definition, more centralized processing of information than do DMEs. Thus, using the extent of centralized information processing as an exclusive desideratum (or odiosum) would automatically yield the conclusion that CPEs are better (worse) than DMEs. Other examples of evaluative criteria that would almost certainly lead to invidious comparisons include the autonomy of enterprises, lack of discrepancy in privately-held wealth, diversity of consumer goods, the relative share of infrastructure in investment, and nominal inflation. The bias induced by each of these criteria should be obvious upon minimal reflection.

It is crucial to note that even though such criteria induce a bias in comparisons, they cannot be excluded from consideration. This follows from the fact that such criteria might be of real importance to the evaluator. Rather, all that can be argued is that any comparative evaluation based primarily on such factors is suspect because of likely invidious intent.

One other source of potential invidiousness, the selection of specimens by the propitiousness of environments, has been implicitly dealt with above. Obviously, to compare one system operating in a resource-rich environment to another system operating in an impoverished environment (e.g., to compare Czechoslovakia with Bangladesh or the United States with Afghanistan) is at best a worthless exercise.

Premature Comparisons. While invidious comparisons between CPEs and DMEs can be biased in either direction, the question of timing comparisons should lead to a one-way bias, but the direction of distortion is not obvious. There are two plausible arguments that can be made here. One is that CPEs have existed only for a few decades whereas DMEs have been around for centuries if not millenia. From this it might follow that CPEs should at present be given considerable benefit of doubt because they have not had sufficient time to "work the bugs out" of their systems. This argument is supported by the current reforms that are taking place within CPEs and which are designed to be performance improving.

The second possible view is that CPEs can be expected to have built-in tendencies for bureaucratization or ossification which would lead to stagnation in the long run. From this viewpoint CPEs should be judged harshly. Even if they are not presently inferior to DMEs, they can be expected to become inferior in the future.

Unfortunately, both of these positions have minimal plausibility and there is insufficient evidence to claim either as being obviously correct. While my own belief is that CPEs probably need more time to engage in self-reform (if only to overcome the Stalinist legacy), I believe that it is best to merely recognize that comparative evaluations are potentially temporally conditional. This means that even if it could be established, at a given point in time, that CPEs were either superior or inferior to DMEs, it would still be worthwhile to reevaluate the situation from time to time.

Neoclassical Criteria

In any assessment of planned economies it is necessary to contend with the economist's natural benchmark of evaluation — the performance of decentralized market economies. At the practical level this task is extraordinarily difficult, as most economists would agree. It is standardly presumed, however, that at the conceptual level comparisons between centrally planned and decentralized market economies are relatively straightforward and result in an unfavorable evaluation of planning, at least under ideal competitive conditions. In fact, this opinion is not, and can not be, founded on rigorous analysis.

Rather, this theoretical conclusion is based on fairly casual arguments which never hold strictly. Given that these statements are at odds with conventional wisdom I shall elaborate on them in detail in the present section. The procedure used is to present the competitive analysis first in its most favorable form and contrast it with a comparable analysis of planning. This purely Utopian approach leads to the conclusion that markets and planning do not differ substantially in terms of potential performance, but that different performances can follow from different goals, with the result that the comparative evaluation is reduced to a purely normative process. This basic conclusion also holds when the Utopian ideals are departed from, as long as this departure is conceived of symmetrically. The net result, in my opinion, is that any theoretical evaluation that rates either central planning or markets as being unambiguously superior is the result of either an unfair theoretical construct or the use of a particular criterion of evaluation.

The textbook ideal of a perfectly competitive market system is well known and thus needs only brief treatment here. The premises are that for all goods (only private goods exist) there are many buyers and sellers (potentially, at least) who thus act as price takers. The buyers and sellers are motivated by selfish interests, i.e., consumers have well-defined, smooth, convex, preferences, and producers (firms) maximize profits constrained only by smooth, convex, technologies (which are free of any externalities). The model is normally closed by assuming that firms are owned by stockholders, so that profits become income for consumers directly. These conditions, together with a few technical assumptions, guarantee the following results:

1. A competitive equilibrium always exists. A competitive equilibrium is defined as a specification of prices (one for each good), a consumption plan for each consumer, and a production plan for each producer, such that
    a) each consumer's consumption is the "best" affordable at the given prices,
    b) each firm's production maximizes profits at the given prices, and
    c) there is balance of supply and demand for each good at these same prices.
2. All competitive equilibria are Pareto optimal. Pareto optimality means that there is no other feasible set of consumption and production plans that could make even one consumer better off without making at least one other consumer worse off.
3. If it is possible to redistribute consumers' initial endowments of commodities (including productive factors) and stocks in firms, then any feasible Pareto optimum can be attained as a competitive equilibrium.

These results are known as the existence, optimality, and unbiasedness properties of the competitive price system. The last two properties are called the two fundamental theorems of welfare economics.

There are at least three bases on which the two fundamental theorems of welfare economics can be criticized. These are (1) the realism of the environmental assumptions; (2) the use of the Pareto criterion; and (3) the assumed nature of the price system itself. These are listed in order of their commonality, and are taken up in this order.

Critiques of the environmental conditions assumed for the competitive model are quite well known, and are generally referred to as the "market-failure" literature. Examples of these exceptions include: if technology is not convex, natural monopoly might arise, which would result in non-competitive behavior; monopolistic behavior can also result from highly concentrated initial endowments of any one good; externalities of any form, including public goods, can vitiate the Pareto optimality of competitive equilibria. The list is really very extensive, but these are the most significant environmental difficulties commonly discussed.

One environmental feature that is potentially very important but infrequently discussed is the predicate of the second fundamental welfare theorem that endowments are transferable. Two basic problems exist here. One is that endowments are often not observable, which makes their transfer a moot issue. For example, endowments include both innate and acquired skills. Second, even if skills can be observed it makes little sense to speak of transfering them. At best, what can be proposed is to give one individual rights to the proceeds of a second individual's use of the second's skills. The problem with this, of course, is that it creates an externality that obviates optimality.

The Pareto criterion is commonly accepted by economists. I have argued elsewhere [6] that the reasons for this are less than compelling, but they are nonetheless worth considering here.

It seems that the primary reasons for accepting the Pareto criterion are that it is fairly weak and that it is compatible with the use of most more stringent criteria. In particular, if one were to begin with any sort of social welfare function that is smooth and strictly monotone in individuals' utilities, then the solution to the maximization of that social welfare function would inevitably result in a Pareto optimum. Hence, Pareto optimality can be considered as a precondition for attaining the maximum of any such social welfare function.

Given this weak nature of the Pareto criterion, how can it be objected to? Consider a hypothetical situation of two systems and assume for simplicity that these are operating in identical environments. Assume further that the first system is Pareto optimal but that the second one is not. Now consider a plausible norm function that gives considerable importance to equality of consumption. Then, if the first system's Pareto optimal equilibrium is more unequal than the second system's inefficient outcome, it is quite possible that the second system is still judged to be superior to the first.

Simply put, the Pareto criterion ignores many factors that might be relevant to evaluation. In addition, the possibility clearly exists that the Pareto criterion will conflict with other criteria, in which case a trade-off necessarily exists between these. A good example of this potential conflict is between Pareto optimality and equality. Thus, the Pareto criterion is far from being neutral and hence unobtrusive.

Finally, the practice of using the theory of perfectly-functioning DMEs suffers from the presumed nature of the price system itself. The price system is assumed to function iteratively and autonomously. Somehow, initial prices exist on the basis of which supply and demand decisions are made. If demand and supply do not balance, then prices are adjusted and the process continues until equilibrium is reached. The next question is, when is the equilibrium reached? Actually, equilibria might never be attained. Rather it can only be shown that it is approached. If the equilibrium could be approached very rapidly, this problem might be dismissed as inconsequential, but this raises another problem: the more rapid the rate of adjustment of prices, for given supply and demand conditions, the more likely is the price system to be unstable. This instability means that prices will move away from equilibrium levels, not toward them. It can thus be concluded that Pareto optimality is a criterion satisfied by DMEs only hypothetically, even under ideal conditions.

A specific example of how the criterion of efficiency might be misleadingly used is found in the study of comparative productivity. By definition one system is more productive than another if it gets more output per unit of inputs used than does the other. Given that outputs are desirable and that input usage is costly, productivity is probably the closest thing to an innocuous desideratum there is. It is quite natural, then, that Abram Bergson conducted pioneering research [3] on the comparative productivity of the economies of the United States and the USSR. His findings were unambiguous: using either United States or Soviet price indices, productivity in the United States is far greater than in the USSR. Further, the size of the difference is so large that it would be impossible to argue that measurement errors were at fault.

At first blush, it would seem natural to conclude that, in terms of productivity, the CPE of the USSR is inferior to the DME of the United States. In fact, there is nothing wrong with this conclusion as long as it is not interpreted too zealously. There are, however, at least three reasons to consider tempering the significance of the productivity gap: first, the productivity measurers are based on price indices, which are not actually perfect measures of relative values in either country; second, the central planners in the USSR do not believe that relative prices should serve the purpose of reflecting relative values of outputs or inputs; third, productivity is not an all-inclusive measure of performance — in particular, it does not capture notions of equity, stability, full-employment, or working conditions. At a minimum, then, it would be necessary to determine whether or not the USSR is buying better performance in any of these areas by incurring lower productivity. If it is, then this lesser productivity does not necessarily translate into lesser efficiency.

A further theoretical problem in the comparison of DMEs with CPEs is the well known result that the competitive price mechanism is informationally efficient, meaning that it is impossible for any alternative system to achieve Pareto optimality (in classical environments) while using less information than does the price system. Unfortunately, it is normally not emphasized that the price system actually uses an infinite amount of information to achieve Pareto optimality (this follows from the infinite number of iterations required to achieve equilibrium). To be blunt, this seems to be a very shallow form of informational efficiency. The usual presumption is that an iterative central planning procedure would need to use more messages than the price system, per iteration. From this it is concluded that CPEs are informationally less efficient than are DMEs. Again, the significance of this result is dubious at best.

Criteria Based on Systemic Characteristics

At this point it is useful to list the political virtues and liabilities that might be attributable to CPEs. The expression "might be" is used because one appraiser's virtue can be a vice to a different observer, in addition to the fact that potentials are much easier to establish than are realizations.

As for virtues, it is clear that central planning has an unequaled potential for control and coordination. In its broadest and best sense, control refers to the establishment of explicit objectives and assuring that actions are taken which are consistent with these objectives. By contrast, in a DME, actions are taken autonomously by individuals, and the resulting outcomes might well be inconsistent with any explicit social objectives. Thus, a CPE has the potential to be socially rational while a DME can be anarchic.

Similarly, a DME leads to coordination of individuals' decisions, when equilibrium is attained, but this coordination is an unconscious result of market processes. In a CPE, however, coordination of decisions is itself an objective, and can be attained (perhaps imperfectly) without waiting for an equilibrium to materialize. In reality, this trait of quicker coordination is but one aspect of the greater control via central planning.

That a CPE offers greater promise for control and coordination is in part a desideratum because it could lead to improved performance. Examples include: (1) the capacity for a superior in a planning apparatus to recognize externalities and other interdependencies among subordinates, which can then be resolved administratively; (2) the ability of planners to assess the preferences of the system's members and act on these (true democracy?), rather than giving people votes in the market place in proportion to their income or wealth; (3) the ability to allow politics to either supplement or supplant economics in decisionmaking; (4) the capacity to explicitly consider future generations in present decisionmaking; (5) the ability to provide security to individuals irre-spective of their initial endowments or the vagaries of markets; and (6) the potential to address the questions of exploitation, alienation, market instabili-ties, etc., regardless of profitability.

Of course, many of these attributes are overlapping, but they are listed separately to allow for different emphases that might be desired. Further, all of these desirable attributes are listed as potential because there is no guarantee that they would be forthcoming solely because central planning is used. In order to realize these benefits, planning would have to be done correctly.

It is also worth noting that the above list of the benefits of planning are all simply negations of imperfections of markets. Similarly, the benefits of markets are often taken to be the avoidance of the potential pitfalls of planning. Thus, we shall simply list the perceived problems of central planning.

The possible liabilities of central planning include the following: (1) central-ization can lead to a concentration of power which can then be misused to the detriment of individual rights or social interests; (2) in a CPE, mistakes made centrally can cause more damage than can small, decentralized mistakes; (3) a planning apparatus may become heavily bureaucratic, thwarting the exercise of power from both above and below; and (4) in moving away from a DME, self-interest is lost as a prime motivator for such implicit goals as efficiency, rapid growth, innovation, and consumer sovereignty.

Obviously, neither of these lists is exhaustive, but they do indicate the types of political considerations that may be important in evaluation. Also, these lists of the potential benefits and costs of a CPE affirm the notion that any given attribute might be either a desideratum or an odiosum, depending on the political perspective of the evaluator.

Conclusions: What to do?

By this point the reader may have concluded that the evaluation of CPEs, as compared with DMEs, is hopeless. This is too extreme a position to take. Rather, I would argue that the comparative evaluation of CPEs is subject to a crucial trade-off: either it can be done quickly and definitively, or it can be done correctly. Obviously, I believe that the latter is the preferred option. Simply put, the conclusion is of such importance as to make errors too costly.

The primary reason for avoiding quick judgments on the relative merits of CPEs as compared with DMEs is the present inadequacy of our knowledge about their true performance. We do not have sufficient empirical evidence to warrant drawing conclusions at this point in time, and our knowledge about potential performance is even less satisfactory.

Further, our present theoretical understanding is insufficient on two grounds: we have not yet come to adequately understand how economic systems affect performance; and there is nothing like an emerging consensus on how to evaluate differing performances. My own reaction to this situation is to conclude that the field of comparative economic systems offers increasing returns to further research. In the meantime, what can the reader do in order to arrive at an evaluation of CPEs? First, it is necessary to decide that one cannot go to the experts for the answer. With this out of the way, the student must remember that the process of evaluation is necessarily subjective, comparative, and tentative.

These features require the following methods to be used in arriving at a personal evaluation:

(1)   A personal decision on the norms to be employed, keeping in mind that this process is subjective.

(2)   A review of relevant evidence, both empirical and theoretical, on the performance of alternative economic systems. This requires an attempt to separate the effects of environmental and systemic factors on the observed performances.

(3)   A decision on the net effects of the systemic factors on the resulting performance differences among the systems being considered.

(4)   An application of the norms attained in (1) to the effects derived in (3). This is the net result of the evaluation.

(5)   Acknowledgement of the tentative nature (due to analytic shortcomings and historical vagaries) of the conclusions obtained in (4).

By following this procedure, any intelligent observer can come up with a legitimate, albeit personal and tentative, evaluation of CPEs. The topic is, after all, too important for the student to do any less.

Notes

1.   The existing literature on comparative evaluation consists primarily of a large number of works focusing on either sectoral comparisons or specific performance criteria, and a few extensive pair-wise comparisons. Given the volume of this literature I do not attempt even a summary. Good introductory discussions can, however, be found in [7, Ch. 10], [8, Ch. 10], or [14, Ch. 14].

2.   The original charge of this paper was to discuss the usefulness of optimization techniques in systemic evaluation. The prerequisites for applying optimization techniques are that choice sets, constraints, and objective functions be fully specified. Given that such a specification is not yet possible for the field of Comparative Economic Systems, I have adopted the more modest goal of elucidating the nature and purpose of the enquiry. My belief is that optimization techniques will eventually prove useful in systemic evaluation, but this remains to be shown.

3.   One aspect of authority that I am slighting is its variable - sum nature. Effective organizational design can at times increase each member's control or authority. For example, a central planner can increase his or her authority, by use of an effective coordination structure, while at the same time giving more control to the periphery. Cf. [15] for supporting evidence.

4.   Any ranking of alternatives leads naturally to an identification of either optimal or acceptable subsets. The terms best and optimal used here and below implicitly allow for either possibility. This presumes only that choices made are consistent with preferences (rankings) when these exist.

References

1.   Arrow, K., *Social Choice and Individual Values* (2nd ed.). New Haven: Yale University Press, 1963.
2.   Becker, L., *Property Rights: Philosophic Foundations.* Boston: Routledge & Kegan Paul Ltd., 1977.
3.   Bergson, A., "Comparative Productivity and Efficiency in the USA and the USSR." In A. Eckstein (ed.), *Comparison of Economic Systems.* Berkeley: University of California Press, 1971.
4.   Blaug, M., *The Methodology of Economics.* Cambridge: Cambridge University Press, 1980.
5.   Conn, D., "Toward a Theory of Optimal Economic Systems." *Journal of Comparative Economics.* 1(4): 325–350, Dec. 1977.
6.   Conn, D., "Economic Theory and Comparative Economic Systems: A Partial Literature Survey." *Journal of Comparative Economics.* 2(4): 355–381, Dec. 1978.
7.   Ellman, M., *Socialist Planning.* Cambridge: Cambridge University Press, 1979.
8.   Gregory, P., and R. Stuart, *Comparative Economic Systems.* Boston: Houghton Mifflin Co., 1980.
9.   Hurwicz, L., "On Informationally Decentralized Systems." In C. B. McGuire and R. Radner (eds.), *Decision and Organization.* Amsterdam: North-Holland, 1972.
10.   Hurwicz, L., "The Design of Mechanisms for Resource Allocation." *American Economic Review.* 63(2): 1–30, May 1973.
11.   Koopmans, T. C., and J. M. Montias, "On the Description and Comparison of Economic Systems". In A. Eckstein (ed.), *Comparison of Economic Systems.* Berkeley: University of California Press, 1971.
12.   Montias, J. M., *The Structure of Economic Systems,* New Haven: Yale University Press, 1976.
13.   Neuberger, E., and W. Duffy, *Comparative Economic Systems: A Decision-Making Approach.* Boston: Allyn and Bacon, 1976.
14.   Nove, A., *The Soviet Economic System.* London: George Allen and Unwin, 1977.
15.   Tannenbaum, A., et al., *Hierarchy in Organizations.* Jossey-Bass, 1975.

3 SOME OBSERVATIONS ON INTERSYSTEM COMPARISONS

Alec Nove

Introduction

This is something of an intellectual minefield. It is all too easy to stray off the narrow path of reason, and the results can be unfortunate. There are several causes of ideological prejudice, but the more important ones are conceptual and statistical in character, and relate to the meaning of figures, the weights which one could or should assign to certain positive and negative features of this or that system, and perhaps also the quantification of unquantifiables. What is the relative importance of security of employment in a trade-off with consumer choice, for example? Particularly difficult is to relate one's analyses to what must be ultimately a very important standard or criterion: human satisfaction, welfare, and these sometimes have only a partial connection with per capita income or similar measurements. A corporal who has been promoted to sergeant is a much happier man than a major who has not made it to colonel.

In a recent article in the *Slavic Review* [1], Steven Rosefielde discussed various forms of statistical exaggeration in the Soviet Union in the thirties, and pointed to spectacular forms of waste, huge public works (in particular a major canal) which were of very little use. Wasteful grandiose schemes were indeed no rarity under Stalin's rule. It may (or may not) be appropriate to make some allowance for this in assessing rates of growth. However, Rosefielde proceeded on the silent assumption that waste of this sort does not occur in Western market economies. Yet, as Davies and Wheatcroft pointed out in their comment on Rosefielde's piece, this is surely improper [2].

Each and every system generates some waste. If Stalinist grandiose constructions are in this category, what can be made of the follies indulged by rich businessmen, William Randolph Hearst, for example? If some investments in the USSR can be shown to be irrational and pointless, what of those Western investments (say shipyards on the Clyde, here in Scotland) which had to be abandoned and scrapped soon after completion? I shall be arguing that much is indeed wrong with the conventional measurement of Soviet growth and of Soviet output statistics, but it is wrong to ignore altogether the irrationalities of our own system. Thus, to take a quite different example, if we were to criticize (quite properly, too) the confusions of Soviet agricultural prices, we must in no circumstances imply that farm prices in the West accord with any sort of economically rational criteria, as they most certainly do not.

I recall also a conference at which a participant drew on the blackboard a curve representing the production possibilities frontier, and then argued that, because of the inevitably imperfect vision of the central planners, Soviet-type economies cannot reach the frontier. Imperfect information, especially about the future, is something we all have to live with, and no one in the real world has ever seen a production possibilities frontier, and would be hard put even to define it operationally. Thus, let us suppose that there are forty entrepreneurs, and that half of them are above and half below the average of skill and efficiency. To reach the frontier must it be assumed that all of them are above average? This whole approach appears to me fruitless, if not absurd. Western economies evidently suffer today from underutilization of both human and technological productive capacity. Soviet-type economies are usually able to ensure full employment, indeed suffer from the defects associated with excess demand and physical shortage. Both East and West suffer from inflationary pressures, which can get out of hand also in the East, as was the case in Poland. However, the effect of high and unpredictable rates of inflation must be very seriously to distort the operations of the capital market, making long-term considerations risky and unprofitable and encouraging the search for security. Thus, a British pension fund has found that the most advantageous use for its money is to invest in old-master paintings and keep them in cellars. Since Soviet investment decisions did not and do not significantly depend on calculations of profitability, they do not become distorted by uncertainty about rates of inflation — though needless to say they are adversely affected by other aspects of the system of centralized planning.

Then one must make some brief reference to another major obstacle in the way of intersystem comparisons. Let us suppose that all statistical and conceptual obstacles are overcome, that there is no index number problem, and that we can say for certain that output per capita in the Soviet Union is exactly 48.5 percent of that of the United States (the figure is purely the product of my imagination). What role can then be assigned to systemic factors? I have developed this theme elsewhere. [3]

What allowance should be made for natural conditions, such as soil fertility, reliability of rainfall, accessibility of coal seams, navigability of rivers, proximity of iron ore to coking coal and other factors which have nothing whatever to do with centralized planning or Marxism-Leninism? What of social-historical factors, which undoubtedly contribute to differences in productivity and in growth within the same system (e.g., compare West Germany and Japan with Great Britain, or Romania with East Germany)? These factors may be unquantifiable, but we ignore them at our peril. Peter Wiles once wisely remarked that, if we omit something, we give it a weight of zero. Even the most blinkered econometrician, faced with Japan's remarkable economic achievements, would scarcely refuse to take into account Japan's social and political culture in explaining these achievements. Conversely, it makes no sense for us to urge the adoption of the Japanese model in Great Britain, or in the Soviet Union.

The Limitations of Econometric Models

The efficiency, and indeed the dynamic qualities, of Soviet and capitalist systems have been the subject of attention from econometricians. We have, for example, "Sovmod," from the Wharton School at Pennsylvania, various computations of factor productivity, x-efficiency, technical progress, and the measurement of the contribution of imported technology to Soviet growth. The USSR's own Institute of Mathematical Economics has sought to elaborate optimizing models for use by Soviet planners, and tries to devise ways of using programming and the computer to overcome problems that plague centralized planning. In Great Britain we have had the model of the British economy devised by the London Business School and by the Treasury, which influence Mrs. Thatcher's policies, and the rival Cambridge model on the basis of which Wynn Godley and his colleagues recommend import controls as a solution to British problems.

Far be it from me to criticize efforts at quantification or to denounce econometrics. Obviously, statistical analysis is highly desirable. What is less clear is the validity and usefulness of some econometric models. The key question is the way in which certain relationships are specified. Let me illustrate by reference to two examples.

What is the contribution to Soviet growth of imported technology? How does one even start to quantify this? Let us suppose that we know the rate of growth from 1960 to 1980, in total and by sector, and that we have particulars also of imports of machinery plus purchases of know-how in total and by sector for the appropriate years (i.e. with the needed allowance for time-lag), plus information on installation of domestically-produced machinery and Research and Development. The first question that arises is: how does one identify the contribution of technology and Research and Development, domestic and imported (most of it is, of course, domestic) to the rate of growth of these years? One can, of course, allow for the quantitative increase in the labour force, but what of quality, i.e., improved education and qualifications, plus any improvements in organization or planning techniques? (or, of course, conversely, for any decline that may have occurred as a result of faulty reorganizations, or increased vodka consumption. . . .). And since all imported technology is utilized alongside, or together with, Soviet machines and Soviet labour, how can its specific contribution be identified and measured? Suppose that we know that the Soviet chemical industry (say) has grown at above-average rates, and that its share of imported technology has been high. It is probable that the reason both for the high growth and the share in imported technology is that it has benefited from a high priority in the investment plan, and the same high priority has caused it to benefit from best-quality Soviet inputs, the allocation of the best managerial skills, and so on.

This is but one instance of a much more general problem: how to identify the separate contribution of one of several inputs to a given result. It is too easily forgotten that the Cobb-Douglas function is an artificial construct, with limited validity, and that the residual contains a miscellany of items: training, technical progress, managerial efficiency, work incentives, and so on, and that some of these are literally embodied (embedded) in labor and in investment in capital equipment.

Discussion of the contribution of Western technology to Soviet growth is further confused by two other matters. One is the time factor. The other is a failure to distinguish between backwardness and a rational reliance on the international division of labour. Let me enlarge briefly on these two themes.

Let us suppose that a major Soviet investment project, say a pipeline or long-distance electricity transmission, requires an imported machine, not made at all in the USSR, if it is to operate. In the short run, the effect of denying this machine may be to halt the entire project, causing billions of dollars or roubles to be lost through the resultant disruption and delay. Reagan's advisors, anxious to maximize economic damage, may wish to calculate the disruptive effect of unexpected cuts in deliveries, but surely this is not what any economist means by the words marginal productivity.

The point, of course, is the word unexpected. The machines were ordered and were embargoed at the last minute. Let us imagine that a few years earlier, the Soviet planners were considering whether to import them, or to develop domestically produced substitutes. If they had indeed decided to import them, this must be because they had calculated that this was cheaper and/or technologically superior to any available domestic alternative. If they had known in advance that the desired technology would be embargoed, they would presumably have spent more on Research and Development and on producing these or similar items at home, at higher cost and with some delay. The gain from importing the technology could then be measured as the difference between these two alternatives. That the difference was thought to be positive, i.e., that the planners considered it advantageous to decide to import, logically follows from the fact that they did so decide. However, we cannot cost an alternative that was not in fact chosen, and so it is inherently absurd to try to quantify this difference.

The second point is related to the first. A decision to purchase a machine or a patent in another country is not, of itself, evidence of backwardness. There is trade on a massive scale between the most advanced countries, each buying many kinds of machines from others. This is a consequence of international specialization. Has anyone tried to compute the contribution of imported technology to the growth of, say, the French or the Italian economies? And what conclusions would or could be drawn from such a study? When, as was once the case, the USSR or Czechoslovakia tried to make within their borders virtually every kind of machine, this was rightly treated as an economically unsound effort at autarky. Their greater dependence on imports in the last decade is surely evidence of rational economic thinking, though it does render them more vulnerable to embargos. This is, of course, not to deny that there is indeed technological backwardness in the USSR, or that much is not wrong with the quality and effectiveness of Soviet machinery. These matters are the subject of sometimes very sharp criticism in the Soviet press. However, a recent issue of the *Harvard Business Review* noted that West Germany buys far more American patents than does the Soviet Union, a fact which tells us precisely nothing about the relative quality of West German or Soviet Research and Development.

Yet one suspects that misapplied or misunderstood econometric models may be used by Reagan's experts as part of their strategy to wage economic war on the Soviet Union. These models cannot be blamed for another assumption which seems to underlie these experts' advice: that East–West trade somehow benefits "them" more than "us," though the reasoning totally escapes me. How can gains from trade be compared without detailed information on price, quality, delivery dates, interest rates, etc.?

But let us return to the West, and to the London Business School and Cambridge models. Their chief weakness lies in the fact that certain relationships which are specified rest upon a set of assumptions which are not necessarily more plausible than an alternative set, and the outcome can be decisively affected thereby. Thus the Cambridge, or Godley, model incorporates a set of somewhat arbitrary assumptions about the consequences of British import controls: the scale of reprisals by other countries, the supply response of British industry, the effect on the domestic price level and on wage demands by trade unions, are all seen in a very optimistic light. The policy implications become highly dubious if these assumptions are questioned. It is, of course, a matter essentially of judgment, of hunch. The danger is that the unwary may be over-impressed by the econometric apparatus and the formulae, that they be "blinded with science."

The Cambridge model did, however, acquire a reputation for correct gloomy prediction, and it has been recently deprived of funding, for reasons which give rise to suspicion. The more so as the officially-supported monetarist models are open to severe criticism. They too arbitrarily specify some relationships and ignore others. One glaring gap is the lack of any real (as against pseudo) supply-side economics, i.e. concern for the forces which affect the fate of specific industrial sectors' productive capacity. Thus, how can one estimate the supply response, or the stimulus to imports, which would follow from reflation, unless one had information about productive capacity (and competitiveness) of the sectors most likely to be affected. Similarly, the effects of changes in the exchange rate — for example devaluation — are bound to be greatly affected by the capacity (both physical and mental capacity) to take advantage of opportunities. As Schumpeter and Keynes knew, opportunities can be missed.

Twenty years ago I attended a seminar in an American university at which a speaker presented an econometric model of considerable sophistication. Two of its elements were "real wages" and "output." It did not occur to the author of the model that they were in any way connected, that real wages are unlikely to rise if output (at least output of wages goods) falls. In the first prewar years, the British (Labour) government rationed domestic investment, setting up a permit system and denying permits to those firms producing mainly for the home market, while at the same time encouraging British producers of machinery to maximize their exports, i.e., to re-equip and modernize competitors abroad, in apparently total lack of awareness that this might affect future growth rates and competitiveness. The Harrod–Domar model deals with aggregates such as savings and investment, but not at all with the composition of output, even when this (obviously so in a closed economy) must affect growth in the future. At least Marx's simple two-sector model distinguished between producers' goods and consumers' goods.

Oddly enough, a theoretical approach popular among some left-wing economists is also deficient in these respects. Sraffa and the neo-Ricardians have some interesting things to say about the theory of value and factor productivity, on a highly abstract level. But Sraffa's model excludes all interesting problems of micro-economics (no problem of matching supply with demand, or in realizing whatever is produced; i.e., we seem to have perfect information and perfect foresight, and Jean-Baptiste Say is alive and well). The model is static, techniques are given and appear to be unaffected by relative prices, and the distribution of income between wages and profits depends on power and bargaining. Yet in the model investment is financed out of profits, and there seems to be no unemployment of material and human resources. In which case how can wages (real wages) rise without prior investment to make possible the production of the goods of which real wages are the counterpart? And how can investment be profitable if wages are so depressed that the workers cannot purchase the resultant flow of goods? I am baffled as to why these ideas have proved so popular in some quarters. I am all for attacking neo-classical general equilibrium orthodoxy, but surely on grounds of its irrelevance and unreality, and not by means of a theory even more abstract and irrelevant.

Contemporary Western orthodoxy includes the revival of the concept of crowding out. It is held that state expenditure (e.g., on investment) must have the effect of reducing the amounts available to private enterprise. Fifty years ago this argument puzzled Keynes, since if this were so, then any investment, private or public, could crowd out other investments. In Britain, with massive unemployment, this bordered on the ridiculous, in 1982 as in 1932. This approach, paradoxically, only makes sense in Eastern Europe. There, for reasons analyzed at length by Kornai [4] and other writers, there is a physical supply constraint, and investments are delayed because the resources needed to complete them are unavailable; thus, the diversion of funds to any project adversely affects others. In the West, at a time of recession and great underutilization of capacity, this is surely nonsense. Asked to explain it, an intelligent colleague pointed to the contrast in assumptions made in micro and macro economics. In the former, opportunity-cost rules under silently assumed conditions of full resource utilization, while the latter makes quite different assumptions. Which has not prevented both from being taught by the same economists.

Econometric models of their nature cannot readily handle quality. They also have problems with human motivation. It has to be assumed that any set

of human beings will respond identically to the same stimuli. The mathematical methods used find the assumption of maximization convenient, though it
is an untestable axiom. We are familiar with the now sizeable literature around
the alternative assumption of "satisficing." Similar controversies arise in respect of the behaviour patterns of management in Eastern Europe, and there
too the outcome of various measures (e.g., reforms to incentive and bonus
schemes) can have results quite different to those which the authors of the
measures anticipated.

There is seldom one identifiable maximand. Nor is money income the sole
or even necessarily the main motive governing action. Kornai very correctly
points to the motive of professional satisfaction, of doing one's job properly
— whether it is that of manager, university professor, a civil service depart-
mental head or theatrical producer, or whatever. In any hierarchy one is also
concerned with pleasing one's superiors. There are other objectives, other
constraints, and some of these matter and, therefore, affect behavior more than
others. Thus, again borrowing a thought from Kornai, because of the consequences of long-lasting shortages, the producer or supplier can usually safely
neglect the desires and interests of the purchaser (be he/she another manager
or an ordinary citizen), and the purchaser knows that it is inadvisable to make
use of his legal powers, whatever they may be, in an effort to get satisfaction
from the supplier, since the longer term consequences of loss of the latter's
goodwill could be disastrous. Therefore, the effects of reform measures designed to stimulate quality and increase the influence of the consumer over the
producer have often been disappointing.

Similarly the efforts repeatedly made to check excess demand, especially
excessive investment starts, have as repeatedly been frustrated. The reasons are
once again complex and multiple. Motives for trying to incorporate one's
projects in the investment plan are very strong. They arise primarily from
commitment to and knowledge of the needs of the sector (or area) for which
one is responsible. Success may, by increasing the size of one's empire, also
enhance one's standing, influence, salary. The point is made correctly that
investments in practice are often free to their recipients (as in the case for
government-financed investments also in the West, for instance in roads,
schools, hospitals, colleges). The imposition of a charge has little effect, because in some cases it is merely a transfer from one state pocket to another,
and/or the charge is incorporated in the officially-fixed prices of the goods
concerned. And if in the end the rate of return is well below that planned, or
is negative, it is unclear who should be held responsible for this. In some
instances the extra charge can actually act as a stimulus rather than the
reverse. In the Soviet economy, for instance, some plans are expressed in
aggregate gross roubles, and (until 1982, when there has been a change to

"normed value-added") there was every incentive for enterprise management to overstate costs in the process of getting their prices confirmed.

But at the same time there was a tendency to underestimate the costs of investment projects, at the stage at which approval was sought from higher authority. A number of Soviet sources have noted that such understatement is of the order of 30–40 percent or even more. It is also clear that it will be easier to obtain investment funds for projects already begun, and hence the attempt to start as many as possible. For all these reasons, the efforts of the central planners to cut back the number of projects so that they match the resources available have seldom met with success. Soviet econometric models therefore need to have built into them a behavioural-institutional pattern which does not lend itself to quantitative-mathematical treatment.

Recent Soviet work on excess demand, for instance a fascinating article by Belkin and Ivanter [5], examines with care the sources of financing of such demand. Sure enough, one does not need to be a monetarist to appreciate that, in the end, the surplus money (surplus, that is, to the goods supposedly available to buy with it) must find its way into enterprise bank accounts and citizens' liquid assets. The Soviet critics direct their attention to bank credits, to the fact that some payments by enterprises into the state budget are fictitious, in the sense that the gaps they leave in the enterprises' accounts have to be covered by credits from the State Bank. Credits can also be obtained on the basis of stocks held. These stocks are sometimes composed of unsaleable and unwanted goods, or stocks of hoarded materials. Finally, wages are paid out in full even when the goods planned to be made by the workers concerned are not in fact made (e.g., because materials fail to arrive), consumers' goods plans are significantly underfulfilled, while incomes rise in close conformity to plans which envisage a closer balance between effective demand and actual supply than is ever realized. Price adjustments, if made, are insufficient to bridge the gap. Needless to say, a monetarist explanation of such phenomena would be even more superficial than purely monetarist accounts of inflation in the West. Nonetheless, it would be interesting and instructive to examine how money supply, including bank credits, percolates through the economy in East and West.

In the Eastern model, incomes are planned and controlled, prices are controlled, investment demand is planned, producers' goods are (mainly) administratively allocated, output is matched by planned and rationed inputs, and control by the banking system is supposed to ensure that no extra payments are made or unauthorized demands on resources occur. Yet the action of intermediate units of authority (ministries, regions, management, local party secretaries, etc.) continuously reproduces a situation of excess demand, imbalance, shortage. To this the financial flows make some contribution, worthy of careful study. One hypothesis, put forward by Igor Birman [6], is that the budget itself is in deficit, because part of the revenues take the form of advances from the banking system. This is a variant of the explanation advanced by Belkin and Ivanter, who also — but in a different way — assert that the budget surplus does not really exist.

There is a growing literature on comparative economic systems. One would like to see some on the comparative futility of orthodox economic theory. Marx's political economy, primarily designed to analyse production relations and "lay bare" exploitation under capitalism, at best is no guide to economic rationality under any sort of socialism, and frequently actually misleads. Thus, it has contributed to a longstanding neglect of use-value, and of much-needed valuation of land, capital (past labour) and of time. While Western economics, when it does not seek shelter from the real world in mathematical abstractions, has spawned theories, such as crude monetarism and the equally crude "rational expectations" assumption, which are actively contributing to the deepening of an already alarming crisis.

It is left principally to intelligent journalists to make the obvious point that, while one firm or one country might benefit from higher competitiveness as a result of a fall in its labor costs, there is bound to be an adverse effect on demand if incomes are depressed (and unemployment increases) in all countries. Indeed, far from benefiting capitalists at labour's expense, as Soviet analysts claim, the current Western orthodoxy greatly increases the number of bankruptcies and reduces profits, and destabilizes the third world much more effectively than decades of Soviet propaganda could possibly do. Reaganomics must be seen in the Kremlin with a sort of joyful incredulity, indeed as a relief from observing the flounderings and disorders of their own economy. The patent inadequacies of Western conventional theory, and the disarray of many a Western economy, are aspects of intersystem comparisons which we certainly should not overlook.

Diseconomies of scale and their statistical consequences

But when all is said, and all allowances made, the fact remains that the Soviet model has run into serious practical difficulties, and their theories seem to be either irrelevant or act as an obstacle to the search for a solution to these difficulties. This is not the place to analyse them at length. Many if not most are, in one way or another, consequences of diseconomies of scale. It was an illusion, but one firmly rooted in the Marxist tradition, that it is possible to envisage society, or "the associated producers" meaningfully deciding what and how to produce and distribute to satisfy society's needs. It is another well-established illusion that this could be "done simply, without this so-called value," to cite Engels's *Anti-Duhring*.

The immense complexity of the task of operating a modern industrial economy, in the absence of "horizontal" or market-type relations between its parts, is now evident to all. Less evident to some incorrigible dogmatists is that the elimination of commodity production necessarily implies centralization, and that centralization necessarily requires a complex bureaucracy to coordinate and manage the separate parts. For who below the level of the centre can judge what are the "needs of society" and ensure that the needed means are provided? And how indeed is the center itself to judge? If the object is to maximize, or even just to increase, "the socially useful effect," or use-values, how are they to be determined and measured? By whom, by what criteria, in what units?

The sheer scale of the center's task — millions of different products, hundreds of thousands of units of production and distribution — excludes any serious consideration of detail by the center, save in a very few top-priority sectors (oil, say, and nuclear submarines). The micro economy is, *de facto,* decentralized. The product mix is to a considerable extent determined by the producers, but there is no horizontal (market) link with the users. Responsibility is to one's hierarchical superiors, up the production line of responsibility. Matters are exacerbated by two other factors of great practical importance: one is the chronic existence of shortages, which gives power to the supplier over the customer. The other is the existence of what might be called administrative monopoly for producers' goods. There may be ten or twenty producers of (say) ball-bearings, but the user can only obtain them from the source designated by the material-supply plan. The result is, inevitably, a tendency to adjust the product mix to plan-fulfilment statistical aggregates, rather than to the needs of the user.

Other consequences, which we will not examine here, include the unintentional stimulation of waste, as when a plan target expressed in tons causes metal goods to be unnecessarily heavy, or when plans for the construction industry are measured in terms of roubles spent, which encourages the profligate use of expensive building materials. Examples of these two "deviations", culled from the Soviet press, would fill a sizeable book. There are also inconsistencies in the plan itself, arising from the impossibly large task of coordinating the activities of numerous planning and administrative bodies.

Efforts to cope with the sheer scale of the needed computation by the use of computers and programming techniques have not had much success. Kantorovich earned his Nobel prize, and other Soviet mathematicians too are among the world's best. Kantorovich had some trouble reconciling his "objectively determined valuations," which reflect relative scarcity and opportunity-costs in relation to the chosen programme, with a dogmatically understood labour theory of value, but this does not appear to have been a significant obstacle, compared with two others, one theoretical and one practical.

The theoretical problem concerns the definition of the objective function for the economy as a whole. What is one maximizing, and why? Soviet discussions on this question are well worthy of study, but they remain on an abstract plane. The other is, yet again, scale. Simply to collect the information needed to program the computer would take far too long, "thousands of years" according to one Soviet academician, even if those who supplied the information would be wholly truthful. Many socialists have no notion of how vastly complex the economic system is, once disaggregated into its micro parts and aspects. Two (far simpler) examples might help to get this into perspective. Even a moderate chess player can do well against a chess-playing computer (unless the computer is given far too much time to "think," and even then it would lose against a good player); yet a chess-board has only sixty-four squares, the rules have remained the same since the sixteenth century and the objective function is clear and unambiguous. The trouble is, as Botvinnik, the former world champion, has pointed out, that the number of possible moves on a board during a game of average length are represented by the figure of 10^{128}, "or more than the number of words spoken by all humans since the building of the pyramids." [7] There are said to be 34 billion possible variations in a Rubik cube, so that no computer can cope with it — though 15-year-old boys and girls have been able to solve the cube in minutes. Furthermore, neither chess nor Rubik cubes contain the quality dimension, which is rather important for goods and services.

Value, Volume, Price

Which brings me to a point which seems to me of key importance: value, evaluation, the meaning of value (monetary) aggregates. Here the ambiguities of Marx's labour theory must be referred to. While recognizing that, to have value, goods must possess use-value of some sort, Marx's whole emphasis was on quantity of labour, i.e., human effort, albeit "socially necessary" at the average level of technique existing. This he needed for his theory of exploitation, but it has its inconveniencies. Thus, a French Marxist, Alain Lipietz, noted that (roughly) the volume of output in France trebled from 1950 to 1975 with no significant increase in either the size of the labour force or labour's share in national income, so that (according to him) the value of output and of labour-power was unaltered! A Soviet economist very properly pointed out that one cannot aim at maximizing labour-values, because this can be achieved only by maximizing human effort, while (naturally) one wishes to obtain a given result with least effort. One recalls also the analytical confusion caused by the concept of "unequal exchange," when an hour of labour in India is thought somehow to be of equal value to a much more productive hour of labour in the United States or Japan. These, it may be said, are examples of misapplication of labour-value theory; one ought not to use it to measure growth (when value by definition would equal the increase in the volume of human effort), or for international comparisons. Agreed. So let us not blame Marx, and turn instead to Soviet prices and what they represent.

Let us take two examples: a drilling machine and a pair of trousers. Their prices are determined by a central pricing bureau by reference to costs. Demand plays no role, either in theory or in practice. Consequently, nor does the evaluation by the user of their qualities, in relation to other machines or clothes.

Marxists are sometimes fond of talking about "the contradiction between exchange-value and use value" under capitalism. This contradiction is resolved, in the capitalist model, in the marketplace. Value in use (the speed, reliability, accuracy of the drilling-machine, the styling and other qualities of the trousers) affect the desire to pay, therefore the price, therefore the profitability of production, and therefore also the behaviour of the producer. Allowing for all the familiar distortions of the real (as distinct from the ideal) market, the fact remains that utility is a significant factor which has its effect on price. Managers and ordinary consumers have a range of choice, and their preferences do (within limits, to be sure) affect both price and output.

Soviet prices can be seen in one of two ways. Either as cost-plus prices, which, as Valovoi once pointed out in *Pravda*, "measure effort and not result." Or they can be regarded as "planners' evaluations." That is to say, the planners decide that the machine is worth 10,000 roubles, the trousers are worth 10 roubles. One refers back to Marx's notion of "the associated producers" deciding between alternatives on the basis of "socially useful effect."

I have already asked the question: how? who? How is it that Marx did not ask himself such questions? Agnes Heller answered as follows: "because in his opinion the category of interest will be irrelevant to the society of the future, there will therefore be no group interest or conflict of interest." [8] This is almost a classic instance of utopian reductionism, using the latter term to designate reducing complex phenomena, such as human disagreement about the use of resources and of time, to their alleged essence, this being a function of class divisions in society. Such an approach in no way helps us to see clearly how, in a socialist society, use-value can be identified.

There are, it is true, some dimensions of quality and use-value which can be centrally determined, because they are precisely measurable: calorific content of fuel, say, or tensile strength. However, in most instances it cannot be a remote center which can determine *ex ante* the quality-in-use of this or that good or service. Returning to the two examples, it is at the factory where the drilling machine is to be used that qualities can be evaluated. Is it accurate enough for the jobs it must do? Is it convenient for the worker to use? Does its effectiveness measure up to its cost, are spare parts available for needed repairs and maintenance? Does the wearer of the trousers, boyfriend or girlfriend like it?

It is not a matter of counterposing planners' preferences and consumers' (users') preferences. One can seldom envisage planners *qua* planners having microeconomic preferences. Soviet planners undoubtedly desire the production of an effective drilling machine, as well as the sort of trousers that cause their wearers to be pleased. If, in the process of trying to fulfil plans in roubles or in tons, what is actually produced does not accord with user requirements, this is almost invariably unintentional, a consequence of a malfunction, one which is itself a consequence of diseconomies of scale. The center does not and cannot know what sort of drill or trousers are required by their would-be users. Their requirements cannot be directly communicated — no market — and so are, so to speak, lost in the process of aggregation.

All this has profound consequences. As Brezhnev and many more junior personages have repeatedly said, the final result is what matters. Yet production is all too frequently concerned with statistical effect, which causes particularly unfortunate results in the case of intermediate goods and services. Let me give a few examples taken at random from the Soviet press. Transport services are planned in ton-kilometers. Therefore, every effort is made to avoid carrying light loads for short distances, while heavy loads are carried for long distances, although it is evident that economic use of goods transport would be achieved by minimizing journey lengths. There are repeated reports of agricultural service organizations (providing repair services, pesticides, and other chemicals) performing not the work needed to ensure a good harvest, but that which counts most towards the plan-fulfilment measure applicable to these organizations.

As we have seen, construction firms increase their output and their productivity by spending as much as possible, since this is how these are measured. *Per contra,* economy of materials has had the paradoxical effect of reducing growth rates and productivity, whether these are measured in tons or in roubles. While the Soviet and Western definitions of national income (or GNP) differ, the former omitting many services, both count any activity which falls within their respective definitions, regardless of its actual usefulness. Suppose we build a steelworks and do not use it, or Soviet lorries proceed on long and useless journeys — this is included in our respective statistics as output.

As I stressed at the beginning, waste is by no means a purely Soviet phenomenon. However, they seem to have far more stimuli towards what might be called operational waste, i.e., toward economically inefficient means to achieve given ends. They have no effective means of overcoming the so-called contradiction between use-value and exchange-value; there being no link between use-value and price, no direct influence on price on the part of the consumer-/user, far less user choice, no operationally functional means of determining use-value. The planners can be influenced in their decisions of course, by observed shortages, complaints, fear of riots, or reports from the retail trade organs. But the link is not with or through price. Such a link does have its defects, just as competition engenders waste (and lack of competition engenders indifference to customer requirements). Nonetheless, I suggest that two conclusions or hypotheses be put forward.

One hypothesis is that there is a much bigger difference, in the Soviet system as opposed to our system, between the volume of activities undertaken and the final result. This finds some statistical expression in two ways. First, living standards in a Soviet-type economy are substantially lower than may be deduced from comparisons of national incomes, GNP or aggregate industrial production. The second is the known and frequently-commented fact that to produce a given product (machinery, for example) the Soviets use much more metal than the Americans. This is the natural and logical consequence of the setting of quantitative plan targets for intermediate goods and services.

The second hypothesis is that the final product tends to be ill-adapted to the users' needs because microeconomic criteria are geared to plan-fulfilment aggregates. This affects both capital goods and consumer goods. Many reports speak of the additional expense incurred by firms in adapting machines and components to the purposes for which they are needed, while the citizen frequently has to make do with substitutes. In such cases, the monetary value of the goods concerned ought to be amended downwards. (These considerations apply with particular force to the USSR, and need modification when, as in Hungary and Yugoslavia, the role of market forces is significant.)

How far downward? We do not know, and we have no methodology to help us. Or rather, such methodology as exists (hedonic indexes, for instance) cannot be (or is not) applied in practice. Let me illustrate the problem with an example, couched in somewhat abstract form, but of evident practical significance. Let us assume that a Soviet-type economy is reformed along Hungarian lines, and that, in consequence, users can now have a much wider choice, and prices are influenced by demand and reflect use-value. Quality rises, there is more concern with user satisfaction. What statistical effect would this have? Most if not all of the gain would be statistically invisible. Suppose that citizens bought a thousand shirts at ten roubles each, but the design was unattractive and the shirts shrank after being laundered. Suppose, after a successful reform, the citizens buy a thousand shirts that please them better, which do not shrink, but which still cost ten roubles each. Growth: zero. Welfare: up.

A not irrelevant aside concerns price indices and new products. In all countries, this creates a measurement problem. How does one compare the prices of different models through time? In an index based on 1960, what is the 1960 price of a good which was not made at all in that year? The outcome is, at best, an approximation. Hedonic indexes would fully reflect changes in quality characteristics where the model changes, but the weights to be assigned each quality characteristic are somewhat arbitrary, and all the relevant details are seldom known to the non-official (or perhaps official) statisticians.

There is also the very important factor of consumer demand. If a new model is dearer, but its quality is proportionately higher and the consumer prefers the better-quality model, then the price index would and should be unaffected. It is quite another matter if the new model is introduced primarily to evade price control, and production of the cheaper version is stopped even though it is in demand. Under conditions of a sellers' market, this is a device which can succeed. Prices thus go up even while it is claimed that they do not, the price index understates price increases, the volume index similarly overstates the volume increase.

This happens both with producers' goods and consumers' goods. In a recent article, using Soviet sources, I argued that the machinery and construction price indices were distorted, that actual prices and costs were rising, and that consequently the apparent rise in the volume of investment financing probably represented an actual fall in the real terms. [9] Despite some criticism [10], the evidence supports me, as witness the following extract from an article in E.K.O. (the journal of the Siberian Institute of Economics), No. 3 of 1982, by K. Val'tukh. After referring to "an absolute decline in productive capital investments in real terms" in the quinquennium 1976–80, he goes on: "In monetary terms the volume of capital investments . . . appears to have risen (in 1976–80). However, the costs rise *(udorozhaniye)* was even faster. The real volume of investments is determined not by its financing but by its results" (pp. 19–20). Many examples may be cited to show that new machines are much dearer than the ones they replace, with a disproportionately small effect on productivity. The customer has these expensive machines foisted on him and has no choice. Meanwhile, the official index for machinery shows that prices have been falling, since the index is based on that segment of production which continues unchanged through time.

True enough, in the Western economies one finds instances of spurious innovation, though because the motive is neither evasion of price control nor pressure to reach aggregate plan targets, the effect on price and growth statistics is probably neutral; and the existence of real or potential competition limits the power of the producer. Thus, Western firms would simply reject a new machine which is so expensive that its use causes costs of production to rise. All in all, we should therefore expect aggregate Soviet price and volume indices to show some distortion, respectively downward and upward, and quantities and values of any but a totally homogeneous product would tend to overstate their "socially useful effect."

Of course, human satisfaction is a multidimensional thing. Thus, success in obtaining a good in short supply affords a pleasure which is not available to those of us who can buy this good freely in the shops at any time. Nor can we experience the feeling of pride in having a pass to a special shop, where goods can be found which ordinary mortals cannot buy, if the said ordinary mortals can also buy them. (What use, then, is a pass to the special shop?) This is no trivial or laughing matter. One of the many causes of the relative stability of the Soviet regime, despite the many shortages, is that a large proportion of the citizens have developed all sorts of connections and links through which they succeed in obtaining scarce goods and services, by all sorts of devious routes.

Job Security, "Producers Preferences"

Finally, what of the important factor of unemployment, and its converse, security of employment? Evidence from emigres supports the view that the Soviet citizen greatly values a virtual guarantee of a job. The chronic shortage of labour confers certain advantages on the worker: management is unable to enforce strict discipline, and sometimes resorts to side-payments and unearned bonuses in order to persuade workers to stay. Work tempos are slack, indeed a sort of go-slow is tolerated, despite official propaganda. This is one cause, among others, of comparatively modest productivity and living standards. Some reformers in Eastern Europe advocate a moderate amount of unemployment, partly to achieve greater flexibility (how, under full employment, does one adjust to the unexpected), partly to make it easier to discipline the labour force. They argue that this is essential for greater efficiency, and so for higher living standards. There may indeed be a trade-off here. But more seriously, unemployment in the West has reached threateningly high levels, and the spread of labour-saving technology combined with cyclical factors can bring about a social crisis which the pursuit of private profit can only exacerbate. What then? People may in the end tolerate misemployment and low wages if unemployment plus social disorders appear to be the alternative.

Perhaps one could end by referring to the French thinker, Andre Gorz. In a recent book, challengingly entitled *Adieux au proletariat,* Gorz strongly criticizes the traditional Marxist notion that the working class would redeem mankind, and that large-scale industry is the route to the liberation of Man.

No, (he argues), large-scale industry is alienating. "Small is beautiful;" small-scale should be preferred, or do-it-yourself, save in those cases where economies of scale are of great importance — like the generation of electricity. In my own new book, [11], I develop the theme of "producers' preferences."

While the user should have the determining voice in deciding *what* to produce, the producer's voice needs to be heard in deciding *how*. I use the argument in connection with agriculture: if peasants or farmers prefer the family unit and dislike large state and collective farms, then, unless the latter are overwhelmingly more efficient, their preferences should be decisive, and they should not be expropriated or collectivized forcibly by a socialist police. Such arguments have a wider application.

Work satisfaction is, in its own way, as important as consumer welfare. Does this point towards some kind of self-management? What is there to learn from the performance of the Yugoslav economy, and the attitude of its workers? And what of the environment, of ecology, of resource conservation? In respect of these last three questions the Soviet record has hitherto been anything but creditable, as numerous articles and discussions attest (the last one in the journal E.K.O. No. 3, 1982). This is explicable partly by the priority of production, partly by the fact that the Soviet system finds it no easier than does ours to internalize externalities.

References

1. Rosefielde S., "The First 'Great Leap Forward' Reconsidered: Lessons of Solzhenitsyn's *Gulag Archipelago.*" *Slavic Review,* vol. 39, no. 4 (December 1980), pp. 559–587.
2. Davies R. W., and S. G. Wheatcroft. "Steven Rosefielde's *Kliukva.*" *Slavic Review,* vol. 39, no. 4 (December 1980), pp. 593–602.
3. Nove A., *The Soviet Economic System.* London: George Allen and Unwin, 1980, pp. 372–380.
4. Kornai J., *Economics of Shortage.* Amsterdam: North Holland, 1981.
5. Belkin and Ivanter. *Voprosy ekonomiki,* no. 6, 1982.
6. Birman I., *Secret Incomes of the Soviet State Budget.* The Hague: Martinus Nijhoff, 1981.
7. *Pravda,* November 24, 1977.
8. Heller A., *The Theory of Need in Marx.* London, 1978, pp. 124–125.
9. Nove A., "A Note on Growth, Investment and Price Indices." *Soviet Studies,* vol. 33, no. 1 (January 1981), pp. 142–145.
10. Cohn S., "Response to Alec Nove." *Soviet Studies,* vol. 33, no. 2 (April 1981), pp. 296–299.
11. Nove A., *The Economics of Feasible Socialism.* London: George Allen and Unwin, 1983.

4 IS MARKET SOCIALISM EFFICIENT?

Deborah Duff Milenkovitch

Introduction

Is market socialism efficient? Why focus on this seemingly narrow neoclassical question? There are two reasons. First, efficiency is the question the profession has asked about socialism, and the neoclassical paradigm is the method of obtaining an answer. While there have been some explorations in the general literature on socialist planning, and some attention paid to issues of equity, the literature on market socialism as an alternative to centrally planned socialism and to capitalism has focussed on efficiency. Second, there is both substantive and methodological confusion about market socialism.

There are two different systems labelled market socialism, and two different theories of market socialism based on them. One is worker managed socialism (which has its counterpart in Yugoslavia) and the other is decentrally planned socialism (which has its counterpart in Hungary). Each theory addresses the

The author would like to thank Alice Amsden, David Arsen, Stuart Brown, André Burgstaller, Duncan Foley, Nicholas Rango and Andrew Zimbalist for their comments on earlier drafts, and Patricia Chick, Saul Estrin, Diane Flaherty, Estelle James, Frederick Pryor and Stephen Sacks for helpful suggestions. All remaining errors are the responsibility of the author.

same question, Is market socialism efficient? Each goes about getting its answers by means of very different simplifying assumptions.

The use of the term market socialism to describe both focusses on the aspects which differentiate both of them from capitalism (social ownership of the means of production) and from central planning (the use of price and quantity information from the periphery to solve the allocation problem). However, it obscures the differences between the two and obscures the different analytical methods by which each reaches its conclusions about efficiency. By focusing on efficiency we can disclose the dissimilarities in both system and method.

Part one introduces the two forms of market socialism and outlines the methodology employed to assess efficiency in each. The second part explores efficiency in the worker managed economy, while the third section addresses efficiency in the decentrally planned economy. Finally, the last section emphasizes the importance of comparing the two theories and suggests aspects in our present theoretical constructs that should be modified for more fruitful and satisfying conclusions.

Theories of Market Socialism

Lange's Theory of Market Socialism

The second half of the nineteenth century witnessed a keen fascination with socialism and the possible organization of the socialist economy. Particular controversy surrounded Marx' and Engels' writings on the subject implying that the market, value and price had no role to play in the socialist economy.[1] At the same time, the marginal revolution in economics was in full sway, pointing to the indispensible links between prices — the ratio of opportunity costs — and optimal resource allocation. The twentieth century has seen many efforts to subject socialism to marginal analysis, both to prove that socialism is efficient, and that it is not.

As early as 1908, Enrico Barone[2] applied the formal general equilibrium analysis of Walras and Pareto to the socialist economy. He concluded that the socialist economy had the same problem to solve as did the private enterprise economy. For identical tastes, technologies, endowments and environments, the optimal allocation of resources (at which no one could be made better off without making someone else worse off) was identical. At the optimal allocation, the ratios of opportunity costs are identical for the socialist and the private enterprise economy. In addition, these imputed prices have the same characteristics as the market prices formed in a competitive, free market economy.

Von Mises[3] continued the debate in the 1920s, arguing that while the nature of the solution was clear, it would be impossible to achieve in a socialist economy. It was obviously not possible to solve the millions of equations implicit in Barone's approach. Nor could socialist markets solve the problem. With no private ownership of the means of production and no competition between producers because the state would be the sole producer, there would be no markets for producers' goods. Without markets for producers' goods, there would be no prices for such goods and, hence, no knowledge of the opportunity costs. Therefore, there was no possibility for rational choice among the means of production. Socialism could not be efficient.

In order to refute von Mises' claim that rational calculation was impossible in the socialist economy, Oskar Lange wrote his famous essay, "On the Economic Theory of Socialism,"[4] in 1936. He described the operation of a market socialist economy not as a blueprint for socialism nor as a proof of socialism's superiority over capitalism (although he suggested both lines of argument) but to prove the possibility of rational calculation and efficiency in a socialist economy.

Lange postulated an economy in which information about consumer preferences for leisure and goods and information about the production function are dispersed at the periphery. This information is both too costly for the center to collect and too important for the center to ignore if its goal is optimal resource allocation. Optimal resource allocation requires three conditions.[5] First, there must be an exchange optimum, which requires that the subjective rates of substitution in consumption for each pair of goods be equal to the rates of substitution in exchange. This obviously requires knowledge of the preferences of individuals. Second, there is the condition of technical efficiency, which requires being on the production possibilities frontier. This is obviously not possible without knowing the production possibilities of each producing unit. Finally, when the subjective rates of substitution between pairs of goods are just equal to the objective rates of transformation of all pairs of goods, the economy is said to be at the optimal resource allocation. At this Pareto optimal point, given the initial endowments of resources, preferences and technology, no one can be made better off without making another individual worse off. The task for the socialist planners is how, if information about preferences and technology is dispersed at the periphery, to get to that allocation.

Lange proposes the establishment of ordinary markets for labor and consumer goods, allowing for both individual choice and consumer sovereignty in determining the output mix and the labor supply. His Central Planning Board supersedes consumer sovereignty in setting the rate of investment. Lange's key point is not to prove the suboptimality of atomistic determination of the rate of saving, although he points to elements of such a proof, but rather to establish a framework of preferences. Given preferences, endowments, technology and environment, he then shows that it is possible to obtain rational prices in a socialist economy.

Lange posits three sets of agents: socialist enterprise managers who operate existing plants, socialist industry managers who make decisions about the entry and exit of plants, and the Central Planning Board which determines the rate of savings and functions as the Walrasian auctioneer in the markets for intermediate goods. Enterprise managers follow three rules: (1) accept existing prices as parameters; (2) discover the lowest possible short run marginal cost curve for the enterprise; (3) produce at that output at which marginal cost equals price. The industry managers follow the same rules except that their task is to identify the long run marginal cost curve for the industry. The Central Planning Board adjusts prices whenever demand and supply are not in equilibrium. It also determines the rate of saving in any given period and, hence, the supply of capital. It adjusts the price of capital so that the demands of the industry managers are brought into equilibrium with the supply. Profits (if any) and capital rental fees are the income of society as a whole and are disposed of by the Central Planning Board in accordance with some collective choice mechanism.

Lange thus provides a scheme for obtaining the rational allocation of intermediate goods in a socialist economy. Lange's scheme, viewed as a means of obtaining equilibrium, has at least one conceptual advantage over the actual market economy. The Central Planning Board can be viewed as the Walrasian auctioneer.[6] Unlike the private market economy with no auctioneer, no transactions would take place until the Central Planning Board announces the equilibrium prices.

Lange succeeded in demonstrating the compatibility of efficiency and socialism in a static world in which managers follow the rules. What happens when externalities, absence of competition, self-interested behavior and dynamic uncertainty are introduced will be examined in the third section of this essay.

Certainly Lange's market socialism does not follow the classical definition of a market economy, namely commodity production, in which individual producers, motivated by profit, produce for exchange. If this is market socialism, in just what sense is it a market economy? Do we mean the existence of actual markets for labor and consumer goods? Or the existence of consumer sovereignty over the leisure and goods choices? Do we mean the replication of the competitive market solution, as Barone's example suggests? Or the

establishment of a means for eliciting the production and preference information in informationally decentralized environments? Or is it the establishment
of an elicitation scheme which, like the price and quantity information in
competitive market economies, is informationally efficient and decentralized?[7]
Whatever the precise sense in which Lange's socialism is a market economy,
the term itself is bound to be confusing because we do not know precisely what
is meant and because it certainly is not a market economy in the everyday,
commodity production sense of the term.

The Theory of Worker Managed Market Socialism

There is another market socialism, the worker managed socialist economy.
The concept of the worker managed economy has dual, and very distinct,
philosophical origins represented in the writings of Proudhon and Gramsci.[8]
Proudhon starts from the notion of the equality of every member of society.
If each member of society has an equal share of the social wealth and equal
conditions for producing it, then workers enter voluntary contracts of association among equals. When these associated producers exchange their products
on competitive markets, products requiring equal amounts of labor and capital
will be exchanged equally. No advantage accrues to anyone from unequal
exchange of equivalents. Proudhon sees production for exchange on the market as central, along with society's provisions for ensuring equality in the
production process itself through equal access to capital.

Gramsci starts from the centrality of the activity of production to human
life. He does not view the division of labor per se as alienating. The division
of labor means that each person's task is equally necessary and that collabora-
tion among producers is a necessary aspect of life. For Gramsci, it is the
work-place that is focal. It serves as the basis of political organization as well.
Each factory would send delegates to industrial and regional councils which,
in turn, send delegates to national councils where the national economic plan
is prepared. The market had no place for Gramsci. Such a system provided
equality, in the sense that each person was equally necessary in the production
process, freedom in the ability to express the social aspect of one's human
nature fully, and solidarity with one's fellow men through membership in the
immediate and in the larger community of producers.

Elements of both Proudhon's notion of the worker-cum-capital joined in
mutualist association producing for exchange in the market and Gramsci's
concept of worker as producer collaborating with his fellow men in the workplace and joined in solidarity with other workers through interlocking councils
are to be found in the experience of Yugoslavia, the only worker managed

economy. The market concept prevails in the system established by the economic reforms of 1965[9] while the system of delegates to negotiate national planning targets was more prominent in the system described by the Constitution of 1974.[10] This essay will treat only the market oriented version of worker managed socialism.

The worker managed enterprise of the Yugoslav type is closely related to the producers' cooperative and the kibbutz. There are, however, important and instructive differences. In a producers' cooperative, the members own the equity capital and are both the workers and the full risk bearers. In the kibbutz, the assets belong to the community as a whole. However, the concept of community is broader than that in a producers' cooperative and is usually conceived of as having an existence that extends beyond the individuals in it at any point in time. Unlike the producers' cooperative, present members of the kibbutz may wish to invest for the benefits of the community as a whole including future generations. Unlike both the kibbutz and the producers' cooperative, the workers in a socialist worker managed enterprise do not own the assets. Assets are owned by society as a whole and entrusted to the worker managers. Workers have the right to usufruct, that is, to use but not to deplete the assets, for the duration of their employment with the firm.

In all three cases workers, organized into firms, make the decisions and reap the rewards. The worker managed enterprise fits somewhat uncomfortably between the kibbutz and the producers' cooperative. It neither owns the assets like a producers' cooperative, although it bears some of the risk and is a residual income recipient, nor does it have the same sense of community and willingness to invest for the future as does the kibbutz. As we shall see, the institutional arrangements pose problems concerning the motivation for the worker managed enterprise to add either to its stock of capital or to its labor force and, hence, concerning both its efficiency and its long run viability.

Is Market Socialism Efficient?

The primary question addressed to both types of market socialism is, is it efficient? Over what environments is market socialism efficient? But the simplifying assumptions adopted in each case are quite different. Langean socialism assumes that the enterprises operate efficiently by establishing rules for managers to follow which are identical with efficiency. Langean enterprises are efficient because the managers are directed to be efficient. The theory then asks how the dispersed information about technology and preferences can be elicited so as to permit the establishment of a socially efficient resource allocation. Worker managed socialism assumes that product markets coordinate the activities of individually technically efficient agents in such a way that the outcome is, from a social viewpoint, both technically efficient and Pareto efficient. It asks, over what range of environments is the worker managed enterprise itself technically efficient? If market prices correctly reflect the social scarcity of goods and services, when will the worker managed enterprise equate the value of the marginal products of its factors of production to the social scarcity price of those factors?

With this overview of the two theories of market socialism and the two sets of simplifying assumptions made to assess efficiency, we now move to the systematic examination of efficiency in the worker managed economy.

Worker Managed Market Socialism

I will first treat the theory of the worker managed firm in the short run, the long run and finally in general equilibrium. I will then look at the problem of risk bearing. Next I will examine the macroeconomics of the worker managed economy. I will briefly survey the empirical evidence on the microeconomic and macroeconomic predictions of the model. The last section presents a critical assessment of the strengths and limitations of the methods used to assess the efficiency of an economy composed of worker managed enterprises.

The Short Run

Framework of the Analysis. The primary method used to establish the efficiency of the worker managed economy has been to compare its behavior with that of the capitalist entrepreneurial firm. I will here make the additional comparison with the Langean socialist enterprise. The capitalist entrepreneurial firm is the familar firm of microeconomic theory. The capitalist firm, by assumption, maximizes total profits. In a competitive environment with no uncertainty and no externalities, the capitalist firm uses resources efficiently and an economy composed of such firms is both technically efficient and Pareto efficient. The Langean socialist firm, by assumption, follows the three rules noted above and as a consequence always produces efficiently, i.e., where price is equal to marginal cost. In a competitive environment with no uncertainty and no externalities, the Langean firm uses resources efficiently and an economy composed of such firms is both technically efficient and Pareto efficient. The worker managed firm is managed by workers who share the earnings equally. The objective of the firm is, by assumption, to maximize dividend per worker, with the size of the labor force a choice variable. It is the objective function which differentiates the worker managed firm analytically from the capitalist firm. The object of our inquiry is to determine the technical and Pareto efficiency properties of an economy composed of such enterprises.

In standard neoclassical theory the elements to be specified in the model are tastes, technology, resource endowments, and environment. Resources are all held by individual agents and all resources are hired on markets. In the worker managed economy, by contrast, no individual agents own the capital and the hiring of labor is prohibited. An enterprise is assumed, and an objective function for that enterprise is specified. The major elements of a model of the worker managed enterprise, and some of the assumptions commonly employed, are as follows.

Objective function of the enterprise.   The objective function of the enterprise is to maximize dividend per worker, at one moment or over time; or, to maximize the utility of the workers, at one moment or over time; or, to maximize global profits.

Production function of the enterprise.   The production function of the enterprise specifies constant, increasing or decreasing returns to scale, the elasticity of substitution among inputs, and the number of inputs and outputs considered.

Institutional constraints on labor supply.   The constraints on labor or supply involve the nature of the contract concerning terms of entry of new workers or exit of old workers; legal possibilities for multiple classes of workers, specifically, hired labor; and number of hours.

Institutional constraints on capital supply.   The constraints on capital supply are sources of capital (internal or external financing); the existence of owned assets or time limited claims on income streams by workers; and risk sharing provisions for both gains and losses.

Utility function of the workers.   The utility function of the workers specifies homogeneity or non-homogeneity; possibilities of coalitions; nature of risk aversity; nature of work aversity; and individualism or altruism.

Environmental characteristics.   The environmental characteristics include the degrees of environmental uncertainty; the market structure in product markets; and the market structure in factor markets. This is not intended to be an exhaustive listing of all possibilities or of all dimensions of modelling the different elements but a quick guide to the major variables and assumptions used in the voluminous literature.[11] The main motivation for the different models is to establish, as generally as possible, the conditions under which the worker managed enterprise is technically efficient. Technical efficiency requires each enterprise to use the factors of production in such a way that the last unit of each factor employed in each use produce the same value of output regardless of where employed. Otherwise, the total value of output could be increased by switching a factor from a lower valued to a higher valued use. Technical efficiency requires the value of the marginal products of each factor to be identical.

The Short Run: One Variable Factor. Benjamin Ward[12] was the first to examine the theory of the worker managed enterprise. In the course of writing a dissertation on the novel system of worker managed enterprises in Yugosalvia, he developed a simple model of the worker managed enterprise. His model can be described as follows: objective function: maximize dividend per worker; production function: $Q = f(K, L); Q_L > 0; Q_{LL} < 0$; labor restrictions: none on number; hours not variable; equal pay; capital restrictions: fixed at K_o with a price r per unit; utility function: not specified (implicitly, a direct function of income per worker); and environment: certainty; product market competition with price at p; implicitly, unlimited supplies of labor.

The principal novelty is in the objective function. Ward asked (1) how a firm with such an objective function would respond to a change in the price of the product? and (2) how these results would compare with those of a postulated capitalist twin enterprise located in a twin economy, identical in every respect except the objective function of the enterprise? Both enterprises are, by assumption, operating in environments in which a locally efficient response is also efficient from a social viewpoint. Ward's formulation of the question, focusing on the objective function of the enterprise and the comparison with the capitalist twin firm as the standard of optimal resource allocation, set the methodology for subsequent inquiry.

The objective is to maximize, with respect to L,

$$Y/L = \frac{pQ - rK_o}{L} . \text{ The first order condition is}$$

$$(Y/L)_L = L\,pQ_L - (pQ - rK_o) = 0, \text{ or}$$

$$pQ_L = \frac{pQ - rK_o}{L} . \tag{4.1}$$

In other words, the firm will take on labor until the value of the marginal product, pQ_L, just equals the dividend per worker, $(pQ - rK_o)/L$. For any given values of r, K_o and p, there is a unique L. Firms will not take on more labor, even if it becomes available at a wage less than the dividend per worker, because of the requirement that the firm must allow all workers to share equally in the dividend. Although workers might be willing to work for lower remuneration than the dividend per worker, this is not legally allowed. This restriction on payment means that there is no mechanism for market clearing in labor markets in an economy of worker managed enterprises. Most of the inefficiencies of the labor managed enterprise follow from, or are worked out through, this restriction.

Ward then asks, how would the firm, initially in equilibrium where the value of the marginal products of the factors equals the opportunity cost of the factors, respond to an increase in product price? Obviously, since this raises p, it raises the value of the marginal product of the last worker. It also raises dividend per worker. Unless $r = O$, the increase in dividend per worker will be more than the increase in the value of the marginal product of the last worker. As a consequence, dividend per worker is higher than the value of the marginal product of the last worker. The worker managed firm will reduce the labor used until the marginal product of the last worker is just equal to the dividend per worker. Since output varies directly with the single variable input, labor, we have in the short run a negatively sloped enterprise supply schedule. As the price of the product rises, the quantity produced declines.

This result is troubling both in terms of its microeconomic and macroeconomic implications. Negatively sloped supply schedules are potentially, but not necessarily, a source of market instability. If the industry is composed of firms with negatively sloped supply schedules, the industry's supply schedule may be negatively sloped as well. If the industry's negatively sloped supply schedule is less steep than the demand schedule, then any equilibrium is unstable. If, however, the supply schedule is steeper than the demand schedule, equilibrium can be attained. The macroeconomic implications of the negatively sloped short run supply schedules are that increases in aggregate demand to expand employment will cause prices to rise and employment to contract. New macroeconomic policies must be designed.

What are the microeconomic efficiency properties of the worker managed enterprise's response? The capitalist firm will respond to an increase in product price by increasing output. Further, its response is technically efficient since the value of the marginal product of the single variable factor, labor, is equal to labor's social opportunity cost, w, the market clearing wage. The Langean socialist firm's response will be identical to that of the capitalist in competition, and is efficient.

The worker managed firm, however, will not be technically efficient in the same environment. Assume that labor is originally fully employed at a dividend per worker just equal to the full employment wage rate in the twin capitalist economy and paying the same market-clearing charges on capital as in the twin economy. If the price of one product were to rise in the labor managed economy, the workers in the firm whose price had risen will, as we have seen, discharge some of their number. The remaining workers will earn a dividend d' higher than that of workers in firms whose prices did not rise. Since the value of the marginal product of the last worker must be equal to the dividend, and the dividend rates differ across firms, the value of the marginal products of labor must also differ. This result, the consequence of restrictions on the operation of the labor market in the worker managed economy, and of the assumption of a significantly positive elasticity of substitution between labor and capital is not only technically inefficient, it is also inegalitarian. The paired problems of technical inefficiency and inequality, and the potential instability of the economy as a whole, are the central insights of Ward into the worker managed economy.

The Short Run: Multiple Inputs.   If these results are general, then they are quite disheartening for enthusiasts of the worker managed version of market socialism: technical inefficiency, inequality and possible instability. But perhaps the results follow from the very specific case explored by Ward.

Domar[13] extended the analysis to the case of multiple inputs and outputs. Considering a simple example, with only one additional variable input X, the objective function becomes

$$\text{maximize } Y/L = \frac{pQ - rK_o - PxX}{L},$$

$$\text{where } Q = f\,(K_o,\,L,\,X) \tag{4.2}$$

To determine the equilibrium conditions for the firm, we set the derivatives of the objective function with respect to L and X respectively equal to zero, yielding:

$$pQ_L = \frac{pQ - rK_o - PxX}{L}, \tag{4.3}$$

the familiar requirement that the marginal product of labor equal the dividend per worker, and $pQ_X = Px$, the requirement that the marginal product of a hired factor equal the price of the hired factor. We can now see that the specific response of the firm to an increase in product price will depend on the elasticity of substitution between L and X. If L and X are strict complements (zero elasticity of substitution), then a rise in product price will have the same results in terms of labor use and output as in the one variable factor case. If L and X are perfect substitutes (elasticity of substitution is infinite), and if both are in use initially, an increase in product price would dictate dispensing with L and using only X. The output of the firm would increase until the value of the marginal product of X equaled its price. Of course, if all the workers were dispensed with, it would be difficult to imagine a worker managed enterprise. If there were some positive, but not infinite, elasticity of substitution between X and L, the impact of an increase in the product price would be indeterminate. One set of factors would indicate reducing L and output; another, increasing X and output. To the extent that there is substitution between inputs, the stark negatively sloped supply schedule of the single variable case is mitigated.

The Short Run: Variations in the Labor Supply Rules. Another way of relaxing the assumptions of Ward's model is to consider different rules for varying the labor membership. One common assumption is to limit L so that it can not be lower than L_o, the initial membership, on the grounds that workers would not discharge one another, although they might fail to hire new workers. In this case, faced with an increase in product price and a constraint on L_o, the enterprise would, in the absence of substitutable inputs, stay at the same output level; with substitutes, it would employ more X and increase output in response to an increase in product price.

Another possibility for varying the labor membership is to make explicit rules for entry and exit from the firm[14] which require the consent of the discharged workers as well as of the remaining workers. In that case, consent might be obtained by making side payments. In general, imposing such restrictions improves the technical efficiency and eliminates the fundamental unfairness of discharging workers arbitrarily. However, unless the rules of entry and exit are such as to cause the marginal products of the factors L and X to be identical across all uses, efficiency will not be attained. The only way, in general, to accomplish efficiency is by mimicking the capitalist's response. One way to do this is to allow the initial number of workers to admit others on discriminatory terms (Meade's inegalitarian labor cooperative[15]). This amounts to one group of workers hiring another.

Yet another possibility is to consider the labor force fixed at L_o but to vary the number of hours worked (or, alternatively, the intensity of work). If the firm's members were initially supplying the utility-maximizing number of hours (or level of effort), when the price of the product rises, the returns at the margin exceed the disutility of supplying the last unit of time or effort, so the workers will increase their supply.[16] The supply schedule is, however, still less elastic than if firms were free to hire new workers from other firms at the initial uniform dividend rate, their reservation wage, and the allocation of resources will be inefficient.

In short, if the enterprise is free to hire labor, then worker managed firms will hire labor up to the point where the value of the marginal product of labor is equal to the price of the hired factor. The worker managed firm will be as technically efficient as the capitalist or Langean socialist twin firm. But will it still be worker managed? Only by some of the workers. If additional labor can not be hired, hours and effort can vary, mitigating the inefficiency and negatively sloped supply schedule effects. However, the basic conclusion remains: unless the dividend per worker falls to the market clearing wage rate, or unless hired labor is a separate factor of production, the value of the marginal product of labor within the enterprise will not equal the value of the marginal product of labor elsewhere. Technical efficiency will not be achieved in the worker managed economy in the short run.

What is the source of this inefficiency? In essence, an increase in product price creates a quasi-rent in the short run. A rent is any payment over and above the price that is just necessary to call forth the supply of factors, originally applied in the analysis of the supply of natural resources. By extension, the term has come to cover payment over and above what is necessary to induce any factors of production to supply their services to production. A quasi-rent is a temporary excess of factor payments above the supply price of the factor. In the short run, with capital fixed and labor variable, for the capitalist firm, the appearance of quasi-rents does not cause inefficient use of factors because in no case is the quasi-rent shared by the variable input, labor. In the Langean socialist firm, the quasi-rent is likewise not shared by any variable factor, and does not influence the use of resources. In the labor managed firm, the variable factor appropriates the quasi-rent, and wishes to share it among as few members as possible. This is the source of the inefficiency.

Imperfect competition.   Despite these inefficient results, Vanek[17] has argued that in a realistic environment of imperfect competition, the worker managed economy may be more efficient. Let us examine his claim.

Given the same elasticity of demand, the worker managed monopoly is more restrictive in output than is the capitalist monopoly. The reason is not difficult to see. The equilibrium conditions for a worker managed monopoly require that $MR \cdot Q_L = (pQ - rK_o)/L$, namely, that the marginal revenue product equal dividend per worker. If a capitalist firm facing the wage rate w is making a profit, then for the capitalist,

$$MR \cdot Q_L = w, \text{ and}$$

$$pQ - rK_o - wL > O.$$

Therefore, $\frac{pQ - rK_o}{L} > w = MR \cdot Q_L$. The worker managed firm facing the same marginal revenue schedule and operating at the capitalist's output and labor input level would have a marginal revenue product below the dividend per worker and would not be in equilibrium. The worker managed monopoly in the short run will restrict output and employment below that of a similarly situated capitalist monopolist and will charge a price higher than that of the capitalist. Vanek reaches this conclusion, but argues that in the long run, in imperfect competition, the results are nonetheless favorable for the worker managed economy. The rest of his argument will be developed in the next section on long run partial equilibrium.

Long Run Partial Equilibrium

Perfect Competition. Does the situation improve when the firm has two variable inputs, capital and labor? Vanek[18] claims that the worker managed firm is more efficient than the capitalist firm in competitive markets in the long run because the worker managed firm does not expand beyond the constant returns to scale output. Let us consider the firm's response when the product price changes initially and stays at the new level and the individual firm increases its capital stock. This is the analysis of the firm's long run partial equilibrium.

Applying our result from the multiple input case, we see that the worker managed firm will hire all hired factors up to the point at which factor price equals the value of the marginal product of the factor. When product price increases, the value of the marginal products of capital and labor both increase. The worker managed firm's response (like the capitalist's) is indeterminate in the long run unless some further specification of the production function is made. It is common to make the capitalist's problem tractable by specifying a production function which has first increasing, then constant, then decreasing returns to scale. At the point where increasing returns become decreasing, there are constant returns to scale. Such a production function generates the capitalist's U-shaped long run average cost curve, with the long run marginal cost curve intersecting it at the minimum average cost, as pictured in microeconomic theory books. This enables us to find the capitalist's unique response, the output and the quantities of capital and labor used. However, as Estrin[19] shows, further specification of the production function is necessary to make the problem tractable for the worker managed enterprise.

The capitalist enterprise has as parameters product price, capital price, labor price and technology, and solves for Q, K, and L. The worker managed enterprise has one less parameter because there is no exogenously given price of labor but an endogenously determined dividend per worker. We have to redesign the problem to solve for one less solution variable. Estrin resolves this dilemma by constructing a production function with increasing returns to scale becoming decreasing returns to scale, where the level of output at which constant returns to scale is encountered is, by construction, constant. This may be visualized as a set of isoquants with capital and labor on the axes, as the case where I_1 in figure 4–1 represents the constant returns to scale level of output. The worker managed enterprise will have no incentive to expand beyond that scale because it could always increase dividend per worker by reducing scale and going back to the constant returns level. For the worker managed enterprise, Estrin's approach amounts to specifying the scale of output and solving only for factor proportions, thereby reducing the number of solution variables by one, as required. The profit maximizing capitalist facing the same production function as the worker managed firm sets output so that long run marginal cost is equal to the new price. This objective would dictate going beyond the scale of constant returns, to isoquant I_2.

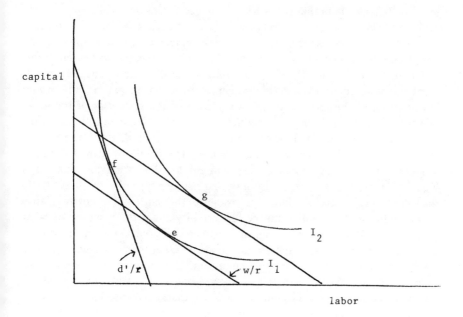

Figure 4–1

We have now established the scale of production for the worker managed firm. We next need to consider factor proportions. Initially, the capitalist and the worker managed firms are in equilibrium with dividend $d = w$, and profits equal to zero, at e in figure 4–1. The relative factor prices are $d/r = w/r$. With an increase in product price, which raises the dividend per worker to $d' > w$, the worker managed firm will move from e to f, the point on the same isoquant where the ratio of the value of the marginal products of the factors is equal to the ratio d'/r. Since d' is greater than d, the factor cost line is necessarily steeper than at e. While the marginal product of capital ($= r$) is identical in both the capitalist and the worker managed firms, the marginal product of labor will vary across firms in the worker managed economy. Without entry, there is no equilibrating mechanism in the long run, any more than in the short run, to equalize labor earnings or values of the marginal products of labor. The capitalist firm will respond, however, in such a manner that the marginal products of both capital and labor are equal across all uses, hence efficiently, at the higher output level I_2.

In the long run, the worker managed firm produces too little output, using too much capital and too little labor relative to its capitalist twin. We can now see that Vanek's claim that the worker managed firm is more efficient than the capitalist firm in the long run because it does not expand beyond the constant returns to scale point is incorrect. The socially efficient solution to the long run partial equilibrium problem is to produce where the marginal cost equals price, which is where the capitalist firm is producing. But to the extent that investment decisions made by individual agents are based on partial equilibrium information, in the absence of the knowledge of the responses of the other players to the initial change in product price and on the assumption that the original product price will be sustained, both the capitalist and the worker managed firms will make erroneous choices. The capitalist firm will be too large, while the worker managed firm will employ the wrong combination of factors. There is not only no basis for saying that one type of error is less costly than the other, but also the failure to recognize that both will be costly relative to an environment in which market uncertainty about the response of other players is reduced. Since in Langean socialism decisions about the expansion or contraction of the industry are not made by enterprise managers but by a single industry manager, this particular source of error is avoided. To the extent that the Langean economy is decomposable into self-contained industries which purchase primary inputs on factor markets and sell final output to consumers and have no intermediate goods transaction between one another, the industry managers would have all the information necessary to reach correct decisions, on the basis of marginal cost and demand schedule information. To the extent that the economy is not decomposable, then the Langean Central Planing Board would have to develop vectors of future prices, which will be discussed below.

Imperfect Competition.   What about Vanek's[20] claim that there is less ineffi-ciency in imperfectly competitive markets in labor managed economies than in capitalist economies? We have already established that with identical input prices, technology and marginal revenue schedules, that worker managed monopolists will operate at an output below that of the capitalist monopolist, charging a price higher than the capitalist. In the long run, when capital stock and scale can be adjusted, we see that the worker managed firm will use inputs that have a higher cost, valued at their market clearing price in an economy in equilibrium, than would the inputs the capitalist would have used had he been producing the worker managed firm's output. Figure 4–2 shows the

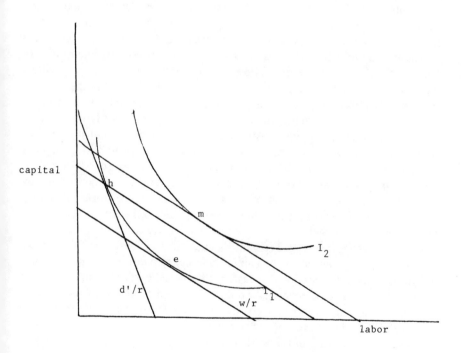

Figure 4–2

worker managed firm's long run equilibrium and factor use relative to the capitalist monopolist. If the worker managed monopolist has positive profits, the dividend d' is greater than w. Therefore it will produce (providing demand suffices to attain this scale of output) on the constant returns to scale isoquant I_1 at the point where it is tangent to d'/r. The capitalist monopolist facing the same elasticity of demand will, as we have seen, produce a larger output, on isoquant I_2. It will produce at a point m, where the marginal products of the factors are proportional to the factor input prices w/r. If w and r represent the opportunity costs of factors in equilibrium, we see that the social cost of the inputs used by the worker managed monopolist at h is greater than the social cost of the inputs the capitalist would have used to produce the same output, at e.

Vanek argues that the situation is not as bleak as it might appear at first glance, for if the worker managed firms are smaller, there may be more of them in an imperfectly competitive environment and, therefore, the demand schedule facing each of them is lower and more elastic. Vanek's[21] argument, which Meade[22] finds "persuasive," is still incomplete. From the first proposition, that the worker managed firm will produce a smaller output for a given elasticity of demand (about which there is no controversy), it is not possible to leap to Vanek's conclusion. It does not follow that the attractiveness for entry will be higher in the worker managed economy, resulting in more firms in the industry than would enter in the parallel capitalist economy. If we had the same number of firms in the worker managed as in the capitalist imperfectly competitive industry, each faces the same elasticity of demand as the capitalist imperfect competitors. In that case, each worker managed enterprise will produce a smaller output and sell it at a higher price, using socially more costly combinations of inputs than would occur in a capitalist imperfectly competitive industry. Therefore, a larger number of firms is necessary in the worker managed imperfectly competitive industry than in the capitalist industry merely to offset the inefficiencies of factor use. Suppose a sufficiently large number of firms existed in the worker managed economy so that the total output in the industry was equal to total output in the capitalist industry. Output and price would therefore be equal to the capitalist case, but the social costs of inputs employed in the worker managed economy would still exceed the value of inputs used in capitalism as long as there are positive profits in the imperfectly competitive industry. Thus a larger number of somewhat smaller firms is not sufficient to establish the superiority of the worker managed economy under conditions of imperfect competition. The larger number must be sufficiently large so that the higher quantity and lower price at the industry level offset the social costs of inefficient input combinations if there are any positive profits. Only in such a case could we unambiguously say that the worker managed imperfectly competitive markets are superior to those in capitalism. Vanek has given no reason why this would be so, and has not established his claim for the superiority of the worker managed economy.

In Langean socialism imperfect competition creates no efficiency problem because of the assumption that socialist managers are efficient, i.e., that they set output so that marginal cost equals price. Whether this assumption is helpful for understanding socialist behavior will be explored in the section on decentrally planned socialism.

General Equilibrium

General equilibrium in the competitive capitalist economy occurs when entry has taken place and all desired adjustments have been made. All quasi-rents are eroded, all firms are making zero profits, and all product and factor markets are in equilibrium. General equilibrium in the competitive worker managed economy has the same characteristics. All the firms will be producing at point e in figure 4–1. In this state of affairs, from the outside, we can not distinguish between the capitalist, the Langean socialist, or the worker managed enterprise. What appears in the short run as a sharp difference between firms' behaviors becomes in general equilibrium a merging of identities. In general equilibrium in competition, all three firms and the economies founded on them are equally efficient.

While entry can resolve the problem of quasi-rents, it cannot resolve the problems the worker managed economy or the capitalist economy encounters when there are imperfections in the product or factor markets. When a monopoly is making positive profits, entry will not erode that position. The worker managed monopolist will not only have lower output and a higher price than the capitalist monopolist, but also a less efficient use of inputs to produce the target output. Any degree of product market imperfection that allows positive profits to persist generates a technically inefficient use of inputs in the worker managed economy as well.

Factor market imperfections will also not be resolved by entry. Vanek[23] has drawn particular attention to a factor market imperfection in Yugoslavia, namely, the subsidization of the price of capital. Vanek argues that the failure to charge market clearing prices for capital prevents the worker managed economy from being efficient. It is helpful to develop his argument by identifying two distinct types of inefficiency: (1) that which results at the margin if the price of capital is below the social opportunity cost; and (2) that which results from the failure to collect the market clearing rental price on capital. In the first case, capital will be artificially cheap and there will be excess demand.

There must either be rationing, implying (since it is non-price rationing) that the values of the marginal products of capital are not equal across uses and, hence, technical inefficiency, or there must be forced saving to provide equilibrium in capital markets, implying a higher rate of accumulation than is consistent with the preferences of society and, hence, Pareto inefficiency. In the second case (even if the market clearing price of capital were charged at the margin, thus ensuring the equality of the marginal products of capital across uses), society's failure to collect the inframarginal capital rental income results in another kind of inefficiency. The uncollected rental income is appropriated by workers in the firm, just as in the case of quasi-rents.

For the worker managed economy to be efficient in general equilibrium two conditions must be met. In product markets there must either be competition or the extraction of monopoly rent. In factor markets the market clearing price must be charged for all non-labor inputs, so that the price of each factor is equal to its social opportunity cost and so that no rental income finds its way into the hands of the worker managers.

Ward's conclusion that the worker managed economy is inefficient is robust for technologies in which there is a significantly positive elasticity of substitution between labor and other inputs. The worker managed economy is efficient only when its outcomes mimic those of competitive capitalism. This can happen in only three ways: (1) Despite different objective functions and institutional environments, the capitalist and the worker managed economies exhibit the same behavior in general equilibrium with competition on product and factor markets. (2) Even if the economy is not in equilibrium, efficiency obtains if the worker managed economy mimics the capitalist factor markets and property relations. If the worker managers who are appropriating any rent or quasi-rent can either hire labor or lease the rent-generating endowments on competitive markets, efficiency results. In either case, there are exclusive property rights over sources of rent. Whether labor hires the property or property holders hire labor does not affect the efficiency of the outcome nor diminish its basic resemblance to capitalist, rather than worker managed, institutions. (3) Since, as we have seen, it is the appropriation of rental income by exclusive groups of workers which results in inefficiency, if we make a rule that no rental income accrues to the enterprises, efficiency results. This rule would play the same function that the rule plays in Langean socialism: the rule is itself synomymous with efficiency and thus tautologically defines efficiency, rather than deducing it from any set of propositions about the behavior of agents. (In reality, the difficulties of collecting rental income are several. The collection of rent requires valuing capital equipment, but capital in place is unique and has no competitive market price. Quasi-rent arises from changes in demand which generate windfall gains and losses and from the supply of Schumpeterian entrepreneurship which creates a new product or technique of production and which will be eroded by imitation. One wishes to eliminate the windfall rents but not the returns to entrepreneurship. But in fact there is no way to disentangle the two. Horvat gives a serious discussion of the possibilities of reasonable approximation of extracting rent in the worker managed economy.[24])

Financing the Worker Managed Enterprise

Up to this point, we have treated capital as a hired factor with a parametric price r. But the enterprise must finance its capital requirements in some manner. Given the simplest assumptions about worker preferences, namely, identical time preferences and identical time horizons of employment there would appear to be several possibilities. (1) Internal financing by the collective. Each worker has a claim on the income stream generated thereby during his employment, but no claim thereafter, and no claims upon the assets as such. We may call this a system of unvested claims. (2) Individually supplied financing through financial intermediaries. (3) Individually supplied financing directly in the enterprise with vested claims on income streams. These claims may be sold upon retirement or at some other point, with or without restrictions. This corresponds to the producers' cooperative. (4) External financing with an obligation to pay off the loan. (5) External financing by perpetual debt.

We shall see that with internal financing and non-vested claims, the rate of investment is suboptimal. Repayable loans are the same as internal finance in this respect. External finance and perpetual debt generate inefficient risk-bearing unless the debt or equity holders are also the enterprise decisionmakers. Only vested claims yield optimal rates of investment and optimal risk-bearing.

Rate of Investment with Non-vested Claims. As Pejovich[25] and Furubotn and Pejovich[26] have shown, internal financing without vesting of assets will result in a suboptimal level of investment. Suppose there are two kinds of assets, owned financial assets — bank accounts — which pass through financial intermediaries to the enterprise in the form of loans, and non-vested claims. Suppose that at the rate of interest of five percent, the demand for and supply of financial assets are in equilibrium. This is the optimal rate of investment, since the marginal rate of return is equal to the pure time preference. The financial institutions serve as intermediaries between the population and the enterprises. Suppose this possibility is withdrawn and that individuals now have only the option of investing in their enterprises in non-vested claims, or current consumption. In order to be willing to invest at the same rate as before, individuals will have to receive the same rate of return as before. If, before, the investment yielded a perpetual income stream at the rate of five percent, then for any finite time horizon of employment with the enterprise, there is a rate of return that would produce the same present value as the infinite stream. If the time horizon is one year, the rate of return would have to be 105 percent; for five years, 23 percent; for ten years, 13 percent; and for twenty years, 8 percent. However, the actual returns on the investment are not high enough to pay the necessary rates on the same volume of investment as before. So the equilibrium rate of investment will be lower under the non-vested institutional arrangements than it was under a system allowing individual ownership of financial assets. The rate is suboptimal because both borrowers and lenders would be better off if the restriction on owned financial assets were removed.

If both forms of investment are allowed — individual ownership of financial assets in the form of bank accounts and non-vested claims on income streams — individuals will prefer to own their own assets to investing in enterprises directly. Since there is always some uncertainty about an individual's life expectancy, the worker would, for equivalent present values if he survived the full length of his time horizon, prefer the security of the owned asset. Workers would have no incentive to invest in non-vested assets unless (a) the transactions cost (the difference between the interest paid out and the interest charged) was higher than the premium the individual was willing to pay for the security of owned assets over risky income streams contingent upon life expectancy; or (b) the assessment of riskiness and of the risk premium required by the lender differed between the workers and the bankers. Ignoring these two qualifications for the moment, we conclude that (1) to have optimal levels of investment in the worker managed economy, it is necessary to have owned assets, not non-vested claims; and (2) that this option in turn assures that all assets will be held in the owned form. This conclusion, if accepted, is quite unsettling. Faced with this situation, society may opt for collectively supplied assets based on taxation. Have we solved the problem?

If the collectively supplied assets constitute the development fund, and if the firm which borrows has to repay the funds from its earnings, this is no different from internal financing by the collective. In one case the workers first earn the money and then invest it, while in the other, the workers first invest and then pay off the loan from earnings. In either case, the workers purchased the non-vested assets from their earnings while receiving no claim on the assets but only finite income stream claims. The analytical problem is identical to the original internal investment problem and the result is identical: underinvestment in the economy as a whole. The only way around the underinvestment problem is for the loans to the enterprise to be loans in perpetuity. (For, as we have seen, subsidizing capital leads to its own inefficiencies.) All of the capital invested in the enterprise must come from permanent loans if the rate of investment is to be optimal. But now we have raised a new problem, that of the consequences of perpetual debt for risk-bearing.

Perpetual Debt and Risk-Bearing.   There would seem to be two major ways that perpetual debt could be handled; it could be guaranteed by a government investment bank, the rate of interest being charged being the market-clearing rate in each time period applied uniformly across firms; or the debt might be rolled over in capital markets or in a regulatory agency in manner involving differential risk premia assessed on the firm. In either case, there are still two problems.[27] (1) Are there sanctions sufficiently strong to prevent or to discourage illicit disinvestment by the workers? Would we detect and deter a failure to maintain the value of the tangible assets which are the security for the loans? (2) Are the sanctions against bankruptcy sufficient to keep the firm from engaging in excessively risky gambles with some one else's capital?

Let us consider risk-bearing in the light of perpetual finance. Suppose we start from an initial equilibrium in which every individual receives the same dividend in his place of work and all capital financed from state funds. Now let there be environmental uncertainty about the future, resulting in gains to some enterprises and losses to others when the state of nature becomes known. While there is no upper limit to the fluctuations, there is a lower limit. No one worker can lose more than the dividend. The worker has very limited liability for losses in the value of capital assets, whereas the workers receive 100 percent of the gains from successful risk investment. Gains are reaped by the workers in the firm, whereas the bulk of the losses are borne by society as a whole. There is an incentive to be overly risky from the point of view of society since, with equal odds, the expected value of the gains to the workers are higher than those of the losses. As neoclassical theory shows, risk-bearing will not be efficient unless the recipient of the gains is also the bearer of the losses.

With a debt to equity ratio of infinity, it is unlikely that lenders will lend their money on the same terms as at a lower debt/equity ratio. Either they would require a premium that rose as the debt/equity ratio rises, representing the increased bearing of risk,[28] or they would demand some say in the enterprise management. In the former case, the workers in the enterprise may find the premium too high and may opt for investment in non-vested assets, with the attendant suboptimal rate of investment. In the latter case, the concept of worker management is diluted.

What this line of argument demonstrates is that it is not possible to have simultaneously socialism (defined as the absence of vested claims), worker management, efficient risk-bearing and an optimal rate of saving. With self-interested human behavior, the only institutions and environment which produce efficient outcomes is the private ownership of the factors of production and competitive product and factor markets.

It might appear that the adoption of efficiency as the criterion determines the conclusions about the institutional forms and environment compatible with efficiency. The conclusions, however, depend equally on certain implicit assumptions. I will return to this point below.

Macroeconomics of the Worker Managed Economy

We have already observed the striking differences between the capitalist and the worker managed model at the microeconomic level. It is not surprising, therefore, that the macroeconomics of the worker managed economy shows similar anomalies.

How will worker managed economies behave? The main systematic effort to establish the macro model has been by Vanek. He presented a very optimistic picture in his 1969 article[29] which was elaborated more systematically in 1970[30] and amended in 1972[31].

Vanek sees two main differences between the worker managed economy and the capitalist economy. First, the low elasticity of supply of the worker managed economy distinguishes it. This, however, cuts two ways. On the one hand, it makes it difficult to devise an effective macroeconomic policy which will restore full employment by manipulation of aggregate demand. Changes in aggregate demand would have a stronger effect on price than on employment and output variables. On the other hand, if an economy were at the full employment level, it would not easily be drawn from that level by changes in internal or external demand conditions. A drop in demand would cause prices to drop and the earnings of workers would decline, but employment and output would be maintained. Second, while output levels in a worker managed economy do not respond as much as in a capitalist economy, price levels would respond more. This means that if there were also downward wage or price rigidity, the worker managed economy would be more subject to inflationary pressures than a capitalist economy. This is because the nominal variables bear more of the adjustment in the worker managed economy than the real variables. In the capitalist economy the adjustment is more evenly divided between wage and price variables which may be downward rigid, and employment and output variables, which can vary down as well as up.

The main conclusions concerning the macroeconomics of the worker managed economy are: (1) the state must take a positive role in the formation of new enterprises, both for reasons of facilitating structural adjustments between sectors at the microeconomic level and for reasons of establishing full employment (which could be regarded as structural adjustment between the employed and the unemployed). (2) The worker managed economy would have more stable employment and output levels in the face of variable domestic and foreign demand than the capitalist economy, and in that context it would be possible to focus on the long term full employment path, with fewer needs to adjust for responses to exogenous shocks. (3) An open economy fostering competition would aid the process of microeconomic efficiency without rendering the employment levels as susceptible as in the capitalist economy to the vagaries of foreign demand changes. (4) There is the possibility of greater susceptibility to inflation than in the capitalist economy with identical downward price rigidities.

The macroeconomic findings are considerably less developed than the microeconomic findings, indicating that the vast majority of effort has been expended on micro issues. The possibility is raised, however, in points (2) and (3) that the macroeconomic properties may result in behavior that is microeconomically more efficient than the similarly situated capitalist economy. These possibilities need further systematic exploration.

Empirical Findings and the Implications

The major source of data for testing the hypotheses that follow from the models of the worker managed enterprises and the economy as a whole is, of course, Yugoslavia. An important summary of the empirical evidence on a variety of propositions, concerning the Yugoslav economic system has been compiled by Estrin and Bartlett.[32] Only a few topics will be touched on here.

What is the evidence on microeconomic efficiency? Until 1965, market considerations were strongly limited in Yugoslavia by political constraints. Prior to 1965 there were effective national wage guidelines and policies which determined both income levels and employment levels of the enterprises, if not in detail, at least the range. Capital was allocated among different regions and industries according to centrally determined criteria. A high rate of taxation on profits meant relatively low retained earnings. Subsequent to 1965, the market elements increased in Yugoslavia significantly.[33] Wage and employment guidelines were withdrawn, profits taxes eliminated, interest charges payable to society on the value of capital equipment were eliminated, and capital allocation was transferred to a profit-maximizing banking system which functioned as a genuine financial intermediary. In the context of such a change in the economic system, a key empirical method is to observe changes between the pre–1965 and the post–1965 period.

Estrin has examined income dispersion from this point of view.[34] Theory would suggest an increase in the intersectoral dispersion of income after the reforms of 1965 as market factors and enterprise autonomy became more prominent. Data on the average gross monthly earnings in 22 industrial sectors show that the dispersion, measured by the coefficient of variation, doubled between the two periods. In the first period 95 percent of the average gross incomes of all sectors were within 25 percent of the mean, while in the post–1965 period, the interval was 50 percent of the mean. By international standards, Yugoslavia's intersectoral coefficient of variation, at its highest levels, exceeded those of Sweden, France, Poland, Hungary, Greece and the United States and was similar to that of Japan, and smaller than that of Spain. The same pattern of increasing intersectoral coefficients of variation held for the eight skill groups (four white collar and four blue collar) into which Yugoslav workers are classified by educational qualifications, implying that the changes in average income dispersion were not caused by shifts in the skill groups mix between sectors. Data for ten particular jobs across twenty-one sectors show the same pattern of increasing coefficients of variation after the reforms, implying that changes in intersectoral income dispersion were not caused by shifts in the composition of job mix between sectors. Finally, the coefficients of variation of intersectoral incomes within the republics were greater than for Yugoslavia as a whole and were not associated with the levels of economic development. All of these findings point to the differences in industry level variables, not skills, jobs, region, or development level, as the cause of the intersectoral differences.

Estrin, Svejnar and Mow[35] seek to determine the causes of these differentials. Two different hypotheses are put forth. One, associated with Vanek and Jovicic[36], Miovic[37], Rivera-Batiz[38] and Staellerts[39], implies that Yugoslavia's distributional problems are primarily the consequence of inappropriate policies for the allocation and pricing of capital. If this is so, the implication is than an appropriate capital allocation and pricing policies would resolve the distribution problem with its implications of associated inefficiencies. The alternate hypothesis put forth by Estrin, Svejnar and Mow is that income differentials arise whenever firms face different conditions on product markets, factor markets, or technology. They attempt to distinguish empirically between these two different explanations of income differentials. They conclude, after careful analysis, that imperfections in the capital market alone cannot account for the variations in observed earnings. Even if capital were properly allocated to ensure the equality of marginal products and the factor capital were charged its scarcity price, income differentials would remain because of different degrees of product market imperfections, different degrees of factor market imperfections (monopsony), and differences in the technological efficiency of production. Any of these can result in dispersion of residual surplus among enterprises and, hence, differential incomes and differential marginal products of labor. Estrin[40] develops a set of equations which test the various hypotheses. Numerous estimation procedures establish a robust and significant relationship between earnings and product markets, factor markets and technology. The weight of evidence is clear. The income differentials are not the result of a single faulty policy and are not amenable to simple solutions.

A second key prediction of the theory concerns the impact of worker management and a system of non-vested claims on voluntary enterprise savings. The theories of Furubotn and Pejovich would predict, in the presence of bank loans at negative real rates of interest (as was probably the case in Yugoslavia), that there would be no voluntary savings in the enterprise and that all capital would be borrowed. That would certainly be true if bank funds were infinitely available — at a negative real interest rate, in any system, there would be an infinite demand for credit. But in reality there is a finite volume of credit. At negative real interest rates it pays to borrow to invest, even if it is in the form of non-vested assets which must be paid for out of current and future earnings. Thus, in this environment, Furubotn and Pejovich's model would not predict a low rate of voluntary enterprise savings. If the rates on alternative financial instruments for individual investors (savings accounts) are also negative, the only positive valued investment alternatives are in real assets, either household assets or at one's place of work. Thus, the observation of positive enterprise saving does not refute the Furubotn–Pejovich hypotheses in the Yugoslav environment.

The primary empirical study by Tyson[41] would appear to be inconclusive on these points. Tyson proposes a permanent income hypothesis to explain Yugoslav savings behavior, and her data are consistent with the three conclusions which would follow from such a hypothesis: (1) a higher percentage of savings as per capita income rises (an increasing marginal propensity to save); (2) a lower variation in per capita income than in per capita net revenue (this is the corrollary of (1)); (3) nontrivial rates of retioned earnings. While the data are consistent with Tyson's permanent income hypothesis, they are also compatible with Furubotn and Pejovich's argument in the environment of negative real rates of interest on both loans and privately held financial assets and limited opportunities for investment in real assets in the private sector. Present evidence does not enable us to distinguish between the permanent income and the Furubotn–Pejovich hypotheses.

Observations on Methodology

Neoclassical theory has both positive and normative aspects. The positive aspects of the theory generate hypotheses which identify outcomes likely to be observed if the specified environments are present. For example, if there are imperfections in product or factor markets, or if disequilibrium obtains, the theory of the worker managed economy predicts inequality of labor income across uses, whereas the theory of the capitalist economy would not. However, the normative aspect of the theory moves beyond prediction and provides a framework for evaluating empirical findings. It implies that the occurrence of such inequalities means that the marginal products of labor are not identical across uses and that the economy is inefficient.

The evidence of income differentials is consistent with the predictions of the positive theory and is subject to a normative interpretation of inefficiency. However, need such consistency between theory and evidence force the conclusion that the worker managed system is undesirable in value terms? Before accepting such an interpretation, several dimensions of the theoretical argument should be examined.

Omitted variables.   The objective function is too simple. In addition to the observed outputs (products), we are also obtaining unobserved outputs of a subjective individual or collective nature, such as work satisfaction, stability of employment, solidarity, democracy, etc. The production of important social values is neglected in applications of the neoclassical approach which look only at the quantities of output of the tangible goods. One should be cautious of drawing sweeping generalization from such analysis.

Misspecification of the objective function.   Horvat[42] has argued that firms might really maximize profits. If firms do maximize profits, and if the environment is reasonably competitive, then all the theorems of neoclassical analysis concerning efficiency apply. Such an argument is consistent with the sociological literature cited by Estrin and Bartlett[43] and with the observations of Comisso[44] suggesting that managers dominate the decision process through their control of information flows and the knowledge of the technical variants proposed. (Managers might also "satisfice" subject to a constraint of meeting workers' wage expectations, or may maximize growth through retained earnings. In all probability managers do have a very large voice in the determination of decisions, in the sense of being the source of the various resolutions that are presented to the workers. But this does not establish that managers' interests will dominate over the workers' interests in the decisions adopted. To reach such a conclusion is to confuse formal and real authority over decisions.)

The strongest objection to adopting a profit maximization hypothesis is the existence of labor income differentials across sectors, by average incomes, by skill groups, and by specific jobs. Profit maximization implies no significant differences in earnings for identical factors. The weight of existing evidence, which points to a strong tendency for income differentials to increase after the market reforms, is not easily consistent with a profit maximization hypothesis. It is, however, consistent with the hypothesis that firms maximize dividend per worker, especially in the presence of known product and factor market imperfections. The burden falls to those who accept the profit maximizing hypothesis to explain its consistency with observed wage variations.

Erroneous comparison. The conclusion of inefficiency rests on the comparison with the competitive capitalist firm. The adequacy of the comparison depends, in the most narrow sense, on two assumptions: first, that the production functions are identical in the worker managed and the capitalist firm, and second, that identical inputs are supplied by the worker managed and the capitalist economies. Objection to both assumptions can be raised. (1) The incentives for shirking in the worker managed enterprises are reduced because the workers, not the capitalists, receive the profits. If, in addition, workers supply more effort when they share the profit, more effort will be forthcoming as a result of shifting the returns from the capitalists to the workers. (2) Whereas workers in the capitalist firm may collude in a slowdown, in the worker managed enterprise, the same peer pressure will be brought to bear on those who deviate from the collectively decided effort level. It is no longer necessary to hire monitors. Each worker will have an incentive to see that fellow workers are not free riders. Therefore, to produce a given output, fewer monitors will be needed in supervisory positions, which alone would change the inputs necessary to produce a given level of output. (3) The choice of techique in the capitalist firm may be selected for ease of monitoring.[45] Where it is necessary to monitor, the technique chosen by the capitalist is the least costly, but were the need to monitor not present, another quite different technique might have been chosen on grounds of technical efficiency. (4) There could be positive effects on labor productivity and innovation from involving those at the production level in problem solving in a way that capitalist arrangements typically do not engage them. (5) There could be higher subjective levels of satisfaction or the lowering of stress associated with work which result in more productive effort by the workers without an offsetting increase in disutility or the need for higher remuneration.

If the production function of the worker managed enterprise should be technically more efficient than under capitalism, or if the workers supply additional inputs without requiring additional remuneration or suffering increased subjective disutility, then we should have to rethink our conclusions about the efficiency of worker managed systems. Our conclusions were based on the assumption that the production function and the inputs were identical in capitalism, worker managed socialism and in Langean socialism. The worker managed system could have a more efficient production function and could elicit additional inputs form the workers. It could also have an objective function which results, because of the differences in marginal products of labor across uses, in lower technical efficiency than if the marginal products were identical. To draw general inferences from this single dimension of relative inefficiency may lead to an important distortion of the comparative economic performance of worker managed socialism, competitive capitalism and Langean socialism. In addition, it is possible that the macroeconomic characteristics of the worker managed economy which provide for more aggregate output and employment stability are conducive to greater efficiency.[46]

All this suggests the need to expand the method originally outlined by Ward. Existing empirical findings are subjected to possibly erroneous normative generalizations because of assumptions that may be unwarranted. Rather than continue down the existing path, it is more fruitful to direct attention to the empirically relevant dimensions of economic behavior hitherto ignored and to incorporate these findings into our analysis. I will return to these points in the last section.

Lange's Decentrally Planned Socialism

Lange, as we recall, developed his theory of market socialism to refute von Mises' claim that socialism and efficiency were incompatible. In an informationally decentralized environment, with knowledge of preferences and production possibilities dispersed, Lange proposed the establishment of ordinary markets for labor and consumer goods, allowing for both individual choice and consumer sovereignty in determining the output mix and the labor supply. The Central Planning Board sets the rate of investment. There are two sets of agents governing the production process: enterprise managers who operate existing plants, and industry managers who make decisions about the entry and exit of plants. These managers follow three rules: accept existing prices as parametric; discover the lowest marginal cost; set output where marginal cost equals price. The Central Planning Board operates as the Walrasian auctioneer to establish the equilibrium prices for intermediate goods.

Lange's proof of the compatibility of socialism and efficiency is persuasive in a world characterized by: (1) managers who follow rules; (2) convexity of preferences and technology, which yields competition and a unique, stable equilibrium; (3) absence of externalities in production or consumption, which guarantee that the equilibrium is Pareto optimal; (4) static equilibrium. Lange showed how, in this environment, to solve the rational allocation problem. Once the solution is found, with both prices and quantities known, it makes no difference for the implementation of the plan whether the enterprise managers follow the rules of price and marginal cost, or whether they follow quantity directives.[47]

Three of these assumptions are quite standard for neoclassical theory and the consequences of relaxing them can be applied in a fairly straightforward manner. The motivational assumption is more complex. It is equivalent to assuming efficiency at the enterprise level. The conclusion that Langean socialism is superior to worker managed socialism in terms of efficiency rests on a tautology. We do not have a theory of the behavior of managers in Lange's system from which to derive conclusions about efficiency. It is not helpful to make such a strong assumption, with such important implications for the conclusions, without empirical or theoretical justification.

In the absence of such a theoretical or empirical justification it seems more appropriate to proceed with a neutral assumption, such as equivalently self-interested behavior on the part of both the worker managers and the Langean managers, or equivalent degrees of altruism. I will assume, for the moment, self-interested behavior on the part of both sets of managers, since it is in terms of self interest of a pecuniary nature that the theory of the worker-managed firm has been developed above and that the literature on the decentrally planned economy has evolved.

Socialism, Efficiency and Self-Interest

If we assume a self-interested orientation on the part of the socialist managers, we are left with the questions Bergson[48] raises: Why will managers follow the rules? How will the system directors know whether the managers are following the rules? How will the system directors know which managers are more effective at following the rules, i.e., at locating the minimal marginal cost schedules?

In a competitive static environment with informational dispersion, there is no problem. The formal literature on optimal incentives in informationally decentralized environments[49] shows that it is possible to induce peripheral managers to allocate resources in such environments in accordance with any set of preferences transmitted through the center (such as consumer preferences) without the center's surrendering its control of any arbitrary share (less than 100 percent) of profits. It suffices to give managers any monotonic function of profits as an incentive. If the managerial abilities are differentially distributed among the population, the center can appoint those managers with the best profit records, for in a competitive static environment, they are the ones who have found the least costly methods.

If we relax the condition of competition and allow monopoly, all three economic systems, capitalism, Langean socialism and worker managed socialism, will depart from Pareto optimality. The possibilities of effective public policy in all three cases lie in the ability of the center to extract accurate information from the periphery about the true marginal costs. For the purposes of comparison, I focus attention on whether this is easier to do in an environment of Langean socialism, capitalism, or worker management.

One consideration affecting the willingness to reveal information is the range and intensity of shared values between center and periphery. This is often expressed in terms of community and cooperation. A family can be viewed as a proto-community in which there is cooperation for the attainment of individual and collective goals. A capitalist economy, by pitting individual interest against individual interest and group interest against group interest encourages more conflict and self-interest than cooperation and community. By contrast, a worker managed economy makes shared interests and joint problem-solving necessities within the enterprise.

The process of compromise within a nonhierarchical structure of equals makes individuals and the community at large aware of both the private and the social consequences of any particular action. Purely self-interested behavior is not condoned within the community. Decentrally planned socialism is essentially a single bureaucratic organization. What is the influence of a single state organization with concentrated bureaucratic authority on social perceptions and behavior? Under what conditions does it foster a sense of community and cooperation? Alternatively phrased, under what conditions does it encourage competition between the bureaus? These questions have been ignored.

If we relax the assumption of no externalities in production and consumption and allow for divergence between social and private costs and benefits, this will not adversely affect attaining equilibrium. A state of equilibrium may be attained, but it may not be technically efficient and certainly will not be Pareto efficient. The standard remedy in any market economy to the problems of externalities is the use of subsidies and taxes, but to develop optimal taxes necessitates the acquisition of sufficient information about the nature of preferences and the true performance potential at the periphery. We thus return to the question whether acquiring such information is more likely to occur under Langean conditions than in the capitalist or the worker managed economy.

Socialism, Efficiency and Uncertainty

What happens when we introduce uncertainty? Meade distinguishes between two types of uncertainty.[50] *Environmental uncertainty* arises due to objective uncertainty as to which of two states of nature will prevail at time $t + 1$. Environmental uncertainty includes any actions taken by individuals outside the sphere being analyzed which are treated as exogenous to the problem at hand. Even if there is no environmental uncertainty and all the information necessary to reach correct decisions exists within the system in time period t, in a dynamic economy with environmental certainty there can still exist *market uncertainty*.

Marked uncertainty exists if the individual agents who must make decisions in time period t about outcomes in $t + 1$ do so without full information as to the actions of the other agents in time period t which will affect the realization in $t + 1$. For example, the decisions taken by the individual enterprises in long run partial equilibrium analyzed in the section on the worker managed economy, would result in faulty social resource allocation because they were made in the absence of information about the responses of other firms. The formal solution to the problem for any market economy is to generate not just a vector of present prices but a complete vector of future equilibrium prices as well. The salient question would be, in what respects would these distinctive economic systems differ in their capacities to generate the price vectors?

If we now relax the assumption of environmental certainty, a new problem arises. How can we induce appropriate risk-bearing by the individual firms at the periphery? The formal solution is to generate a set of contingency contracts specifying deliveries at all points in the future depending on the actual state of nature, against contract payments made in the present.

Let us assume there is no difference in the assessment of contingencies between periphery and center. As Hildebrandt and Tyson show[51], if the center and the periphery also share identical attitudes toward risk bearing, it will be possible to induce the periphery to follow centgrally transmitted preferences about risk-bearing while preserving central control of profits. Intuitively, the argument can be seen in terms of risk and insurance. If the state of nature depended on the toss of what was perceived by both center and periphery to be a fair coin, and if center and periphery are both risk neutral, there would be no demand for insurance against adverse outcomes. The Central Planning Board's preferences for risk neutrality, meaning that it would not wish to divert resources from production into insurance from risk, would be effected by the peripheral agents who would not seek to buy insurance. If, however, center and periphery do not share the same attitudes toward risk, the Central

Planning Board must persuade the periphery to take decisions bearing the centrally preferred degree of risk. If the risk aversion of the periphery is known, the Central Planning Board can induce the periphery to bear any desired level of risk-bearing by varying the profit share that goes to the periphery. (There are additional problems in eliciting truthful information about the risk aversion of the periphery which will not be pursued here.) But to get the periphery to bear appropriate risks, the Central Planning Board surrenders its ability to control the distribution of profits in society.

Thus, when we introduce uncertainty, the only way to maintain the socially desired level of risk-bearing is to surrender social control over the profits. This conclusion is not surprising, for our analysis of the worker managed socialist economy showed a similar tension around risk-bearing by enterprises venturing social capital.

These points were made by Hayek in 1940[52] and 1945[53] and von Mises in 1951.[54] Von Mises distinguishes between the problems of a stationary economic system and one with dynamic uncertainty. "Under stationary conditions there no longer exists a problem for economic calculation to solve. The essential function of economic calculation has *by hypothesis* already been performed."[55] The rest is mechanics. From von Mises' point of view, the essential function of economic calculation is weighing the "desire for profit" against the "risk of loss."

Without private ownership of capital, self-interested individuals will not adequately weigh the costs and benefits of any given investment decision. The contemporary experience in the two economies most closely approximating our models of worker managed socialism and Langean socialism, Yugoslavia and Hungary respectively, suggest that the problem of appropriate risk-bearing with social capital is important. On one hand, there is too little risk-bearing, resulting in low rates of productivity change because the penalties for lack of innovation and efficiency are too weak. On the other hand, there is an excessive appetite for social capital, especially for the purchase of high technology or high prestige Western capital goods which yield immediate satisfaction and gains for the enterprise while imposing costs on society as a whole. This appears to be socialism's biggest dilemma: How to structure the decision matrix regarding rewards and penalties attached to the use of social resources? It is precisely this question that is the focal point of discussion in both Yugoslavia and Hungary in the 1980s.

Conclusions

The term market socialism is often used to describe both Langean decentrally planned socialism and worker managed socialism. It draws attention to the ways in which they both differ from capitalism and from central planning. A single term, however, obscures the differences between the two systems. A single term obfuscates the different analytical methods by which each reaches its conclusions about efficiency. Perhaps we should consider abandoning the term altogether in the interests of intellectual clarity.

The question remains: How to construct a theoretical orientation that is more adequate for studying and comparing different economic systems? Three steps need to be taken initially to address this question.

First, it is necessary to develop a theory of the behavior of agents in decentrally planned socialism which can be productively juxtaposed to the worker managed economy. The existing literature examines but one kind of structurally induced motivation, self-interested managers responding to the pecuniary rewards of a centrally designed bonus scheme. But planned social-ism is essentially a single bureaucratic organization, and the agents in an organization have complex motivations involving promotion, power and pres-tige. How do the bureaus and bureaucrats work in a bureaucratic system?

Second, we need a better theory of what goes on within the different types of enterprises. Will the production function be the same for a traditionally managed enterprise with a socialist manager as for a worker managed enter-prise? Will the supply of inputs forthcoming be the same? What is the nature of work, authority and initiative in the traditional versus the worker managed enterprise and how will this affect the efficiency of outcomes? Blind assump-tions of identical processes of production and supplies of effort across systems without theoretical or empirical justification undercut the strength of any conclusion.

Finally, the ability of any informationally decentralized system to formulate optimal policies in environments of uncertainty, monopoly and externalities depends on the willingness of the periphery to provide truthful information to the center and to use social resources responsibly. The more peripheral agents see themselves acting as self-interested individual agents rather than also as a part of the whole, the less information they will reveal. How do the values and beliefs of the system itself influence the values and beliefs of the agents operat-ing at the center and at the periphery of the societal entity?

In the end, the arguments of neoclassical analysis reduce to a single ques-tion: Is market socialism efficient? To answer this question, the neoclassical perspective has thus far invoked a set of assumptions: (1) that production functions are identical across systems; (2) that inputs supplied are identical across systems; (3) that the motivation of agents and the willingness to provide truthful information is identical across systems; (4) that macroeconomic per-formance is identical across systems or, if not, has no impact on microeco-nomic efficiency. These assumptions force the various forms of the argument to the same conclusion: Since efficiency obtains under conditions of competitive capitalism, only systems that mimic competitive capitalism can be efficient.

There is an internal consistency in such an argument. Dissatisfaction arises, however, at the poverty of the conclusion. Only if we can extract comparative analysis from these assumptions which contain their own conclusion can we make progress in understanding the nature of efficiency in systems which do not mimic capitalism. Otherwise, we need go no further. Answers to all questions about efficiency will be found in a literature haunted by its own self-fulfilling character.

References

1. Engels, F., *Anti-Dühring,* 2nd ed. Moscow: Foreign Languages Publishing House, 1959, p. 427.
2. Barone, E., "The Ministry of Production in the Collectivist State," in F. A. Hayek, ed., *Collectivist Economic Planning.* London: Routledge and Kegan Paul, Ltd., 1935.
3. von Mises, L., "Economic Calculation in the Socialist Commonwealth," in Hayek, ed., *Collectivist Economic Planning.* London: Routledge and Kegan Paul Ltd., 1935.
4. Lange, O., and F. M. Taylor. *On the Economic Theory of Socialism* Minneapolis: University of Minnesota Press, 1938.
5. Mishan, E. J., "A Survey of Welfare Economics, 1939–1959," in American Economic Association and Royal Economic Society, editors, *Surveys of Economic Theory,* Vol. 1. New York: St. Martin's Press, 1966, p. 163.
6. Cave Martin and Paul Hare, *Alternative Approaches to Economic Planning* New York: St. Martin's Press, 1981, Chapter 6.
7. *Ibid.*
8. Comisso, E. T., *Workers' Control Under Plan and Market* New Haven: Yale University Press, 1979.
9. Milenkovitch, D. D., *Plan and Market in Yugoslav Economic Thought* New Haven: Yale University Press, 1971.
10. *See* Comisso. Also Schrenk, M. *et al., Yugoslavia: Self-Management Socialism* Baltimore: Johns Hopkins Press for the World Bank, 1979, and Ardalen, C., "Workers' Self-Management and Planning: The Yugoslav Case," *World Development* 8, 1989, pp. 623–638.
11. See the bibliographies in Frederic L. Pryor, "The Economics of Production Cooperatives: A Reader's Guide," *Annals of Public and Cooperative Economy,* forthcoming; A. Steinherr, "The Labor-Managed Economy: A Survey of the Economic Literature," *Annals of Public and Cooperative Economy* 49, No. 2, April–June 1978, pp. 129–148; and Derek Jones and Jan Svejnar, *Participatory and Self-Managed Firms.* Lexington: Lexington Books, 1982.

12. Ward, B., "Market Syndicalism," *American Economic Review* 48, No. 4, 1958, pp. 566–89.
13. Domar, E. D., "The Soviet Collective Farm as a Producer Cooperative," *American Economic Review* 56, 1966, pp. 734–757.
14. Meade, J. E. "The Theory of Labour-Managed Firms and Profit-Sharing," *Economic Journal* 82, No. 1, Supplement, March 1972, pp. 402–428; Bonin, J. P., "The Theory of the Labor-Managed Firm from the Membership's Perspective with Implications for Marshallian Industry Supply," *Journal of Comparative Economics* 5, No. 4, December 1981, pp. 337–351.
15. Meade (1972).
16. Bonin (1981).
17. Vanek, J., "Decentralization Under Workers' Management: A Theoretical appraisal," *American Economic Review* 58, No. 5, December 1969, pp. 1006–14.
18. *Ibid.*
19. Estrin, S., "Long Run Supply Responses under Self-Management," *Journal of Comparative Economics,* 6, No. 4, December 1982, pp. 363–378.
20. Vanek (1969).
21. *Ibid.*
22. Meade, J. E., "Labour-Managed Firms in Conditiosn of Imperfect Competition," *Economic Journal* 84, No. 4, December 1974, pp. 817–824.
23. Vanek, J. and M. Jovićić, "The Capital Market and Income Distribution in Yugoslavia: A Theoretical and Empirical Analysis," *Quarterly Journal of Economics* 89, No. 3, 1975, pp. 432–44.
24. Horvat, B., *The Political Economy of Socialism* White Plains: M. E. Sharpe, Inc. 1982.
25. Pejovich, S., "The Firm, Monetary Policy and Property Rights in a Planned Economy," *Western Economics Journal* 7, No. 3, September 1969, pp. 193–200.
26. Furubotn, E. G. and S. Pejovich, "Property Rights and the Behavior of the Firm in a Socialist State: The Example of Yugoslavia," *Zeitzchrift für Nationaloekonomie,* Band 3, No. 3–4, December 1970, pp. 431–454.
27. Jensen, M. C. and W. H. Meckling, "Rights and Production Functions: An Application to Labor-managed Firms and Codetermination," *Journal of Business,* No. 4, October 1979, pp. 469–506.
28. McCain, R. A. "On the Optimal Financial Environment for Worker Cooperatives," *Zeitschrift für Nationaloekonomie* 37, Nos. 3–4, 1977, pp. 355–384.
29. Vanek (1969).
30. Vanek, J., *The General Theory of Labor-Managed Market Economies* Ithaca: Cornell University Press, 1970.
31. Vanek, J. "The Macroeconomic Theory and Policy of an Open Worker-Managed Economy," *Ekonomska Analiza* No. 3/4, Summer 1972. Also published in Jaroslav Vanek, *The Labor-Managed Economy: Essays.* Ithaca: Cornell University Press, 1977.
32. Estrin, S. and W. Bartlett, "The Effects of Enterprise Self-Management in Yugoslavia: An Empirical Survey," in Jones and Svejnar, *Participatory and Self-Managed Firms.*

33. Milenkovitch (1971). *See also* S. Estrin, "Income Dispersion in a Self-Managed Economy," *Economica* 48, 1981, pp. 181–94.
34. Estrin, S., "Income Disperson in A Self-Managed Economy."
35. Estrin, S., J. Svejnar and C. Mow, "Market Imperfections, Labor-Management and Earnings Differentials in a Developing Country: Theory and Evidence from Yugoslavia," Working Paper # 276, Department of Economics, Cornell University, 1982.
36. Vanek and Jovićić.
37. Miović, P., *Determinants of Income Differentials in Yugoslav Self-Managed Enterprises.* Ph.D. dissertation, University of Pennsylvania, 1975.
38. Rivera-Batiz, F., "The Capital Market and Income Distribution in Yugoslavia: A Theoretical and Empirical Note," *Quarterly Journal of Economics,* 94, February 1980, pp. 179–184.
39. Staellerts, R., "The Effect of Capital Intensity on Income in Yugoslav Industry," *Economic Analysis and Workers' Management* 15, No. 4, 1981, pp. 501–516.
40. Estrin, S., *Self Management: Economic Theory and Yugoslav Practice* New York: Cambridge University Press, 1983.
41. Tyson, L. D'Andrea, "A Permanent Income Hypothesis for the Yugoslav Firm," *Economica* 44, No. 4, November 1977, pp. 393–408.
42. Horvat, B., "On the Theory of the labor-managed Firm," in Horvat *et al., Self-Governing Socialism: A Reader.* White Plains: International Arts and Sciences Press.
43. Estrin and Bartlett.
44. Comisso.
45. Noble, D. F., "Social Choice in Machine Design: The Case of Automatically Controlled Machine Tools," in Andrew Zimbalist, ed., *Case Studies on the Labor Process.* New York and London: Monthly Review Press, 1979.
46. See, for example, the argument of Robert H. Hayes and William Abernathy, "Managing Our Way to Decline," *Harvard Business Review,* July–August 1981, pp. 67–77.
47. Caves and Hare, p. 103.
48. A. Bergson, "Market Socialism Revisited," *Journal of Political Economy* 75, No. 5, October 1967, pp. 655–673.
49. Hildebrandt , G. G. and L. D'Andrea Tyson, "Performance Incentives and Planning Under Uncertainty," *Journal of Comparative Economics* 3, No. 3, September 1979, pp. 217–231. *See also* Conn, D., "A Comparison of Alternative Incentive Structures of Centrally Planned Economic Systems," *Journal of Comparative Econnomics,* 3, No. 3, September 1979, pp. 261–276.
50. Meade, J. E., *The Theory of Indicative Planning.* Manchester: Manchester University Press, 1970. *See also* Miller, J., "Meade on Indicative Planning: A Review of Informational Problems," *Journal of Comparative Economics,* 3, No. 1, March 1979, pp. 41–55.
51. Hildebrandt and Tyson.
52. Hayek, F. A., "Socialist Calculation: The Competitive 'Solution'," *Economica,* New Series, 7, No. 26, May 1940, pp. 125–49.

53. Hayek, F. A., "The Use of Knowledge in Society," *American Economic Review,* 35, No. 4, September 1945, pp. 519–30.
54. von Mises, L., *Socialism: An Economic and Sociological Analysis* New Haven: Yale University Press, 1951, pp. 137–142. This is an expanded translation of *Die Gemeinwirtschaft,* originally published in 1922.
55. *Ibid.,* pp. 139–140.

Bibliography

Ardalen, Cyrus. "Workers' Self-Management and Planning: The Yugoslav Case," *World Development* 8, 1980, pp. 623–38.

Barone, E. "The Ministry of Production in the Collectivist State," in F. A. Hayek, ed., *Collectivist Economic Planning.* London: Routledge and Kegan Paul, Ltd., 1935.

Bergson, Abram. "Market Socialism Revisited," *Journal of Political Economy* 75, No. 5, October 1967, pp. 655–673.

Berman, K. V. and M. D. Berman. "The Long Run Analysis of the Labor-Managed Firm: Comment," *American Economic Review* 68, No. 4, September 1978, pp. 701–705.

Bonin, John P. "On the Theory of the Labor-Managed Firm under Price Uncertainty: A Correction," *Journal of Comparative Economics* 4, No. 3, September 1980, pp. 331–337.

———. "On the Design of Managerial Incentive Structures in a Decentralized Planning Environment," *American Economic Review,* Vol. 66, No. 4, September 1976, pp. 682–688.

———. "The Theory of the Labor-Managed Firm from the Membership's Perspective with Implication for Marshallian Industry Supply," *Journal of Comparative Economics* 5, No. 4, December 1981, pp. 337–351.

Bonin, John P. and Alan J. Marcus. "Information, Motivation, and Control in Decentralized Planning: The Case of Discretionary Managerial Behavior," *Journal of Comparative Economics,* Vol. 3, No. 3, September 1979, pp. 235–252.

Cave, Martin and Paul Hare. *Alternative Approaches to Economic Planning.* New York: St. Martin's Press, 1981.

Comisso, Ellen T. *Workers' Control Under Plan and Market.* New Haven: Yale University Press, 1979.

Conn, David. "A Comparison of Alternative Incentive Structures of Centrally Planned Economic Systems," *Journal of Comparative Economics,* Vol. 3, No. 3, September 1979, pp. 261–276.

Conte, Michael A. "On the Economic Theory of the Labor-Managed Firm in the Short Run," *Journal of Comparative Economics* 4, No. 2, June 1980, pp. 173–183.

Domar, E. D. "The Soviet Collective Farm as a Producer Cooperative," *American Economic Review* 56, 1966, pp. 734–757.

Dréze, Jacques. "Some Theory of Labor Management and Participation," *Econometrica* 44, No. 6, 1976.

Dubravčić, Dinko. "Labor as an Entrepreneurial Input," *Economica,* August 1970.

Engels, Friedrich. *Anti-Dühring.* 2nd ed. Moscow: Foreign Languages Publishing House, 1959.

Estrin, S. "Long Run Supply Responses under Self-Management," *Journal of Comparative Economics,* Vol. 6, No. 4, December 1982, pp. 263–278.

————. "Self-Managed and Capitalist Behavior in Alternative Market Structures," Working Paper #273, Department of Economics, Uris Hall, Cornell University, 1982.

————. "An Explanation of Earnings: Variations in the Yugoslav Self-Managed Economy," *Economic Analysis and Workers' Management* 13, No. 1–2, 1979, pp. 175–193.

————. "Income Dispersion in a Self-Managed Economy," *Economica* 48, 1981, pp. 181–194.

————. *Self Management: Economic Theory and Yugoslav Practice.* Cambridge University Press, 1983.

Estrin, S. and William Bartlett. "The Effects of Enterprise Self-Management in Yugoslavia: An Empirical Survey," in Jones and Svejnar, *Participatory and Self-Managed Firms.* Lexington: Lexington Books (D.C. Heath and Co.), 1982.

Estrin, Saul, Jan Svejnar and Carolyn Mow. "Market Imperfections, Labor-Management and Earnings Differentials in a Developing Country: Theory and Evidence from Yugoslavia," Working Paper #276, Department of Economics, Cornell University. May 1982.

Estrin, Saul and Jan Svejnar. "Wage Determination Under Labor-Management: Theory and Evidence from Yugoslavia," Working Paper #292, Department of Economics, Cornell University, December 1982.

Furubotn, Eirik G. "The Long Run Analysis of the Labor-Managed Firm: An Alternative Interpretation," *American Economic Review* 66, No. 1, March 1976, pp. 104–124.

————. "The Long Run Analysis of the Labor-Managed Firm: Reply," *American Economic Review* 68, No. 4, September 1978, pp. 706–09.

————. "The Socialist Labor-Managed Firm and Bank-Financed Investment," *Journal of Comparative Economics* 4, No. 2, June 1980, pp. 184–191.

Furubotn, Eirik G. and Svetozar Pejovich. "Property Rights and the Behavior of the Firm in a Socialist State: The Example of Yugoslavia," *Zeitschrift für Nationalokonomie,* Band 3, No. 3–4 December 1970, pp. 431–454.

Hayek, F. A., editor. *Collectivist Economic Planning.* London: Routledge and Kegan Paul, Ltd., 1935.

Hayek, F. A. "Socialist Calculation: The Competitive 'Solution'" *Economica,* New Series, 7, No. 26, May 1940, pp. 125–149.

Hayek, F. A. "The Use of Knowledge in Society," *American Economic Review,* 35 No. 4., September 1945, pp. 519–530.

Hayes, Robert H. and William Abernathy. "Managing Our Way to Decline," *Harvard Business Review,* July–August 1981, pp. 67–77.

Hey, John D. and John Suckling. "On the Theory of the Competitive Labor-Managed Firm Under Price Uncertainty: Comment," *Journal of Comparative Economics* 4, No. 3, September 1980, pp. 338–42.

Hildebrandt, Gregory G. and Laura D'Andrea Tyson. "Performance Incentives and Planning Under Uncertainty," *Journal of Comparative Economics* 3, No. 3, September 1979, pp. 217–231.

Horvat, Branko. "On the Theory of the Labor-Managed Firm," in Horvat *et al., Self-Governing Socialism:* A Reader. White Plains, NY: International Arts and Sciences Press.

————. *The Political Economy of Socialism.* White Plains: M. E. Sharpe, Inc. 1982.

Hurwicz, Leonid. "Socialism and Incentives: Developing a Framework." *Journal of Comparative Economics,* Vol. 3, No. 3, September 1979, pp. 207–216.

Ichiisi, T. "Coalition Structure in a Labor Managed Market Economy," *Econometrica* 45, No. 2, March 1977, pp. 341–59.

Ireland, Norman J. and Peter J. Law. *Economic Analysis of Labor Managed Enterprises.* London: Croon Helm, 1982.

———— and ————. "An Enterprise Incentive Fund for Labour Mobility in the Cooperative Economy," *Economica* 45, No. 2, May 1978, pp. 143–151.

———— and ————. "Efficiency, Incentives and Individual Labor Supply in the Labor Managed Firm," *Journal of Comparative Economics* 5, No. 1, March 1981, pp. 1–24.

Jensen, Michael C. and William H. Meckling. "Rights and Production Functions: An Application to Labor-Managed Firms and Codetermination," *Journal of Business,* No. 4, October 1979, pp. 469–506.

Jones, Derek and Jan Svejnar. *Participatory and Self-Managed Firms.* Lexington: Lexington Books (D. C. Heath and Co.), 1982.

Lange, Oskar and Fred M. Taylor. *On the Economic Theory of Socialism.* Minneapolis: University of Minnesota Press, 1938.

McCain, Roger A. "On the Optimal Financial Environment for Worker Cooperatives" *Zeitschrift für Nationaloekonomie* 37, Nos. 3–4, 1977, pp. 355–384.

————. "Empirical Implications of Worker Participation in Management" in Jones and Svejnar, *Participatory and Self-Managed Firms,* 1982.

Meade, James E. "The Theory of Labour-Managed Firms and Profit-Sharing," *Economic Journal* 82, No. 1, Supplement, March 1972, pp. 402–428.

————. "Labour-Managed Firms in Conditions of Imperfect Competition," *Economic Journal* 84, No. 4, December 1974, pp. 817–24.

————. "The Adjustment Process of Labour Cooperatives with Constant Returns to Scale and Perfect Competition," *Economic Journal* 98, No. 356, December 1979, pp. 781–88.

————. *The Theory of Indicative Planning.* Manchester: Manchester University Press, 1970.

Milenkovitch, Deborah. *Plan and Market in Yugoslav Economic Thought.* New Haven: Yale University Press, 1971.

Miller, Jeffrey, B. "Meade on Indicative Planning: A Review of Informational Problems," *Jour. Comp. Economics,* Vol. 3, No. 1, March 1979, pp. 41–55.

Miović, Peter. *Determinants of Income Differentials in Yugoslav Self-Managed Enterprises.* Ph.D. dissertation, University of Pennsylvania, 1975.

Mishan, E. J. "A Survey of Welfare Economics, 1939–1959," in American Economic Association and Royal Economic Society, editors, *Surveys of Economic Theory,* Vol. I, New York: St. Martin's Press, 1966.

Noble, David F. "Social Choice in Machine Design: The Case of Automatically Controlled Machine Tools," in Andrew Zimbalist, ed., *Case Studies on the Labor Process.* New York and London: Monthly Review Press, 1979.

Pejovich, Svetozar. "The Firm, Monetary Policy and Property Rights in a Planned Economy," *Western Economics Journal* 7, No. 3, September 1969, pp. 193–200.

Pryor, Frederic L. "The Economics of Production Cooperatives: A Reader's Guide," *Annals of Public and Cooperative Economy,* forthcoming.

Rivera-Batiz, F. "The Capital Market and Income Distribution in Yugoslavia: A Theoretical and Empirical Note," *Quarterly Journal of Economics,* Vol. 94, February 1980, pp. 179–184.

Sacks, Stephen R. *Self-Management in Large Corporations: The Yugoslav Case.* London: George Allen & Unwin, forthcoming.

Sen, Amartya K. "Labour Allocation in a Cooperative Enterprise," *Review of Economic Studies* 33, No. 4, October 1966, pp. 361–371.

Schrenk, Martin *et al.* Yugoslavia: *Self-Management Socialism.* Baltimore: Johns Hopkins Press for the World Bank, 1979.

Staellerts, R. "The Effect of Capital Intensity on Income in Yugoslav Industry," *Economic Analysis and Workers' Management* 15, No. 4, 1981, pp. 501–16.

Steinherr, Alfred. "The Labor-Managed Economy: A Survey of the Economic Literature," *Annals of Public and Cooperative Economy* 49, No. 2, April–June 1978, pp. 129–148.

Stephen, Frank. "Bank Credit and the Labour-Managed Firm: Comment," *American Economic Review* 70, No. 4, 1980, pp. 796–803.

Svejnar, Jan. "On the Theory of a Participatory Firm," *Journal of Economic Theory,* Vol. 26, No. 3, April 1982.

Tyson, Laura D'Andrea. "A Permanent Income Hypothesis for the Yugoslav Firm," *Economica* 44, No. 4, November 1977, pp. 393–408.

Vanek, Jaroslav. "Decentralization Under Workers' Management: A Theoretical Appraisal," *American Economic Review* 59, No. 5, December 1969, pp. 1006–14.

Vanek, Jaroslav. *The General Theory of Labor-Managed Market Economies.* Ithaca: Cornell University Press, 1970.

———. "The Basic Theory of Financing of Participatory Firms," in Vanek, *Self-Management: The Economic Liberation of Man.* Harmondsworth, Penguin, 1975, pp. 445–55.

———. *The Labor-Managed Economies: Essays.* Ithaca: Cornell University Press, 1977.

Vanek, Jaroslav. "The Macroeconomic Theory and Policy of an Open Worker Managed Economy," *Ekonomska Analiza* No. 3–4, Summer 1972. Also published in Jaroslav Vanek, *The Labor-Managed Economy: Essays.* Ithaca: Cornell University Press, 1977.

Vanek, J. and Milana Jovićić. "The Capital Market and Income Distribution in Yugoslavia: A Theoretical and Empirical Analysis," *Quarterly Journal of Economics* 89, No. 3, 1975, pp. 432–44. Reprinted in Vanek, 1977.

Vanek, J. and Peter Miović. "Explorations into the Realistic Behavior of Yugoslav Firms," 1977, in Vanek, 1977, pp. 104–34.

von Mises, Ludwig. "Economic Calculation in the Socialist Commonwealth," in Hayek, ed., *Collectivist Economic Planning,* London: Routledge and Kegan Paul, Ltd., 1935.

————. *Socialism: An Economic and Sociological Analysis.* New Haven: Yale University Press, 1951, reprinted in Morris Bornstein, Comparative Economic Systems: Models and Cases. Revised Edition. Homewood, Illinois: Richard D. Irwin, 1969, pp. 61–67.

Ward, Benjamin. "Market Syndicalism," *American Economic Review* 48, No. 4, 1958, pp. 566–89.

Zimbalist, Andrew, Editor. *Case Studies on the Labor Process.* New York and London: Monthly Review Press, 1979.

5 DYNAMIC COMPARATIVE ECONOMICS: LESSONS FROM SOCIALIST PLANNING

Ruud Knaack

Introduction

It is well known that the mainstream of comparative economics has usually concerned itself with the construction of ideal models, which are studied from the point of view of allocative efficiency. This approach neglects a number of important features of economic systems and is also unable to explain the dynamic processes actually observed.

This paper attempts to initiate a dynamic approach to comparative economics based on the experiences of the state socialist countries. The paper begins with a survey of the mainstream approach in comparative economics. Next follows an analysis of the Soviet planning system and an outline of its fundamental problems. These fundamental problems lead to spontaneous changes of the planning system, the second economy, and to conscious change of the planning system, i.e., economic reform. The final section tries to elucidate what lessons may be drawn from these developments in the state socialist countries

The author is indebted to Annegreet van Bergen, Erik Dirksen, Michael Ellman, Pat Ellman, Michael Masuch, Roald Ramer, Hans-Jürgen Wagener and Andrew Zimbalist for valuable comments.

which could lead to the development of a dynamic approach to comparative economics.

Mainstream approach

The Classical socialism debate

Traditionally comparative economics has been studied entirely in the context of neoclassical equilibrium theory.[1] This holds especially for the first important debate in comparative economics, the Classical socialism debate. The debate was centered around the issue whether central planning could successfully replace the market and more specifically whether central planning could meet in its operations the formal conditions of allocative efficiency satisfied by the model of competitive society. This problem was formulated for the first time by Pareto in 1907. Pareto wondered in which way prices could be fixed in a socialist society "in order that the subjects can enjoy a welfare level as high as possible".[1] The result of that analysis may be called the Pareto-theorem of comparative economics: a replacement of the competitive market regime by the social and united organization of production, ultimately leads to the same pattern of production, assuming that the relations of distribution are the same in both coordination mechanisms and that both strive for maximum efficiency. A year later Barone came to the same result.

This result was obtained purely instrumentally. In both the market system and in the planned system, the ultimate goal is the maximization of individual utility by means of, from this point of view, an efficient allocation of factors of production. The efficient allocation is guaranteed in the market economy by perfect competition and in the planned economy by a government whose only task is to look after the citizens so that the same results are achieved as would have been achieved had there been perfect competition. Hence, as far as prices are concerned, the planners play the role of the Walrasian auctionneer. In fact, we are dealing with virtually the same system in which only the method of coordination is changed.

The Pareto-theorem of comparative economics has been heavily criticized. Von Mises [2] argued that, in a centrally planned economy, rational behaviour is impossible because of the absence of a market for the means of production. In fact, Von Mises confuses prices in an ordinary sense, i.e., the exchange ratio of two commodities on a market, with prices in a generalized sense — the terms on which alternatives are offered.[2] As it has been seen already from the work of Pareto and Barone, prices in the generalized sense may be calculated directly from a system of equations.

Von Mises' proposition about the theoretical impossibility of a rational allocation of means in a socialist economy was adopted with amendments by Von Hayek and Robbins. They do not deny the theoretical possibility of rational allocation in a socialist economy, but, on the other hand, they stress the practical impossibility of central planning. The issue has been put very clearly by Robbins: [3] "Planning . . . would necessitate the drawing up of millions of equations on the basis of millions of individual computations. By the time the equations were solved, the information on which they were based would have become obsolete and they would need to be calculated anew."

For the Von Hayek-Robbins argument two solutions have been offered. The first one, the quasi-market solution, is associated with Lange. In this model, the decisions about both output and investment are taken at the level of the individual enterprises on the basis of accounting prices, which would be set by a higher economic authority and varied at intervals according to whether the market situation was one of excess demand or excess supply. This solution was criticised by Dobb [4] who argued that the amount of decentralization envisaged by Lange would be so great as to virtually eliminate centralized planning which is a great advantage of a socialist economy. Instead, Dobb proposed a centralized solution, in which the center constantly compares the productivity of the productive factors on the basis of the prices of a free market for consumers' goods, and at all levels of allocation pushing these factors always toward a more productive use from a lesser one.

After the Second World War, the theory of quasi-market solutions received a new impulse from linear programming. Assuming that the system of equations in a socialist economy is a linear one, the prices obtained by Pareto, Barone and Lange would be linear programming dual prices. [5]

In the classical socialism debate, power relations and property relations were not investigated. At first sight this is surprising because owing to scarcity the appropriation of goods has consequences for the appropriators, for those who are excluded and for the society as a whole. The explanation is that in neo-classical theory, production is not considered as an activity of people, but as a form of cooperation among factors of production. Each factor of production adds an imputable contribution to the final product. This product will be distributed to the factors according to their contribution. Given certain conditions, for example perfect competition and constant returns to scale, the final product will be distributed without any remainder. This has an important consequence. Regardless the property and motivation structure, the entrepreneur is doomed to strive after only one goal, namely the maximization of profit, in order to survive. In any other case, the enterprise would make economic losses. In this situation, therefore, it is possible to be completely indifferent

about responsibility and decision-making authority: "under perfect competition workers can rent capital goods or capitalists can rent workers". [6]

It is clear that the classical socialism debate is far from realistic. We cannot
blame Pareto and Barone for this. When they discussed the working of a
socialist state, no such state existed. But strangely enough, much of the debate
continued along the same lines in the thirties. The socialist economy was still
investigated as a kind of 'capitalism without capitalists'.[3] This approach in the
classical socialism debate has been much criticized by several authors. They
have argued that a theory of socialism can only start from an analysis of the
existing socialist systems.[4]

The systems theory approach

The failure of the neoclassical ideal models to give an adequate description of
the multiplicity of economic organization types in reality gave rise to the
construction of more complex models with the help of the language and
approach of systems theory. These system theoretical models have, like the
neoclassical models, a functional nature. Their object is the specification and
estimation of a production function of the entire economic system

$$R = f(e, s, p_s) \qquad (5.1)$$

in which e denotes the environment, s the system structure, p_s the policies
pursued by the participants under system structure s, and R the results observed during the period of comparison. [7] Until now, work has mainly
concentrated on the specification of the function. Kornai [8] and Montias [9],
in particular, put a lot of effort in the specification of the important elements
and aspects for the system.

Given the impossibility of analysing simultaneously all aspects of the economic system, only partial analyses have been attempted. First, an attempt has
been made to describe the economic institutions with the help of selected
structural aspects. For example, Neuberger and Duffy [10] described the institutions with the help of a set of categories centered round three partial structures, namely the decision-making structure, the information structure and the
motivation structure. In fact, this approach is a form of institutional economics. [11]

Secondly, there is an attempt to build a typology of economic systems with
the help of a set of system theoretical categories which are considered to be
important. For example, Montias [12] classified the state socialist countries in
four ideal types, namely, mobilization systems, centralized-administered systems, decentralized-administered systems and market-socialism systems.

Thirdly, there is an attempt to compare empirically the performance of concrete economic systems. In most cases, it is necessary to restrict the analysis to the comparison of productivity.

The systems theory approach neglects fewer features than the neoclassical approach. This can be clearly seen from the systems theoretical approach to organizations, which are considered rather as coalitions than as teams. In the neoclassical approach, the organization is seen as a homogeneous entity, which, without restriction, may implement any decision taken by the constitutional organs. For that reason, neoclassical theory may neglect organizational and motivational problems. In reality, organizations are not obedient tools, but a group of cooperating individuals, which have some but not all goals in common. Thus, moral and material incentives both negative and positive, play an important motivating role in ensuring the implementation of decisions. [13] In a coalition the formation of goals is a concrete problem in which the distribution of power plays an important role. In this connection, in the systems theory approach the neutral state also disappeared. The assumed neutrality of the state has also been criticized by Eucken. According to Eucken [14], the tremendous power position of the state provokes a self-evident exercise of this power. History shows clearly the absurdity of the proposition that the state is willing not to use this possibility of exercising power.

In fact, however, the system theoretical approach has not contributed more than the development of a heuristic terminology for the description, comparison and analysis of economic systems. In this approach, moreover, the structure of the system is considered as given. In reality, however, the structure of the system is also changing. It is not sufficient, therefore, to specify a social production function. It is also necessary to explain "why a particular society comes to rest in a particular category at a given moment or why and how it comes to combine market, planning and its characteristic form of administration". [15] What is lacking is a dynamic theory of institutional change. In the next sections an attempt will be made to sketch a dynamic approach to comparative economics based on the experiences of the state socialist countries

The fundamental problems of the Soviet planning system

The Soviet Planning System

The Soviet planning system as we know it today was shaped during the period of the First and Second Five Year Plans. It shows in its intended method of functioning a great similarity with the conception of a socialist society formulated first by Kautsky and taken over by Lenin in his *State and Revolution.* "All citizens are transformed into hired employees of the State . . . A witty German Social-Democrat of the Seventies of the last century called the postal service an example of the socialist economic system. This is very true . . . this is the economic foundation we need". [16]

This conception of a socialist society is reflected in the concrete Soviet planning system by the extensive use of ideas like party-mindedness, directiveness and one-man-management. [17] The principle of party mindedness (*partiinost'*) means that the plan is a concrete expression of party policy. Characterizing Soviet planning, Stalin long ago stressed that the mark of planning is its directiveness; that economic activity proceeds in accordance with instructions from above. The principle of one-man-management means that in each economic unit decisions are made not by a committee but by one man. He is responsible to his superiors for the execution of orders.

The basic method of Soviet planning is the material balance method, a double-entry bookkeeping in physical or price units. A material-balance shows, on the one hand, the economy's resources, and, on the other hand, the economy's needs, for particular products over a specified period of time. The method consists of an iterative process of concurrent adjustment of the supply and demand for each commodity, resulting from an exchange of information between the center and the firms, ending with the closing of the balance when the sum total of all allocations matches the total planned supply. It can be proven that under certain conditions the material balance method will lead to a consistent result [18] and to an optimal result. [19]

Imperfections of the Soviet planning system

When the optimum conditions of the Soviet planning system are compared with the optimum conditions of the neoclassical models, surprisingly the same unrealistic assumptions are found, such as strict rationality, no uncertainty, smooth production functions, no unavoidable conflict, etc. [20] In reality these optimum conditions of the Soviet planning system are not fulfilled. The arguments for this have already been given by Von Hayek in the classical socialism debate: namely, that the information required to coordinate systematically the activities of hundreds of thousands of enterprises is lacking.

The partial ignorance of the center results from the impotence of the central leadership to concentrate within itself all the necessary information for the construction of efficient plans. This information is mainly concentrated in the hands of the periphery. In the process of transmitting information a lot of things might go wrong. [21]

First, the subordinates may transmit inaccurate information. This results indirectly from the fact that "each official tends to distort the information he passes upwards to his superiors in the hierarchy. Specifically all types of officials tend to exaggerate data that reflects favourably on themselves and to minimize those that reveal their own shortcomings". [22]

Secondly, the process of information transmission destroys some information. During the process of planning, aggregation by commodities, enterprises and time periods takes place. Each aggregation introduces errors.

Thirdly, information can also be ignored when it reaches the addresses. This may happen when the information does not fit in with the existing pattern of belief. For example, Stalin was surprised at the German invasion of 1941, despite the advance information transmitted by Sorge and others. Sometimes information is ignored because the source is distrusted. In the Stalinist period it often happened that the information provided by specialists was ignored because the political leadership regarded them as politically unreliable. For this reason an entirely fanciful picture of reality could emerge.

Fourthly, the information can be out of date. The economy is continually being affected by events which were not foreseen when the plan was drawn up. This is particularly true with respect to harvest results, technical and organizational innovations, international affairs and demographic factors.

Also data processing problems are creating difficulties for the compilation of consistent plans. [23] First, the planning of production and supply for all the commodities produced and consumed in the economy is regarded as too big a problem to be solved. Accordingly, the authorities concern themselves only with the more important commodities. In the USSR, the sixteen thousand commodity groups which were centrally planned in 1968, represented in an aggregated form the bulk of the twenty million commodities distinguished in the all-Union industrial classification. This reduces the size of the problem from millions to thousands of equations, but it makes the material balances incomplete. It might happen that the requirements of the nonplanned products used as an input into the production of centrally planned products are greater than their output.

Secondly, the material-balances for the centrally planned products might be inaccurate. According to Levine, [24] the number of iterations required for consistency of the material-balances are between six and thirteen. However, because of the great labor intensity involved in the calculation of changes and the insufficiency of time in practice for the completion of such work, sometimes only those balances which are linked by first order relationships are changed.

Thirdly, the planning of production and supply is regarded as too large for one organization and, accordingly, is split among many organizations. The trouble is that not all organizations use the material balance method for securing consistency. For example, in the USSR the organizations other than Gosplan, such as the territorial administrations of Gossnab, predominantly rely on the method of 'planning from the achieved level'. This inevitably leads to mistakes.

Fourthly, given the high level of aggregation of the enterprise plan, the quotas have to be specified through direct contact. This gives rise to considerable difficulties. Suppliers may not wish to supply goods of the type required. For example, when planning is in tons, metallurgic enterprises are not very keen on producing thin steel sheets. Moreover, the producer enterprise may not be able to produce the goods required, because it lacks the necessary inputs, or because the plan, although balanced in aggregate terms, is unbalanced in disaggregate terms. For example, the demand and supply of tubes may appear to be in equilibrium, but the demand for tubes used in oil pipelines may far exceed the supply possibilities.

The partial ignorance of the central planners and the limitations of the planning techniques reveal themselves in disturbances in the production process, frequent changes in the enterprise plans, deliveries which do not come in time and so on. These phenomena, inter alia, cause a tremendous loss of labor time. For the GDR the loss of labor time has been estimated to be more than ten percent. [25] It also happened that certain enterprises are forced to surrender temporarily a part of their labor force to help elsewhere. In the Soviet Union, for example, each year more than eight million factory workers are enlisted in the harvest. From all these arguments we may conclude that the enterprise plans turn out very often to be inadequate, inaccurate and partial. Hence, the enterprises are caught in a decision trap: they are supposed to fulfil nonfulfillable plans. [26]

Managerial strategies

Given the decision trap in which the enterprises are caught, they have to develop alternative strategies in order to meet the demands on them. These strategies can be legal, when they remain within the limits of the planning system, or illegal, when they form a part of the second economy. There are three legal economic strategies at the enterprise level to deal with the frictions in the production process: risk aversion, overtime and investment drive.

A manager who will be rewarded on the basis of plan-fulfillment, but is regularly confronted with bottlenecks and shortages, will develop risk averting behavior to be able to cope with his problems. This risk averting behavior may take different forms. First, the manager might maintain excessive reserves of factors of production including labor. One way of creating reserves is to strive for a slack enterprise plan: such a plan provides for less output than possible or more inputs than are necessary. A slack plan may be obtained by transmitting imperfect information in the process of negotiation with the higher authorities during the formulation of the enterprise plan. Secondly, risk aversion is an important factor hindering technical progress. The technological gap between the state socialist countries and the leading capitalist countries is not caused as much by a lack of research results as by a lack of diffusion of new technology. [27] The diffusion of technology is hampered by the organizational division between research and development and, moreover, by the use of criteria giving high priority to quarterly plan fulfillment.

The enterprise often tries to remove bottlenecks by paid overtime work, especially at the end of the planning year. As a result the wages paid out are often more than the value of the consumption goods produced, leading to inflationary pressures or floating purchasing power.

Enterprises may also try to escape from the pressures of bottlenecks and shortages by huge investment programs. When the foundry is unable to supply enough casting to the metal cutting workshop, it ought to be enlarged. When there is a queueing for the firm's product, investment is needed so that those in the queue can get more. According to Kornai, [28] bottlenecks and shortages are the main source of the investment hunger characteristic of the state socialist countries.

In order to meet the plan targets, an important part of the required inputs has to be obtained through unofficial channels, the second economy. The second economy includes all nonregulated activities of the state and cooperative organizations, as well all forms of private activities. [29] A check carried out by USSR Gossnab revealed that enterprises of the Ministry of Industrial Construction obtain twenty percent of the steel they use and twelve percent of the cement by means of these unofficial circuits. [30]

These unofficial circuits can take several forms. To begin with the unofficial circuit can be characterized by personal relationships. The structural circumstances of central planning based on partial ignorance makes mutual trust a scarce and highly valued commodity which can be obtained through the exchange of personal favors extended at personal risk. From this it follows that the success of the plan director is largely determined by his ability to use the resources of his office for exchanging favors with key officials in the institutions constituting his organizational environment, for example with the local party and state officials. Thus, there emerge cross-institutional cliques whose members dispose of their respective official prerogatives to mutual advantage. It is through and by these local power élites that plans are (partly) implemented and modified. [31]

When these personal relationships are absent, some other methods can be used in order to implement the plans. For example, the management often uses the services of a *tolkach*. A *tolkach* is an unofficial supply agent whose job is to see that the necessary materials, components and equipment will arrive. To do this he makes extensive use of unorthodox means like agitation, nagging, begging and sometimes bribery.

In agriculture, an important role in construction is played by the *shabashniki**, privately constituted construction brigades. In one year in Kurgan Oblast alone, *shabashniki* carried out construction work to a value of seventy million rubles, or fifty percent more than all the official building organizations together. Their earnings are high by Soviet standards, say 2000 ruble per person per season which is about a year's average wage in the USSR.

From the behavior of the enterprises three conclusions may be drawn. First, the behavior of the enterprises makes it clear that the prerequisite for the efficient functioning of the Soviet planning system, namely that all participants in the economy are a part of a team, is not present. The Soviet planning system presupposes that the implementing organizations are pliable and obedient participants. However, in reality all organizations are striving after their own goals, which often lead to conflicts and inefficiencies. Hence, it is necessary to formulate an efficient motivation structure in the state socialist countries aiming at the correspondence of the individual interest and the social interest.

Secondly, insofar as the responses of the enterprises remain within the limits of the official first economy, the administrative uncertainty under which the enterprises have to operate will be aggravated. For example, the greater the external shortage of labor is, the greater will be the desire of enterprises for internal labor hoarding. Obviously, these internal hidden reserves of labor will exacerbate the bottlenecks and shortages elsewhere. Here we encounter one of the vicious circles of the Soviet planning system. The shortage of labor necessitates, from a national point of view, the intensification of the production process. At the same moment the shortage of labor induces the enterprises to hoard labor. Hence, the shortage of labor requires an efficient use of labor and prevents it at the same time. [33]

Thirdly, as far as the responses of the enterprises are unofficial, as far as they are a part of the second economy, the reactions will to some degree correct

*Shabashniki are temporary laborers, who carry out construction work during the summer months. They are organized in privately constituted, illegal but tolerated, construction brigades. The *shabashniki* often work 14–15 hours a day, seven days a week. Usually, they are well disciplined, do not drink, and guarantee quality. In many cities there are unofficial agencies, whose job is to mediate between the seasonal workers and the *kolkhozy* and to obtain the construction materials. Obviously, the *shabashniki* can only operate in an environment in which the official state construction enterprises and the inter-*kolkhoz*-construction enterprises are functioning badly. [32]

the rigidities and mistakes of the first economy. According to Powell [34], the second economy functions as a corrective mechanism, that protects the first economy from extreme and disastrous results. The mutual interweaving of the first and second economy is described by Dolan [35] in what he calls an experimental polycentric model. The properties of the model are investigated with the technique of computer simulation. The experiments reveal that the combined operation of the first and the second economy almost realizes the goals of an optimal plan, while the economic system completely collapses when the first economy operates alone.

Reactions of the political leadership

In the last section it was observed that in the Soviet planning system partial ignorance and inadequate techniques give rise to bottlenecks and shortages, which are intensified by the legal reactions of the enterprises or modified by the illegal reactions of the enterprises. Of course, the bottlenecks and the legal and illegal reactions of the enterprises are well-known to the authorities. They do not, however, interpret these phenomena as consequences of an infeasible planning system and ultimately as reflecting theoretical inadequacies, for the planning system is the whole rationale for their existence. Instead, they see them as consequences of imperfections in the planning system, the under-development of the productive forces or the operations of some external or internal class enemy.

In order to deal with the imperfections of the planning system the central authorities have tried to improve the information structure, the planning techniques and the incentive system. In the seventies in most state socialist countries it was attempted to shorten the information channels by reducing the traditional system of three organization levels, namely ministry, chief administrations and enterprises, to two organization levels. The chief administrations were dissolved and new organizations, associations, were formed above the enterprise level. It may be questioned whether this organizational reform offers a solution to the problem of partial ignorance. Rather, the situation may be viewed as a shift from an external information problem from the viewpoint of the enterprises to an internal information problem from the viewpoint of the associations.

In the seventies the central authorities tried to improve planning techniques in all state socialist countries by ensuring the wide application of mathematical planning techniques, the use of electronic computers and organizational technology and means of communication. On all levels management information and control systems* were introduced. The results of many of these systems were very favorable. It often took not more than 2–2½ years to recoup the costs of a management information and control system. The most effective systems are those regulating technological processes where the investment is recouped on average in one to two years. [37] It was intended that the management information and control systems would form an interconnected whole enabling the planners to control in an efficient way the entire economy. (Following the same train of thought, Lange [38] once thought that the computer could replace the market and could assist the central authorities with the construction of an all-embracing plan. Wiles once called this expectation the replacement of 'perfect competition' by 'perfect computation'.) However, evaluating the Soviet experience, the management information and control systems still have to be considered more as a part of the traditional planning routine, although undoubtedly the systems shortened the process of data processing and for that reason increased the possibility of control by the central authorities. [39]

As a part of the Kosygin reforms (1966–1969) the central authorities tried to mobilize the available resources by the prescription of taut plans. The system for taut plans can be written as

$$B = a.Q_p + b.(Q_a - Q_p)$$

$$a > b > 0 \qquad\qquad (5.2)$$

where B is the value of the bonus, Q_p is the planned value of the bonus forming index and Q_a is the actual value of the bonus forming index. [40] The first term provides an incentive to adopt a high plan. The higher the planned value of the bonus forming index, the higher the bonus. Besides the aiming at taut plans the bonus formula is also based on an overfulfillment logic: bonuses are supplied also when the plan targets are overfulfilled. It is obvious that the general message of the system is 'more is better than less'. Apparently, the system functions best when the plan is overfulfilled. According to Lohmann [41], such a train of thought is only logical assuming that a more efficient allocation is possible than that foreseen in the ex ante scientific official plan.

---

*A management information and control system, or an automated management system (ASU) as the Soviet call them, is a computerized system for information and data processing. These automated management systems are introduced at several levels, namely at the level of the enterprises (ASUP), regional organizations and ministries (OASU), the State Planning Commission (ASPR–automated system of plan calculations), and also at nationwide functional systems for prices, supply (ASU MTS), statistics (ASGS) and scientific-technical progress (ASUNT). It is envisaged that all these systems will be compatible with one another and form subsystems of one national system (OGAS). [36]

The aiming at taut plans did not lead to the intended results. Instead of mobilizing the hidden reserves, it strengthened the inclination of the enterprise managers to avoid risks and to strive for slack plans. (See Koont and Zimbalist in this volume.) It also leads to formal changes of the plans. Ministries wish to report that not only have they fulfilled their plans, but that most of their enterprises have also. If, for instance, enterprise A looks as if it could produce 110 percent of its original plan and enterprise B only 94 percent, then without actually changing anyone's output, it is possible to alter the plan so that both are at, or just in excess of, 100 percent of the revised plan. [42]

As far as the shortages are blamed on the underdevelopment of the productive forces, the remedy of the central authorities is the use of mechanisms directed to the qualitative and quantitative growth of the productive forces. These mechanisms are huge investment programs and the stimulation of technical progress.

The first mechanism used by the central authorities to cope with the underdevelopment of the productive forces is a huge investment program. In the sixties and the seventies the planned share of gross investment in the state socialist countries varied between 25 and 40 percent of the produced net material product. [43] The investment policy was aiming at a rapid mechanization of the primary activities in industry. Notwithstanding this huge share of planned investment, the planned investment fund was regularly surpassed. This is caused by two factors. [44] First, the costs of the investment programs are systematically underestimated. The initiators of investment projects have an interest in underestimating costs since the chances of acceptance of the project are greater if expected costs are relatively small. The discrepancy between estimated costs and actual ones is on average on the order of 20–30 percent and a discrepancy of 50 percent is not infrequent. Secondly, projects outside the plan are often added to the originally approved investments for reason of unforeseen troubles and difficulties such as floods and planning mistakes.

As a result of the huge share of planned investment and the regular surpassing of the planned investment fund, the state socialist countries are characterized by investment tension. The stronger the investment tension the more it is felt that investment demand tries to draw resources away from other fields of utilization thus amplifying general shortages. Again there is a vicious circle. Awareness of shortage is a main motive for expansion drive and investment tension, which in turn amplified shortages. When the investment tension has become too strong, the central authorities will protect the most important investment projects on the basis of an ad hoc priority system.

The second mechanism used to develop the productive forces is the stimulation of technical progress. In Marxist-Leninist thought and in planning practice enormous stress has always been laid on the importance of stimulating technical progress. In contemporary Soviet plans, action on technical progress comes first. This indicates the symbolic significance attached to it. Furthermore, in terms of numbers of institutes and the number of qualified personnel huge inputs go into the research and development sector. In the USSR the pool of manpower in research and development was already in 1966 substantially larger in absolute terms than that in any other country, including the United States. [45] Despite all this, the results are somewhat disappointing. The technology gap between the USSR and the leading capitalist countries is substantial and seems not to have diminished in the last 15–20 years. [46] This might be explained by systemic factors in the Soviet planning system, for example, the already mentioned problems with the transfer from research to production, the stress on short term plan fulfillment and the weak position of users in the administrative economy. [47]

When the problems are blamed on the opposition of a class enemy, the reaction of the central authorities is evident: class struggle from above. In the case of an external class enemy, the felt threat from outside is answered by an increase of arms production at the expense of civil production, which negatively influences the tensions already existing in the civil sector. [48] In the case of an internal class enemy, the central authorities might react in different ways. [49] First, they might complain about the lack of class consciousness. Opponents are reproached for possessing a lower-middle-class and individualistic way of thinking. When the class enemy is becoming too troublesome, the method of political repression is not ignored. Secondly, the political atmosphere becomes more rigid. The necessity of severe discipline is stressed so that nobody can construct his own plan. The control systems become more and more complex and the penalty for white-collar-criminality is raised. In 1961, capital punishment was reintroduced for some economic crimes in the Soviet Union. According to Western estimates, about 2000–2500 death sentences are handed down each year, of which about one third are actually implemented. Recently in the USSR a campaign against corruption has been waged. Thirdly, a process of centralization begins. Because the central authorities do not trust anybody, all the key decisions are taken by themselves.

From this pattern of reaction by the central authorities, two conclusions can be drawn. First, the reactions of the central authorities are not consistent. Some of the reactions are based on the idea that the planning system works well and that the problems originate outside the planning system. Other reactions on the contrary proceed implicitly from the idea that it is the planning system itself which generates malfunctions which through ad hoc solutions have to be corrected. Hence, in fact, the policy of the central authorities wavers between two opinions. In this respect, it is worthwhile mentioning the opinion of Spulber [50], who makes a distinction between central command, the administrative centralized day-to-day management of the economy, and planning, the operation of the economy on the basis of a consistent, reliable and coherent plan or set of plans. According to Spulber, the Soviet system of centralized day-to-day administrative management does not render the Soviet economy one coordinated by a coherent plan.

Secondly, it has been seen that the central authorities pattern of reaction in many cases amplifies the existing difficulties. The Soviet planning system is characterized by an interweaving of vicious circles. As a result of partial ignorance and inadequate techniques the economy is plagued by ever-recurring bottlenecks and shortages. These are amplified by the legal and illegal reactions of the enterprises. The reactions of the enterprises are not effectively curbed by the central authorities. On the contrary, their reactions amplify the investment drive and hoarding tendencies of the enterprises and create in addition a sphere of administrative uncertainty in which the enterprises cannot be sure whether their actions will be positively or negatively evaluated.

It is clear that the problem of the ever recurring bottlenecks and shortages can only be solved by a disentanglement of the interweaving vicious circles. To that end, many efforts have been made. These will be discussed in the next section.

Economic reform

The economic reforms in the state socialist countries were meant to transform the formal economic mechanism to such an extent that regulation through planning could be combined with greater reliance on the market. An easy way to reach this goal is to integrate the second economy in the first economy. This happened on a significant scale in the countries of Eastern Europe. In these countries, therefore, the second economy is identified more with the legal private sector. In Hungary, for example, private workshops are permitted to do repairs on apartments. They quite legally carry out 84 percent of all such work compared with 60 percent carried out illegally in the USSR. Whereas the Soviet Union only makes attempts to dam the second economy, Hungary has enlisted private initiative to an appreciable extent; where a new law on the development of private enterprises came into force in January 1982. This permits the setting up of private businesses with up to one hundred workers.

Another path of economic reform is the enlargement of the decision-space of the enterprises. With different results all state socialist countries have experimented with various ways of decentralizing economic decision-making. The first wave of economic reforms started in the fifties in countries like Czechoslovakia, Hungary and Poland. These reforms suffered a severe setback in the late fifties, not only for economic but also political reasons. The conservative political climate in Eastern Europe resulting from the Soviet invasion of Hungary in 1956 was not congruent with decentralization measures in the economic sphere.

The idea of economic reform was clearly resuscitated in the early sixties. On the economic side the second wave reflected the failure to recover the dynamism of the fifties. For example, in 1963 the NMP fell in absolute terms in Czechoslovakia. On the political side the economic reform seemed less frightening for the ruling elites than before. The chances of an orderly economic system free from radical ideas such as workers' councils were judged to be more favorable.

The economic reforms went in the direction of devolution of decision-making and the increased role of the market mechanism in a broad sense. One of the outstanding features of the second wave was to establish a closer link between internal and external economic activities, with the foreign trade sector undergoing in many instances the most serious reorganization. In most cases, it was not the enterprise which was the direct beneficiary of the devolution of decision-making, but the intermediate branch organization. In the course of this development the intermediate organization underwent substantial transformation: it became an association of nationalized enterprises in which the enterprise function became vested. Hence, the devolution of decision-making was combined with a higher level of organizational concentration. [51]

The steps taken in this general direction in individual countries varied greatly as far as the scale of change was concerned. The gap, for example, between Hungary on the one hand and Romania on the other was in this respect very wide. However, the underlying concept of change was in each country the same: to retain the principle of effective central planning. The differences in devolution of decision-making and the various proportions of direct and indirect steering of economic activities reflected only different views on the applicability of one set of instruments or another within the framework of central planning. In this respect we can better interpret the economic reforms as a form of technocratization than of marketization. [52]

Also, the second wave of economic reform was short-lived. In the GDR where the New Economic Mechanism was proclaimed in 1963, the first changes in attitude appeared as early as 1967. In Czechoslovakia the recentralization measures came after the Soviet invasion of 1968. In the USSR, the Kosygin reform of 1965 was followed after 1969 by a 'galloping recentralization'. [53] In Hungary the loss of momentum showed itself initially in the retention of controls in the beginning of the seventies which had been considered as temporary in 1968. The Polish case was more complicated. The economic reform of 1968 went along with strong deflationary policies. This led to the December 1970 workers revolt and the toppling of Gomulka. New attempts at a gradual reform started in 1972–73, but in 1975 some important elements of autonomy of the associations were withdrawn in an informal way. [54]

The reason for these setbacks was mainly the nonfulfillment of the three prerequisites for any successful economic reform; namely, the reform must be consistent, both in its micro aspect and its macro aspect, and the reform must be embedded in a politically stable environment. [55]

The problem of micro economic consistency has been analyzed by Wakar. [56] He has pointed out that in any economic system the three elements of the stimulation system (the price system, the incentive system and the calculation system) have to form a harmonious whole. The various stimulation systems each have their own particular structure. For example, profit incentives require another method of price formulation and cost calculation than gross output incentives. These conditions have not been met by any economic reform in the Soviet bloc. For instance, in the USSR the price reform was reasonably successful in eliminating the loss-making industries, but did not eliminate the dispersion of the profitability and the turnover rates. Therefore, the profit rate could still not function as an indicator of the overall work of an enterprise. [57]

This also has consequences for the acceptance of the increased role of bonuses related to profitability. Because the profits still did not reflect differences in effort, it gave the non-profit-making enterprises and the non-bonus receiving workers an opportunity to complain about unfair treatment.

Successful economic reform requires macroeconomic consistency, i.e., the macroeconomic situation must be consistent with the reform's successful implementation. Producer goods have to be readily available, otherwise the autonomy of enterprises is largely meaningless. Consumer goods have to be readily available, otherwise material incentives are largely meaningless. In short, to use Kornai's [58] terminology, the central authorities have to pursue a policy of harmonious rather than rushed economic growth. This condition was not met in most countries. For example, in Hungary during the early seventies the markets for both labor and investment rapidly led to problems after the release of the market forces. In the seventies, the ratio of net accumulation to net material product rose from 23.5 percent in 1970 to 27 percent in 1977. This increase, however, was not the result of a deliberate government policy, but by an investment drive of the enterprises resulting in a huge gap between the actual enterprise investment and the planned enterprise investment, [59] Therefore, in 1971 an abrupt credit freeze was imposed to deal with overinvestment and in 1974 new legislation increased central control over investment plans.

The third prerequisite of an economic reform is that the reform is embedded in a politically stable and supportive environment. An in-depth, comprehensive reform that represents a sharp departure from the existing system requires a strong government and an equally strong bureaucratic apparatus which will have enough experience and confidence to prepare the proper grounds for the reform and enough patience to wait out an occasionally lengthly gestation period before the reform comes to fruition. According to Korbonski and Terry [60], this prerequisite might (partly) explain the relative success of the Hungarian economic reform compared with those in the other East European countries. One of the results of the Hungarian revolution in 1956 was the nearly total collapse of the Hungarian party, which forced Kadar to rebuild it from scratch. In the process of doing so, he was able to eliminate the two extremes on the left and the right, thus fashioning a new party that was united in its loyalty to Kadar. While there is some evidence of ongoing internal disagreements within the party, culminating in the removal of some leading supporters of the reforms such as Dezso Nyers, all indications point to the fact that at the beginning of the eighties the Hungarian party remains as united as fifteen years ago. The situation in Poland, for example, was strikingly different. The chief characteristic of the Polish party has been for many years the lack of basic unity. This absence of consensus led to the successive reforms becoming increasingly watered-down compromises, far removed from a comprehensive overhaul of the economic system.

The fluctuations in economic policy in the post–Stalin period in Eastern Europe have been formalized into what Nuti calls an economic and institutional cycle. [61] The cycle works as follows. Measures of economic decentralization do not go far enough. The hard budget constraint is not introduced. Hence, the new system is not strong enough to overcome the built-in accumulation bias of the old system. It may ever worsen it by releasing central control. As a consequence, the economy remains in a state of strain with pressure on resources which does not give the economic decentralization a chance to operate in a congenial environment: inflation and economic disruption are the result. The living standard of the population does not improve significantly, giving the opposition a weapon to end the decentralization process. Central control, both economic and political, is tightened up again.

On nearly all occasions, the dynamic of the cycle is based on the traditional conflict between individual rationality and social rationality. In the East European case, this conflict reveals itself in a contradiction between the goals of the government and the goals of the enterprises. The moment the goals of the government dominate over the goals of the enterprises, the enterprises work more and more inefficiently; the moment the goals of the enterprises dominate, the economy suffers from macroeconomic disequilibria and increasing earnings inequalities.

Lessons from socialist planning

We can distinguish between intended and unintended results of an action. Socialists have always believed that the unintended results would be predominant under conditions of capitalism and that planning would guarantee that the intended results would be increasingly predominant under socialism. Above, however, it was observed that the Soviet planning system is plagued with an array of unintended results, like bottlenecks and shortages, caused by the nonfulfillment of the optimal conditions of the Soviet planning system. This creates a decision-space on the decentralized level.

The problems with which the Soviet authorities are confronted are not unique. In fact, they happen in every situation in which activities are coordinated in a dynamic environment with the help of a 'rational-central-rule'. The class of planning models characterized by the 'rational-central-rule' is called orthodox planning by Van Gunsteren. [62]

Another well-known example of orthodox planning is the 'Planning-Programming-Budgeting-System' (PPBS)*. One aim of this system is to contribute to a more rational and more conscious process of decision-making regarding government expenditures. In practice, PPBS has not been able to achieve this goal. In the literature many explanations have been offered for this. [63]

On the basis of all the experiences with the 'rational-central-rule', for example, in the form of the Soviet planning system or PPBS, it is questionable whether orthodox planning can function at all at the level of a national economy. Van Gunsteren [64] has an outspoken opinion on this issue. "When a proposal does not work as intended one has always a choice. One can say that something is wrong with the proposal or that something is wrong with the world . . . (however), orthodox planning can only work when goals are clear and consistent, when there is a reliable basis of knowledge, when formal organizations serve as obedient instruments, when the field of application is relatively stable and when the plan is sustained by considerable power and consensus. These conditions are seldom met".

From this perspective, it is possible to interpret the origin of the second economy and the economic reform as a reaction to the working of an infeasible orthodox planning system. The fact that the impossibility of the creation of an universal plan creates a decision-space on the decentralized level, which is filled up through horizontal relations, in a formal or an informal way, is called by De Jong [65] the planning paradox.

The market mechanism too has a paradox. Under conditions of perfect competition and constant returns to scale, the individual equilibrium of the

---

*PPBS was introduced in the USA in the early 1960s in the Defense Department for controlling, scheduling and budgeting complex programs in an efficient way.

firm is indeterminate. This gives room for a process of free competition. When one firm can compete on noneconomic grounds better than the others, this will finally lead to a sharp decrease in the number of market subjects. On the basis of these paradoxes of coordination mechanisms we can logically conclude that each real, complex economic system will be characterized by a combination of coordination mechanisms.

Reaching this conclusion, one can immediately ask oneself the question: does there exist an optimal combination of coordination mechanisms? This question is answered in the affirmative by the adherents of the convergence theory. This theory was originally advocated by Tinbergen. [66] According to the Tinbergian school (e.g., Van den Doel [67]), the dynamics of the alleged convergence process can be explained by each society's efforts to overcome inefficiencies. Since there is an optimal economic order which is the same for all societies (Tinbergen) or similar for all societies (Van den Doel) and all societies function in similar environments, then efforts to reduce waste automatically generate convergence.

To the extent that the search for efficiency plays a dominant role in social evolution, this assumption contains an important truth. It may happen, however, that the most efficient set of institutions is not known. In addition, there may be important complementarities between policies or institutions so that substantial gains in one area can only be obtained at substantial costs elsewhere. Moreover, factors other than economic efficiency may be important in determining social evolution. In this connection Nuti [68] points out that no economic decentralization was contemplated, or even discussed in the state socialist countries, until after Stalin's death. Obviously, in the evolution of economic systems political factors play an important role. As far as the similarity of the environment is concerned, it is obvious that the position of countries in the world economy and international politics differ widely and, therefore, the possibilities for the individual countries to pursue an autonomous policy are different. Basically, the conception of an optimal economic order is an application to the economy as a whole of the elementary mathematics of optimization: a social welfare function is maximized given some constraints. In general, we can say that this model is a classical example of a model based on the 'rational-central-rule'. Most of what we already said about the Soviet planning system and PPBS is also relevant for the assumptions underlying the model of the optimal regime.

From the discussion about the modified convergence theory we may conclude that the combination of coordination mechanisms characterizing an economic system may change as a result of the evolution of the political process and of environmental changes; in other words, each system is determined by the 'dialectics of coordination mechanisms'. More precisely, the dialectics of coordination mechanisms is the expression of a dialectical relationship between economic process and economic organization. For example, orthodox planning leads to some unfavourable results on the basis of which some market elements are substituted for some parts of orthodox planning. New problems will, however, arise leading to a substitution of market elements by orthodox planning. Hence, whether one coordination mechanism will be substituted by the other depends, inter alia, on the weighting of each mechanism's advantages and disadvantages by the political process.

Conclusions

The ideal models of orthodox planning and free competitive markets have some features in common. Both models are undercomplex, i.e., when these models form the basis of a government policy, the pursued policy will generate a multitude of unintended results because of the limitations of the model. In the case of the market, externalities, inequalities, unemployment, etc. are observed; in the case of orthodox planning, there are inefficiencies and stagnation. Furthermore, both ideal models are undemocratic in the sense that in both cases worker self-management cannot exist or is meaningless. In orthodox planning this results from planning itself; in the market mechanism it results from the necessity to strive after maximization of profit on penalty of downfall. As a result of the tension between intended and unintended results of the economic process and the tension between formal and factual democracy, economic systems evolve into a more complex organizational form, a combination of planning and market.

However, this combination is neither stable, given the internal instability of both ideal models, nor free of problems. Each real system is based on a practical compromise of principles and requests which exclude each other. "The economy is not a supermarket in which we can make our choice as we like. Every real economic system constitutes an organic whole. They may contain good and bad features . . . The choice of system lies only among 'various package deals' ". [69] Which package deal will be finally chosen cannot be decided in theory. "It must evolve from concrete practise based on conditions peculiar to each country, e.g., its social relations and material development, as well as the country's role in the international economy". [70]

It has been the argument of this paper that the analysis of economic systems, their evolution and their performance, would be enriched by a consideration of what has been termed here the dialectics of coordination mechanisms and the interplay of the political and economic spheres in different periods. Such an approach would constitute the basis for a dynamic comparative economics.

Notes

1. Wagener, H. J., *Economische systemen*, Alphen a/d Rijn 1980, p. 42
2. Lange, O., 'On the Economic Theory of Socialism', in H. Townsend (ed.), *Price Theory* Harmondsworth 1971, p.34
3. Nuti, M., 'The Contradictions of Socialist Economies: A Marxian Interpretation', in R. Milliband and J. Saville (eds.), *The Socialist Register 1979*, London 1979, p. 288
4. For example, J. Drewnowski, 'The Economic Theory of Socialism: A Suggestion for Reconsideration', *Journal of Political Economy*, August 1961; or P.C. Roberts, *Alienation and the Soviet Economy*, Albuquerque 1971.

References

1. Pareto V., *Manuel d'Economie Politique*, Génève 1966, p. 210–211.
2. von Mises L., 'Economic Calculation in the Socialist Commonwealth', in A.Nove and M.Nuti (eds.), *The Socialist Economy*, Harmondsworth 1972.
3. Quoted in O. Lange, op.cit., p.36.
4. Dobb M., *Welfare Economics and the Economics of Socialism*, Cambridge 1976, p. 186–189.
5. Bliss C.J., 'Prices, Markets and Planning', *The Economic Journal*, March 1972, p.94.
6. Samuelson P., 'A Summing Up', in R.C. Merton (ed.), *The Collected Papers of Paul A. Samuelson*, Cambridge Mass. 1972, p. 237.
7. Koopmans T.C. and J.M. Montias, 'On the Description and Comparison of Economic Systems', in A.Eckstein (ed.), *Comparison of Economic Systems*, Berkeley 1971, p.35.
8. Kornai J., *Anti–Equilibrium*, Amsterdam 1971.
9. Montias J.M., *The Structure of Economic Systems*, New Haven and London 1976.
10. Neuberger E. and W. Duffy, *Comparative Economic Systems: A Decision-Making Approach*, Boston 1976.
11. Wagener H.J., op.cit., p. 159.
12. Montias J.M., 'A Classification of Communist Economic Systems', in C.Mesa-Lago and C.Beck (eds.), *Comparative Socialist Systems: Essays on Politics and Economics*, Pittsburg 1975.
13. Ellman M., *Socialist Planning*, Cambridge 1979, p. 77.
14. Eucken W., *Grundsätze der Wirtschaftspolitik*, Bern–Tübingen 1952, p. 136.
15. Spulber N., 'On some Issues in the Theory of the Socialist Economy', *Kyklos*, Number 6 1972, p. 729.
16. Lenin N.J., 'State and Revolution', in A.Nove and M.Nuti (eds.), *Socialist Economics*, Harmondsworth 1972, pp. 26–31.
17. Ellman M., op.cit., p. 17.
18. Montias J.M., 'Planning with Material Balances in Soviet Type Economies', in A.Nove and M.Nuti (eds.), *The Socialist Economy*, Harmondsworth 1972.
19. Ward B.N., *The Socialist Economy: A Study of Organizational Alternatives*, New York 1967.

20. Kornai J., op.cit., p.334.
21. Ellman M., op.cit., pp. 68 onwards.
22. Downs A., *Inside Bureaucracy*, Boston 1967, p. 77.
23. Ellman M., *Planning Problems in the USSR*, Cambridge 1973, pp. 24 onwards.
24. Levine H.S., 'The Centralized Planning of Supply in Soviet Industry', *Joint Economic Committee*, Washington 1959.
25. Vortmann H., 'Beschäftigungsstruktur und Arbeitsmarktpolitik in der DDR', in H.Höhmann and B.Knabe (eds.), *Arbeitsmarkt und Wirtschaftsplanung*, Köln 1977, p.127.
26. Masuch M., 'De Sovjet-beslissingswijze', *Tijdschrift voor politiek economie*, nr. 3 1980, p. 107.
27. Davies R., 'The technological level of Soviet Industry: an overview', in R.Amann, J.Cooper and R.Davies (eds.), *The technological level of Soviet Industry*, New Haven and London 1977, p. 59.
28. Kornai J., *Economics of Shortage*, Amsterdam 1980, Ch. 9.
29. Marrese M., 'The Evolution of Wage Regulation in Hungary', in P.Hare, H.Radice and N.Swain (eds.), *Hungary, a Decade of Economic Reform*, London 1981, p. 54–65.
30. Kroncher A., 'CMEA Productive and Service Sector in the 1980s: Plan and Non-Plan', *NATO Colloquium* 1982, p. 3.
31. Andrle V., *Managerial power in the Soviet Union*, Westmead 1976, pp. 31 and 145.
32. Broekmeyer M., *Het Russische dorp*, Utrecht 1983 (forthcoming).
33. Knaack R., 'Werkgelegenheidspolitiek in staatssocialistische landen', in H.van Overeem (ed.), *Oosteuropese economie*, 's-Gravenhage 1982, p. 83.
34. Powell R.P., 'Plan Execution and the Workability of Soviet Planning', *Journal of Comparative Economics*, March 1977, p. 52.
35. Dolan E.G., 'An Experimental Polycentric Model of the Soviet Economy', in J.Thornton (ed.), *Economic Analysis of the Soviet Type System*, Cambridge 1976, pp. 125 onwards.
36. Ellman M., 'The Scientific-Technical Revolution and Economic Management; *UN-Paper* (unpublished), 1976; M.Cave, *Computers and Economic Planning: the Soviet Experience*, Cambridge 1980.
37. Ellman M., op.cit., p. 6.
38. Lange O., 'The Computer and the Market', in A.Nove and M.Nuti (eds.), *Socialist Economics*, Harmondsworth 1972.
39. Cave M., op.cit., p. 183–184.
40. Ellman M., *Planning Problems in the USSR*, Cambridge 1973, p. 43.
41. Lohmann K.E., *Planübererfühlung: Kritik einer Kategorie der politischen Ökonomie des Sozialismus*, (unpublished), Berlin 1980.
42. Nove A., *The Soviet Economic System*, London 1977, p. 104.
43. Deutsches Institut für Wirtschaftforschung, *Wochenbericht*, 25/81, p. 284.
44. Kornai J., op.cit., p. 196–197.
45. Amann R., 'Some approaches to the comparative assessment of Soviet technology: its level and rate of development', in R.Amann, J.Cooper and R.Davies (eds.), *The technological level of Soviet Industry*, New Haven and London 1977, p. 27.

46. Davies R., op.cit., p. 66.
47. Berliner J.S., *The Innovation Decision in Soviet Industry,* Cambridge and London 1976.
48. Becker A., 'The Meaning and Measure of Soviet Military Expenditure', in *Soviet Economy in a Time of Change,* Joint Economic Committee, Washington 1979, p. 366.
49. Masuch M., op.cit., p. 113 onwards.
50. Spulber N., op.cit., p. 772–773.
51. Brus W., The East European Reforms: What happened to them? *Soviet Studies* 1979, p. 259.
52. Selucki R., *Economic Reforms in Eastern Europe,* New York and London 1972, pp. 43 onwards.
53. Schroeder G., 'The Soviet Economy on a Treadmill of Reforms', *Soviet Reforms in a Time of Change,* Joint Economic Committee, Washington 1979, p. 361.
54. Brus W., op.cit., p. 262.
55. Knaack R., 'Economic Reforms in China', *The ACES-bulletin,* Summer 1981, p. 15 onwards.
56. Wakar A., 'Prices, Incentives and Calculation Methods', *On Political Economy and Econometrics,* Warsaw 1964, p. 621.
57. Knaack R., 'The Role of Profit in the Soviet Economy', *De Economist,* Summer 1980, p. 408.
58. Kornai J., *Rush versus Harmonic Growth,* Amsterdam 1972.
59. Hare P., 'The Investment System in Hungary', in P. Hare, H. Radice and N.Swain (eds.), *Hungary, A Decade of Economic Reform.* London 1981, p. 87.
60. Korbonski A. and S. Terry, *The Politics of Economic Reforms in Eastern Europe,* 1980 (unpublished).
61. Nuti M., op.cit., pp. 256 onwards.
62. van Gunsteren H., *The Quest for Control,* London 1976.
63. van Gunsteren H., op.cit., Ch. 2.
64. van Gunsteren H., op.cit., pp. 7 and 73.
65. de Jong H.W., *Dynamische markttheorie,* Leiden 1981, Ch. 2.
66. Tinbergen J., 'Do Communist and Free economies show a converging pattern?', *Soviet Studies,* April 1961. For a critique, see M. Ellman, 'Against convergence', *Cambridge Journal of Economics* September 1980.
67. van den Doel J., *Konvergentie en evolutie,* Assen 1971.
68. Nuti M., op.cit., p. 256.
69. Kornai J., 'The dilemmas of a socialist economy: the Hungarian experience', *Cambridge Journal of Economics,* 1980 no. 4, p.156.
70. Zimbalist A., 'On the Role of Management in Socialist Development', *World Development,* 1981, number 9/10, p. 975.

6 CENTRAL PHYSICAL PLANNING, INCENTIVES AND JOB RIGHTS

David Granick

Introduction

Centralized physical planning in socialist economies has received bad press among comparative economists. In this chapter, I take the Soviet economy — both before and after the reforms of the mid 1960s — as representing such economies.[1] My concern is with the following question: what portion of the malfunctions which are commonly associated with centralized physical planning might more properly be explained by other economic features, each of which constitutes a set intersecting that set which consists of the feature of centralized physical planning?

To put the issue in a slightly different fashion, I wish to investigate the degree to which the reputation of socialist centralized physical planning is undeservedly maligned as a result of misspecification of a regression function. If the relevant differentials existed (which is not the case in my analysis, where all variables representing the features are treated as discontinuous), the economic malfunctions in Soviet-type economies should be regarded as constituting a function of centralized physical planning, *given* other key features of these economies. But the implicit regression function often used takes centralized physical planning as the only argument of the function — thus causing it to serve as a partial proxy for the other arguments of the true regression, and so causing bias in the estimated coefficient.

In looking at other features I am concerned only with systemic aspects; thus I exclude geography, cultural traditions, demography, random shocks, and the like. Incentives and job rights constitute shorthand descriptions of the other features with which I intend to deal.

The reader should note carefully that I am not concerned with evaluating the net costs (positive or negative) of any of the three economic features under investigation. Rather, I ignore benefits and concentrate on gross costs. Thus my approach may be expected to reduce the gross costs usually associated with socialist centralized physical planning, and this indeed is what is found. But there are no implications from this analysis as to the direction of change in the evaluation of net costs. Only an analysis which also considers benefits could yield a result relating to net costs, and such an analysis would go well beyond the scope of this paper.

Using the definitions that S = set, CPP = feature of socialist centralized physical planning, I = feature of Soviet-type incentives, and JR = feature of Soviet-type job rights, I examine the economic malfunctions which occur in the space $S_{CPP} \cap S_I \cap S_{JR}$ which I shall call S_T, with the Soviet economy having a subset of features that are inside S_T. My objective is to explain the different economic malfunctions observed in the Soviet Union by the fact that the space S_T falls within one or another of the above three sets.

My analytic procedure will be as follows. I shall examine the space that consists of $\hat{S}_{CPP}$ where $\hat{S}_{CPP}$ constitutes the intersection of S_{CPP} and of two other sets, $\tilde{S}_I$ and $\tilde{S}_{JR}$, where $\tilde{S}_I$ is the complement of S_I (i.e., it is not-S_I).

$$\hat{S}_{CPP} = S_{CPP} \cap \tilde{S}_I \cap \tilde{S}_{JR} \tag{6.1}$$

Any malfunctions which are both observed in the Soviet Union and which might logically be expected to occur in space $\hat{S}_{CPP}$ will be ascribed to the existence of centralized physical planning in the Soviet Union.

I then turn to $\hat{S}_I$ which is defined by

$$\hat{S}_I = S_I \cap S_{CPP} \cap \tilde{S}_{JR} \tag{6.2}$$

Malfunctions that are both observed in the Soviet Union and that which might logically be expected to occur in space $\hat{S}_I$ will be ascribed to the existence of Soviet-type incentives, given centralized physical planning.

$\hat{S}_{JR}$ is treated symmetrically to $\hat{S}_I$, with

$$\hat{S}_{JR} = S_{JR} \cap S_{CPP} \cap \tilde{S}_I \tag{6.3}$$

and with malfunctions that are both observed in the Soviet Union and that might logically be expected to occur in space $\hat{S}_{JR}$ being ascribed to Soviet-type job rights, given centralized physical planning.

To summarize, the analysis is concerned only with the set of centralized physical planning in socialist economies, and it divides this set into four subsets whose union covers the entire original set. Thus

$$(\hat{S}_{CPP} \cup \hat{S}_I \cup \hat{S}_{JR} \cup S_T) = S_{CPP} \tag{6.4}$$

My interest is in phenomena that exist in the Soviet Union, whose features are contained within S_T. In order to investigate causation within subset S_T, I examine subsets $\hat{S}_{CPP}$, $\hat{S}_I$ and $\hat{S}_{JR}$ and draw conclusions regarding S_T from these contiguous but nonintersecting subsets (see figure 6-1).

Characterization of Three Economic
Features of the Soviet Economy

I now proceed to a characterization of those three economic features of the Soviet economy which will command our attention.

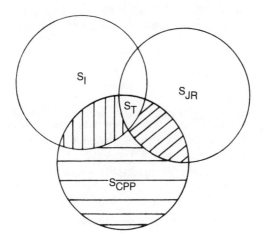

Figure 6–1.   Venn Diagram of Four Regions of S_{CPP}

Socialist centralized physical planning (CPP)

CPP is viewed as constituting the intersection of a particular information system and of a very general form of authority-incentive structure described by an agent-principal model. The information system consists of output targets set for individual enterprises, at that level of aggregation of individual products into subaggregates which is used in output planning; input usage as that is expressed both in wage-fund plans and in materials allocations to enterprises at a rather similar level of aggregation to that of products; and of State-determined current and constant prices which serve as weights in the aggregation process. Various other pieces of information (such as profit targets by enterprise) might be included in the information system if we wish to define CPP more broadly.

Accompanying this information system is an hierarchical authority system that links the Center (Principal) to the Periphery (Agent)[2] and thus provides an authority-incentive backbone for the utilization by the Periphery of the information provided by output targets, input constraints, and prices. All that is required here is the general class of hierarchical authority systems, but let me be more specific. I shall posit that the hierarchical authority system can be properly described as one in which the agent acts in a utility-maximizing fashion, given the procedures set down by the principal, rather than attempting to influence these procedures.[3] The principal, in turn, has two problems: that of selecting and dismissing the managers of the various agent bodies, and second that of devising and implementing procedures that will lead to maximization of the net product[4] produced by the agent, given both the agent's constraints and the predicted reaction of the agent to these procedures.

The Soviet-type incentive system (I)

The incentive system is the second feature of the Soviet economy that enters the forthcoming analysis. This system represents a subclass of the authority-incentive system described by the agent-principal model. This subclass can be described by equations 6.5 through 6.9) below. [1]

Enterprise managers (the agent) attempt to maximize a function (U) of the following objective function:

$$Y_t = \sum_{t=1}^{n} f(B_t,C_t)/(1 + r)^t \tag{6.5}$$

where Y_t = discounted lifetime earnings earned in period (t)
B_t = bonuses received in period (t)

C_t = career level attained as of period (t). This can be measured in terms of base salary in period (t).

r = the rate of time preference of the agent

n = average number of periods before retirement of the enterprise managers

B_t and C_t are each functions both of the behavior of the enterprise managers and of choice variables determined by the principal, while r is a choice variable of the agent. U is an arbitrary constant if the enterprise managers are risk neutral, since utility then varies proportionately to income. Following from equation (6.5), and from the fact that $\sum\limits_{i=0}^{m} C_{t-1}$ determines who are the particular enterprise managers in period (t) whose utility functions are being maximized, we derive

$$A_t = \gamma(U[Y_t], \sum_{i=0}^{m} C_{t-i}) \text{ subject to constraints} \qquad (6.6)$$

where A_t = enterprise behavior in period (t).

The first really substantive element of the Soviet-type incentive system is a proposition concerning how managers are chosen by the principal. It is assumed that the principal uses his power to determine the manager's C_t with the exclusive purpose of influencing A_{t+1} directly through equation (6.6), and thus that he renounces its use to influence Y_t through equation (6.5). This is a strategic decision of the principal, which can be described as the decision to use the principal's power to appoint managers solely in the interest of selecting those managers having the greatest x-efficiency[5] rather than in order to provide incentives for managers or as a mixed strategy.

The principal does not use career movement of enterprise managers as a device for influencing these manager's choice of enterprise action. As a result, bonuses constitute the only instrument variable available to the principal to affect behavior of existing managers in equation (6.6). (6.7)

The result is that the agent, in attempting to maximize his $U(Y_t)$, allows his managerial choice as to the particular aspects of enterprise performance that should be pursued, and to what degree, to be determined by the marginal effects of these different aspects on bonuses (B_t). He will indeed carry out other personal actions — e.g., improvement of his political position, further education — in order to influence his personal $\sum\limits_{i=1}^{n-1} C_{t+i}$; but these actions will be irrelevant to A_t.

Equation 6.8 is the second substantive element of the Soviet-type incentive system.

$$B_t = h(Dm_t/Pm_t) \text{ where } \partial B_t/\partial[Dm_t/Pm_t] > 0 \qquad (6.8)$$

where Dm_t = aspects of enterprise performance in period (t) that are measurable in period (t)

Pm_t = the plan (generally annual) for period (t) for those aspects of enterprise performance in period (t) that are measurable in period (t).

The significance of equation 6.7 is that it is only through plans for those aspects of enterprise performance in (t) that are measurable in (t) that the principal is capable of affecting enterprise behavior in (t). (The exception, in which the principal uses the instrument variable $\sum\limits_{i=0}^{m} C_{t-i}$, affects only the technical efficiency of the enterprise and not the enterprise's choice among actions which are equally efficient from a purely technical standpoint.)

The third and last substantive element of this incentive system is incorporated in the proposition that

period (t) should be of brief duration, certainly not longer than one year. (6.9)

Soviet incentive principles that appear to underlie what I have called the Soviet-type incentive system are the following: The most important aspect of managerial behavior towards which a proper managerial-incentive system should be directed is managerial effort, so as to benefit technical as opposed to economic efficiency. Proper choice of trade-off ratios among the various dimensions of enterprise performance is desirable, but comes second to technical efficiency in a lexicographic ordering.

Enterprise managers are perceived by the principal as operating in a stochastic world and as being risk averse; these two conditions together cause an appropriate form of bonus to yield a higher net payoff to the principal than could be attained through the use of any straight salary paid to the manager. In order to maximize managers' effort, given that managers are risk averse, bonus should be a function of enterprise performance where the function is known beforehand by the enterprise managers; but this implies that the function must be restricted to the quantifiable aspects of performance. Given that managers also have a positive rate of time preference, the measurable performance of period (t) should be rewarded fully in (t), and (t) should constitute as short a period as feasible.[6]

Soviet-type job rights (JR)

This set is a characterization of a vector of arguments included in the social welfare function of Soviet leaders. The assumption is made that this vector

(JR) is lexicographically preferred to all other arguments in the social welfare function. The mathematical way in which this is stated is to treat the vector (JR) as a constraint upon the maximization of a function of the remaining arguments in the social welfare function.

Thus the governing social welfare function $f(X_1,X_2)$ in the Soviet Union is stated as: maximize a function of vector X_1 subject to: vector $X_2 <$ vector Z_2 and vector $X_3 \leq$ vector Z_3. X_3 is the usual constraint vector imposed by the environment. X_2, on the other hand, constitutes a set of constraints that is imposed solely by the lexicographic form of the social welfare function.

The above function can be interpreted in two ways. The first is the obvious interpretation of the social welfare function of Soviet leaders: i.e., that the leaders themselves lexicographically prefer a marginal improvement in any component of vector X_2 (up to the relevant component of Z_2) to any attainable value of vector X_1. The second interpretation is that Soviet leaders believe that the political reactions of the Soviet population to violations of the component-by-component constraints of vector X_2 would be so severe that Soviet leaders feel compelled — regardless of their personal desires — to accept X_2 as a constraining vector. For my purposes, there is no reason to choose between these interpretations.

Of course, as is customary in economics, the statement of the objective function of Soviet leaders, and the constraints under which it is maximized, is not intended as a description of the state of mind of these leaders or of the analytic process by which their decisions are generated. Rather, it is presented as an hypothesis which, it is claimed, logically generates behavior that simulates fairly well the behavior observed in the Soviet economy.

I shall focus on three labor-market components of X_2, all of which refer to the structural *demand equations* for labor in the state sector. It should be noted that they do not refer to the reduced-form equations of the labor market, and thus their constrained values do not constrain the level of observed unemployment or of job mobility.[7] The logic of this approach to labor markets is that Soviet leaders have no way of constraining unemployment or total job mobility except by constraining both the demand and supply functions of labor. Although it is true that the supply function is indeed constrained both by Soviet law and custom, it would seem appropriate to view such constraints as mechanisms employed by Soviet leaders in order to maximize $f(X_1)$ — e.g., gross national product — rather than as self-imposed constraints upon the maximization of $f(X_1)$. It is here hypothesized that Soviet leaders are unwilling to reduce the maximum-attainable $f(X_1)$ in order to keep observed unemployment and observed job mobility within designated limits, although they are willing to accept such a reduction in order to constrain the level of unemployment and job mobility which is forced upon workers by labor demand factors.

The first component of X_2 is expressed in inequality (equation 6.10) below in the form of a two-way categorization of skill and of the physical difficulty of jobs. It can be readily generalized to an n-way categorization.

Inequality (equation 6.10) provides each individual job seeker with the high probability $[(1 - \epsilon_1)]$ of obtaining a job of some sort, and without leaving his own geographic area, within a reasonable period y_1. It does not guarantee that the job offered will match the individual's qualifications, but only that the individual will possess at least the minimum qualifications for the job.

In inequality (equation 6.10), the ratio of job vacancies to job seekers (V_{Z_j}/S_{Z_j}), where both numerator and denominator have similar characteristics, is chosen so that

$$PR \left. \begin{array}{c} f(Z_j) \\ \\ V_{Z_j}/S_{Z_j} \end{array} \right\} < \epsilon_1 \; \forall \; j \qquad (6.10)$$

where

$f(Z_j) = $ unemployment of individual (i) for $> y_1$ calendar days when individual (i) has the characteristics Z_j and is willing to take any job within his own geographic area for which he/she is qualified both physically and with regard to skill.

Variables

$V_{Z_j} = $ number of job vacancies with the characteristics of Z_j

$S_{Z_j} = $ number of job seekers with the characteristics of Z_j

Constants

$y_1 \;\; = $ roughly, thirty

$\epsilon_1 \;\; = $ a very small percentage

Characteristics

$Z_j \;\;\; = Z_I, \ldots, Z_{IV}$

$Z_I \;\;\; = z_1$

$Z_{II} \;\; = z_1 \cup z_2$

$Z_{III} \; = z_1 \cup z_3$

$Z_{IV} \; = z_1 \cup z_2 \cup z_3 \cup z_4$

$z_1 \;\;\; = a \; u \; e$

$z_2 \;\;\; = a \; u \; h$ where the righthand side is a vector of

$z_3 \;\;\; = a \; s \; e$ characteristics whose elements include

$z_4 \;\;\; = a \; s \; h$ all non-zero values

$a \;\;\; = $ an area of the country, and takes values $a_1, a_2, \ldots, a_N$

$u \;\;\; = $ unskilled jobs (or workers), and takes values 0 or 1

$s \;\;\; = $ skilled jobs (or workers), and takes values 0 or 1 e   = physically undemanding jobs (or workers who are both physically capable and desirous of filling them), and takes values 0 or 1

h   = physically demanding jobs (or workers who are both physically capable and desirous of filling them), and takes values 0 or 1

Inequality (equation 6.10) would be an unnecessarily restrictive constraint on the maximization of $f(X_1)$ if Soviet leaders were concerned only with minimum-income guarantees. It is assumed here that they are concerned with such guarantees combined with the opportunity for individual (i) to earn such income rather than to receive it as a transfer payment; the reason can only be sociological since it constrains the maximization of $f(X_1)$.

The second component of vector X_2 is:

$$Pr \mid A_i \mid < \epsilon_2 \tag{6.11}$$

where

A_i = forced and unwilling idleness within his current enterprise of individual (i) for $> y_2$ working days per annum

ϵ_2 is very small

y_2 is a moderately substantial number (e.g., thirty)

"Idleness" is defined as working less than a normal pace

Inequality (equation 6.11) guarantees (i) that he will be given the opportunity of actually earning his paid income, rather than receiving it as a transfer payment made on condition of his physical attendance at the job. Furthermore, when combined with inequality (equation 6.12) below, it constrains any potential employing enterprise (k) — where $k = \epsilon \mid k_1, k_2, \ldots, k_K \mid$ — against maintaining a labor force which is structurally imbalanced; this constraint on (k) is a necessary condition of the guarantee to (i).

The third component of X_2 is:

$$Pr \mid B_i \mid < \epsilon_3 \tag{6.12}$$

where

B_i = dismissal of individual (i) from enterprise (k), or the forcing him to change jobs within the same enterprise, except where the jobs differ only by substituting the characteristic (e) in the new job for (h) in the previous one.

Inequality 6.12 does not apply to those holding managerial jobs, and may not in practice apply to those eligible for pension.

Inequality 6.12 guarantees the right to his existing monetary quasi-rents on the labor market to each individual $i_{a,b,u}$ and $i_{a,b,s}$ — where b = the branch of the economy and is $\epsilon \mid b_1, b_2, \ldots, b_V \mid$ — with probability $> (1 - \epsilon_3)$.[8] This guarantee is provided subject to two limitations: that the government does not alter the average quasi-rents of group $_{a,b,u,e}$ or group $_{a,b,s,e}$ as a whole; nor that individual (i) does not opt out of this guarantee by quitting his job. Furthermore, inequality 6.12 guarantees that individual (i) will not have his work satisfaction reduced against his will by being compelled to perform a different type of work in enterprise (k) or to transfer from enterprise (k) to another enterprise. Such reduction in work satisfaction, however, may occur for a legally limited period.

Not only does inequality 6.12 provide important work satisfaction guarantees to (i), but on the income side it is an important complement to inequality 6.10. Inequality 6.10 provides guarantees only as to the availability of entrance level jobs; it says nothing as to the availability of vacancies matched to the individual applicant's education and job experience. Furthermore, suppose that inequality 6.12 were eliminated as a constraint, and instead Z_j of inequality 6.10 were redefined for inequality 6.10 as $\hat{Z}_j = (\hat{a}\hat{s}\,\hat{h})$ with

$$\hat{s} = \epsilon|u{=}s_o, s_1, \ldots , s_S\}$$

$$\hat{h} = \epsilon|e{=}h_o, h_1, \ldots , h_H\} \qquad\qquad (6.13)$$

and with all combinations of values of a and $\hat{s}$ being expressed in $\hat{Z}_1$, $\hat{Z}_2$, $\ldots , \hat{Z}_j, \ldots , \hat{Z}_J$. In that case, it might well be beyond the powers of the central planners to respect inequality 6.13 together with inequality 6.11 — for this would require a very high degree of concordance between the stock of skills in the labor force and the stock of skill-requirements in the job market. Even if feasible, inequalities 6.11 and 6.13 might constrain the maximization of $f(X_1)$ as much as or more than do inequalities 6.10, 6.11, and 6.12.

Malfunctions Arising from the Three Economic Features

Malfunctions Resulting from CPP

Malfunctions resulting from socialist centralized physical planning (CPP) are those that are both observed in the Soviet Union and that might logically be expected to occur in Space $\hat{S}_{CPP}$ as described in equation 6.1. These numerous malfunctions may be properly ascribed to the particular information system employed for the socialist sector in the Soviet Union.[9] The most important of these malfunctions are identified below.

Inconsistency, as defined in input-output, is inevitable between the various subaggregates in which output planning and materials-balances planning is carried on.

This lack of balance in planning is the most basic of the information system problems. In the balancing process, only limited attention is paid to indirect materials requirements. [2] At first view, this materials-balances approach would seem markedly inferior to proceeding through inversion of an input-output matrix — since this latter approach would permit full recognition of indirect requirements. However, the cost of such matrix inversion would be the need to work with a much higher degree of aggregation than is employed in materials balances — and therefore with considerably greater instability between periods of matrix coefficients. The relative terms of the tradeoff are unclear, but it would seem that either method must result in inconsistent planning.

Given the unwillingness of Soviet planners to incur the costs of holding sufficient amounts of both inventories of intermediate goods [3] and, more important, of reserve capacity for the production of such goods, it seems inevitable that enterprises should be unable to count on receiving the material inputs that they have been allocated.

Given the inconsistency problem of physical planning, the attention of central planners is concentrated on obtaining as much consistency as possible rather than on utilizing the most economically efficient mix of inputs to produce a given product.

Efficiency, as defined by equating the marginal rates of substitution between input subaggregates in the production of different output-subaggregates, is sacrificed in the interest of maximizing the degree of feasibility contained in the national plan.

There exists in the planning of foreign trade a close analogue to the efficiency loss described above, and for the same reason: [4] There is inefficient choice by central planners as to the product-subaggregates chosen for import as opposed to export.

In attempting to achieve comparative advantage, *foreign trade inefficiency* results from the planners' preoccupation with problems of feasibility.

An aspect of foreign trade organization, which is frequently treated in the western literature as an organizational inefficiency, is that the *foreign trade ministry stands as an intermediary* between the Soviet enterprise and its foreign trading partner. Each of these partners must deal with the ministry, rather than with one another.

This results from the fact that foreign trade must constitute a sector in the input-output balancing of the economy, and thus must be granted inputs (exports) and be charged with outputs (imports). In order for centralized physical planning to function, this sector must be represented by some organization which can be given output plans and receive material allocations.

Although this separation of purchaser and seller is usually treated as being particularly harmful to Soviet exports of goods other than bulk products, the organization of Japanese export trade should make one hesitate to draw such a conclusion. In 1972, for example, only 30 percent of Japanese exports of manufactures were handled directly by the producing firm; the remaining 70 percent were handled by trading companies which effectively separated the producer from the purchaser. [5] Even in the relatively technical engineering industry, 47 percent of all 1975 exports passed through the ten largest trading companies [6].

Returning to purely domestic production and exchange, we observe the following difficulty existing to the degree that enterprises are both output maximizers and that they do not engage in semi-legal barter transactions: Each enterprise determines its input mix in the light of its production isoquants and of its particular input allocations. Considering the enterprise's determination of input mix for its individual products as a programming problem, individual enterprises will be faced with very different relative shadow prices for identical input subaggregates. This implies that the *marginal rate of substitution between input subaggregates will differ considerably as between enterprises.* The implication of different MRS remains even when enterprises maximize some combination of output and profit, or even if they are pure profit maximizers.

The implication of different MRS has two effects. The first consists of the interenterprise differences in MRS which were pointed out above; the second effect is a result of the efforts of enterprises to moderate these consequences of being faced with different shadow prices for different input subaggregates.

A semilegal barter economy is created for exchange of goods among enterprises. Not only are allocated inputs bartered, but also above-plan outputs are bartered for inputs allocated to other enterprises.

From a static efficiency viewpoint, and despite the fact that barter is an inefficient form of exchange, this barter economy represents an improvement in its pure form.[10] Whether it represents such an improvement from the viewpoint of dynamic efficiency is unclear, since now enterprises are provided a strong incentive, supplementary to other incentives that would have existed in any case, for attempting to misinform central authorities as to their allocation needs for all inputs. Such semilegal barter also has a tendency to slip over into private corruption.

Still another inefficiency is that embodied in the enterprise response to the "ratchet effect" in planning. Despite efforts of Soviet administrators since 1965 to provide enterprises with incentives to prefer ambitious plans to loose plans, all of the existing evidence points to these efforts failing.[11] Moreover, enterprise managers clearly believe that superior performance in year *(t)* leads to increases in their plan in year *(t + 1)*. Even if this belief on the part of enterprise managers should be incorrect, it is difficult to see how the planners can convince the managers of this — unless the plan for year *(t + 1)* is firmly established prior to year *(t)*, thus deliberately depriving the planning process of the use of important and available information.[12] [12]

Enterprise managers are provided with strong incentives to *misinform planners* as to their production capacities. Such misinformation is always in the downward direction. *Avoidance of any substantial overfulfillment* of current plans is a tactic employed in this misinformation campaign.

Another malfunction is in *investment allocation.* Planners are subject to what appears to be irresistible pressure both from ministries and from enterprises to overcommit the resources allocated for total national investment. Such pressure arises because, when investment funds are allocated out of the state budget, the receiving unit does not pay the opportunity cost of the funds or of the physical resources that it receives.

It should be noted that this problem could not be avoided by financing all investment through loans. So long as it is the planners who are to determine investments — a consequence of physical planning that rests upon the use of input-output and capital/output coefficients — the cost of investments to receiving-units must be low enough so that they apply for these investment funds. If the cost is allowed to become higher than this, planners lose direct allocative control over investments.

Planners are subject to irresistible pressure to overcommit resources allocated for total national investment. The consequence of such overcommitment is a stretchout of construction periods leading to a very high ratio, by international standards, of the value of unfinished investment projects to annual investment expenditures.

Malfunctions Resulting from I

The malfunctions that arise from the socialist centralized physical planning information system, are impressive in both number and significance. But what is of interest for purposes of this chapter is the list of malfunctions in the Soviet economy that are not due to the CPP. Elimination of these other malfunctions could make a substantial difference to the performance of the Soviet economy.

Malfunctions that are observed in the Soviet Union and that might logically be expected to occur in space $\hat{S}_I$ will be ascribed to the existence of Soviet-type incentives, given CPP. Soviet-type incentives lead to one critical malfunction in the Soviet economy, but this malfunction finds expression in a number of major economic areas.

The principal (composed of central planners and ministries) is incapable of internalizing into the utility function of the agent (enterprise manager) any objectives of the principal whose fulfillment cannot be measured within a period of one year from fulfillment. Such *objectives of the principal are externalities to the agent.* These externalities include both the introduction by existing enterprises of new major products and processes in production operations, and the improvement of quality of output. This results from 6.8 and 6.9 above.

Let us consider first the issue of quality — as representing an aspect of enterprise performance that cannot be measured satisfactorily. Since quality is not an argument in the bonus function or wage-fund function of the enterprise, yet the pursuit of high quality uses up enterprise resources, enterprise managers maximize their utility by setting quality of output at some minimum level (δ) below which there are likely to be repercussions either from the principal or from users who refuse to purchase the goods. However, since the Soviet economy is characterized by sellers' markets (as we would expect in a CPP economy), (δ) is quite a low level indeed.

Efforts have been made by planners to measure quality, and to internalize its pursuit into the utility function of managers through setting higher prices for higher-quality goods. But such efforts at measurement have been unsuccessful. [13]

Major new products represent an element in the set of outputs of period (t) that are unmeasured in period (t) but yield a measured result in $(t+i)$. Production of such new products cannot be internalized into the agent's utility function because of the brevity of (t).

The problem is that the introduction of a major new product into an enterprise's production program involves teething costs for the first year or two, when the enterprise's total output is likely to decline relative to what would have occurred without the transfer of capacity to this new product. Thus, costs are incurred by the enterprise in period (t), while the increase of the enterprise's profits and output — which will occur if the price of the new product is set appropriately high by central authorities — will occur only in later periods $(t+i)$.

However, enterprise bonuses in $(t+i)$ are a function of measured performance in $(t+i)$ divided by planned performance in $(t+i)$. Since the plan for $(t+i)$ is intended to be a proxy for standard performance in $(t+i)$, it must incorporate the principal's anticipation of the effect of the enterprise's introduction of the new product in (t) on the same enterprise's output and profit performance in $(t+i)$. If the principal's anticipation is equal to the expected value of this performance, the enterprise gains nothing in period $(t+i)$ from having introduced the new product in (t). Thus, although the introduction of a new major product leads to net additional expected costs to the enterprise in (t), it leads to no net expected benefit to the enterprise in $(t+i)$.

The approach to this problem taken by Soviet planners has been to reduce the opportunity costs borne by the enterprise in *(t)* from having introduced new products in that period [14]. But so long as these costs remain positive, the enterprise continues to be motivated to slow down as much as possible the process of introducing major new products. It is clear that Soviet enterprises have been very successful in this slowdown process[15].

The externalities malfunction, which results from the incentive system, will certainly strike the reader as of minor significance compared to the malfunctions which result from the information system. Nevertheless, it is the incentive-related malfunction that has particularly exercised Soviet administrators in their concern for intensive development and in their efforts to speed the process of technological change.

Malfunctions Resulting from JR

It is those malfunctions of the Soviet economy that are due to Soviet type job rights that have been relatively unexplored in the published literature.

First to be examined is the absence of any equilibrating tendency in the supply and demand for goods at the microeconomic level [16]. Physical planning of both outputs and materials allocations is perforce done at the level of subaggregates of products; prices are set by authorities at the level of individual products, but these prices (or, rather, their relative levels) must in the main remain stable for long periods because of the magnitude of the administrative task of general price revision. Given the combination of planning in terms of subaggregates and of stable prices, no mechanism exists for equating supply and demand of individual products within a planning subaggregate. Producers maximize their output by choosing their product mix within a planning subaggregate so as to equate the marginal rate of substitution of the individual products to their relative prices. But these relative prices are completely uninfluenced by current demand. So long as a sellers' market exists (and this will always be the case for allocated subaggregates if there has been any purpose in the allocation), product mix within a subaggregate will be chosen primarily according to producers' convenience. But even if there were not sellers' markets, there is no mechanism available to equilibrate supply and demand in an efficient fashion. Thus, within the planned subaggregates, there is necessarily chaos at the level of the individual product.[13]

Now it would be perfectly possible for Soviet planners to remove this chaos without creating inflation. It would require the use of two sets of prices, but two sets — although not the proposed two — have in any case been employed since 1928. Let me illustrate one possible procedure.

Maximand for the enterprise: Profit measured in current prices. CON-STRAINTS: The producer is constrained to supply the volume of planned output, measured in constant prices, to holders of allocations. The allocation holders receive their allocations expressed in current prices.

Institutional requirement: Current prices for a given product are uniform, regardless of the purchaser. Such prices are market determined.

It is assumed here that enterprise plans are not so taut that there is only one product mix that will allow the producer to fulfill his plan.[14]

Given the above procedure, the producer would produce that mix of products within the planned subaggregate which equates his marginal rate of substitution in the production of these products to their market-determined current prices. Holders of allocations for the subaggregate would purchase individual products within the subaggregate so as to equate their MRS in the use of these products to their market-determined current prices. Finally, while the current prices of the individual products would fluctuate freely, the average price of the products within any subaggregate would be constrained to any rate of annual price change desired by the planners; this is achieved through the restriction that allocations are expressed in current prices while output plans are fixed in constant prices. Thus, given the allocations of subaggregates, Pareto optimality is achieved in the production and distribution of each product within individual subaggregates.[15]

If such Pareto optimality could be achieved without inflationary pressure, and while respecting the constraints both of socialist centralized physical planning and of Soviet type incentives, how can one explain the fact that Soviet planners have never introduced such a simple and advantageous procedure? If we make the neoclassical assumption that decisionmakers are rational, we are forced to search for some constraints which would be violated by this procedure. Soviet-type job rights (Inequalities 6.10 to 6.12) constitute a set of constraints that provide such an explanation [18]. This is because market-determined changes in the product mix of a given enterprise, which lead in turn to market-determined changes in the labor skills required in that enterprise, are inconsistent with Soviet-type job rights.

Resultant malfunctions, ascribable to Soviet-type job rights given centralized physical planning, are described below. There is no *equilibrating tendency in the supply and demand for goods at the microeconomic level,* although the production and use of these goods are planned at the subaggregate level. The development of vertical integration at the individual enterprise level, with the object of reducing dependence upon suppliers, is in part a result of CPP through input-output inconsistency. While it is true that the enterprise attempts through vertical integration to protect itself against nonreceipt of allocated supplies, this reaction is much more a response to its total lack of control over the product mix that it will receive within an allocation.[16]

There is an *extreme degree of vertical integration at the enterprise level,* developed in order to reduce dependence upon suppliers for the desired product mix within a material allocation. The cost of this development is both the failure to realize economies of scale in production, and the need for individual enterprise managements to supervise an excessively wide range of technologies.

Just as there has been vertical integration at the level of the individual enterprise, so too has there been vertical integration at the level of the ministry and its subordinate *glavki* and Associations. The reason is the same as for enterprises. *Vertical integration within ministries, glavki and Associations,* has developed for the same reason as has integration within an enterprise. An enterprise is more likely to receive the desired product mix within a material allocation if it deals with another enterprise in its own organization than if it is dependent upon a "foreign" organization. A major malfunction of this condition consists of *extensive transportation crosshauls.*

A second category of malfunction is in the sphere of *investment.* Employing a constant elasticity of substitution function for industry, Weitzman [20] analyzed Soviet industrial growth during 1950–69 and found that the best fit CES function had an elasticity of substitution between capital and labor of 0.403 with a standard error of 0.030. It seems a reasonable speculation that this low elasticity is due not only to the high growth rate of capital relative to labor, but also to the placement of investments within industry in a fashion very different from the pattern that would maximize output given the volumes of capital and labor. The malfunction resulting from the overcommitment of investment resources provides a partial explanation of such misallocation of investment, but much more may be explained as a result of Soviet type job rights.

Given Inequalities 6.11 and 6.12, individual Soviet enterprises must operate in such a fashion that individually they neither dismiss nonmanagerial personnel, compel them to work at trades other than those for which they were employed when hired, nor fail to give their employees the opportunity of actually earning the income paid to them. True, the enterprises can take full advantage of natural labor wasteage to eliminate unneeded jobs; indeed, they can encourage such wasteage by concentrating increases in earnings on those trades and skills that are most useful to the enterprise. Nevertheless, compared to enterprises in capitalist countries, Soviet enterprises face major handicaps in adjusting rapidly to changing requirements for different types of labor.

One might expect to see this Soviet handicap reflected in the country's investment policies. With an annual increase in the capital/labor ratio in Soviet industry during 1960–70 of seven percent [21], enterprises operating in a framework other than that of Soviet type job rights might have been expected to devote much of this expanded capital to labor saving investments. Yet examination of Soviet data from censuses of manual trades shows only modest reductions in the percentages of workers engaged in the most labor intensive occupations.

I hypothesize that Soviet planners are reluctant to engage in substantial labor saving investments in existing plants, because it is never clear ahead of time whether such investments could actually be put into use. If it were not possible to eliminate the saved jobs through a combination of natural wasteage of labor and voluntary retraining, the new capital stock would go largely unutilized. Moreover, wasteage/retraining and jobs scheduled for elimination must be matched at an individual enterprise level — rather than at a more aggregative level, such as a locality. Thus investments cannot be directed in what would be the most productive directions, given the relative growth rates of capital and labor.

This hypothesis has been tested by examining the Soviet and American population census questions dealing with occupation, and observing the changes over ten years in the number of respondents who categorized themselves as falling within a given occupation. If the hypothesis is correct, then — ceteris paribus — we should observe a greater degree of occupation change in the United States than in the USSR. This is because technological change can be more readily accompanied by change in occupation in a country which does not have the barrier to forced job mobility which is incorporated in Soviet type job rights.

Table 6–1 presents data showing individuals' self-classification of their occupations in 1959–60 and in 1970. Occupations examined are individually comparable between countries (at least with regard to 64 occupations and to 14 other occupation groups into which the remaining occupations fell), all are manual, and specifically agricultural occupations are excluded.

Section A of table 6–1 — in which the ceteris paribus conditions are ignored — shows that the number of occupations whose labor force declined between the two censuses was substantially greater in the United States than in the Soviet Union. This is consistent with the hypothesis. The net magnitude of decline of the labor force in all declining occupations is counter to the hypothesis, being somewhat greater in the USSR than in the United States. But this latter result is due to a concentration of Soviet declines in seven of the 51 declining occupations — with 62 percent of the total Soviet decline being in these seven occupations; these occupations appear to be primarily unpleasant, and a voluntary net exodus from them over a decade does not seem unreasonable.

The key result is that of the last row of Section A: that the percentage of

Table 6–1 Reduction in Manual, Nonagricultural Occupations in the USSR and in the U.S. during the 1960s [a]

	USSR (1959–1970)	U.S. (1960–1970)
A. Occupations in the sample		
Number of occupations	135	128
Labor force in these occupations as a percentage of the total nonagricultural labor force (earlier census data)	37%	25%
Occupations whose labor force declined between censusus		
Number of declining occupations	51	63
Declining occupations as percentage of all sample occupations	38%	48%
Intercensus decline in labor force in declining occupations as percentage of total labor force in all sample occupations as of the time of the earlier census		
Labor force decline in all declining occupations	−8.9%	−7.8%
Labor force decline in all except three of the occupations which declined in the USSR [b]	−5.0%	−8.0%
B. Inter-census change in		
Total labor force	+16%	+20%
Total non-agricultural labor force	+42%	+24%
C. Capital/labor ratio in industry [c]		
Annual compound rate of growth	+6.8% [d]	+3.3% [e]

[a] I am indebted to my former research assistant, Edward Albertini, for having carried out the necessary classifications of occupations and for doing the calculations.

[b] The excluded occupations are: blacksmiths, loggers cutting and stripping trees, and carpenters.

[c] Labor is measured in hours worked.

[d] Data are for the broad, Soviet-definition of industry for 1960–70 and are CIA estimates [22].

[e] Data are for 1959–69. Labor hours refer to all private business; capital is net fixed, nonresidential business capital [23].

intercensus labor force net decline by occupation in all except three Soviet occupations was five percent in the Soviet Union versus eight percent in the United States. This result supports the labor immobility hypothesis with regard to job rights societies.

Sections B and C of table 6–1 are intended to cast light on the *ceteris paribus* conditions required to appreciate the Section A results. Section B deals with inter-census change in the size of the labor force, since it is easier for a country to avoid absolute declines in the numbers engaged in any given occupation when the overall labor force is growing rapidly. Here we see that, if growth in the total labor force is taken as our standard, the two countries stand on a par. On the other hand, if one uses growth in the non-agricultural labor force alone, the Soviet growth rate was substantially greater than the American. It would seem that one can make a case for the use of either standard; if one chooses the second, the comparative labor mobility case of Section A should be modified.

Section C, however, appears much more significant in its import as to the Section A results. Over the inter-census period, the capital/labor ratio rose by 107 percent in the USSR compared to 39 percent in the United States. Certainly this wide difference should have provided a substantially greater motivation for capital-labor substitution in the USSR — and we might have expected this to have resulted in substantial declines in a wide variety of Soviet occupations. But this is the opposite of what we observe in Section A of the table.

On the basis of the hypothesis tested in table 6–1, I conclude that a major malfunction of the Soviet economy which is due to Soviet type job rights is: Soviet investment is seriously misallocated when judged by the unconstrained criterion of maximizing output growth, given the expected growth of capital and labor. Such misallocation is a major cause of the low capital–labor elasticity of substitution that is observed in Soviet industry when a CES production function is employed. This misallocation is a result of the job rights constraint, which sharply limits the amount of capital/labor substitution possible in individual occupation-skill-enterprise cells.

A third category of malfunction is in the sphere of *education*. The Soviet type full employment constraint (through the form of the Z_j vector in inequality 6.10) requires that labor demand be high relative to supply for each subaggregate of labor skills, with subaggregates overlapping and each including all lower skills in the given geographic area. This requirement implies either that all structural imbalances between labor demand and labor supply must be avoided in each geographic area or, more realistically, that labor supply must be biased in the high-skill direction relative to labor demand. Such a bias makes it possible for all job applicants to be placed rapidly in some job in their locality — but not in a job appropriate to their education and skill level. It is only by working up the career ladder of an individual enterprise through seniority in that enterprise that the individual can be assured of eventually reaching a position appropriate to his/her education and skill; but once such a position is achieved (assuming that it is nonmanagerial), the individual is assured of retaining it (through inequalities 6.11 and 6.12).

At the same time that the capital structure of the Soviet economy, and the resultant relative demand for different occupations and different level skills, has changed fairly slowly, the educational level of the population was changing rapidly. In 1959, 14 percent of the Soviet population over the age of ten had completed secondary education; in 1970, the figure had risen to 24 percent [24]; in contrast, the proportion of seventeen year olds with completed secondary education was 68 percent in 1970 and was expected to be 92–94 percent in 1975 [25]. Furthermore, only one-third of the graduates of general education secondary schools in the early 1980s were going to work directly thereafter; the remainder were receiving further job-oriented formal education of some sort on a fulltime basis [26].

The problem of matching supply and demand by education level is seen most dramatically in the case of graduates of junior colleges *(tekhniki)* working in industry. Such graduates are expected to work in engineering-and-professional posts; but the proportion of such graduates working in all Soviet industry who occupied posts as blue collar workers rose steadily from 20% in 1968, to 25% in 1970, to 30% in 1973 and 33% in 1975 [27]. Of those *techniki* who had studied in evening or correspondence courses, as shown by one investigation, 40 percent continued in their former blue-collar jobs after graduation — and almost half of these jobs were in the lower half of the blue-collar skill grades [28][17]

Even those with higher education, who seem to have no particular difficulties in finding appropriate positions, suffer from low earnings. Data given for the city of Tartu in Estoniia for the mid-1970s suggests an annual rate of return on private investment in higher education[18] of 0.6 percent for men and 0.3 percent for women [30], compared with 3 percent on savings accounts. One would expect that the social rate of return on total investment in higher education, as well as in junior-college education, must be substantially negative.[19]

The result is that, if one considers education — at least that beyond the ten-year standard secondary education — from the standpoint of an economic investment whose payoff is only in increased output, then total investment in the Soviet economy is inappropriately biased in the direction of investment in human capital. However, it should be remembered that this is so only given the job-rights constraint on changes in the structure of physical investment. Moreover, such overinvestment in human capital — dictated by the full employment constraint — leads to considerable psychological disappointment among Soviet youth who have learned skills which they are unable to use on the job. Total Soviet investment is biased in the direction of over-investment in human capital — given the constraint that exists on changes in the structure of physical capital. Both the constraint and the bias are results of the Soviet-type job rights pattern.

Summary

This chapter has taken off from an approach inspired by Neuberger and Duffy [31], who suggested that the study of comparative economic systems be approached along the complementary but distinct lines of information, decision-making and motivation. For my purposes here, I have collapsed these three sets of relations into the two of information and incentives — placing various aspects of decision-making into one or the other of these two sets.

I have attempted to categorize various malfunctions of the Soviet economic system according to their cause. Throughout, I have assumed three causal aspects: the information system (socialist centralized physical planning), the incentive system, and a major argument in the social welfare function (Soviet-type job rights). I have treated the analyzed malfunctions as due either to the information system alone, to the incentive system given the information system, or to the job-rights argument of the social welfare function given the information system.

I believe that the two aspects of this chapter that are new to the literature are the following: (1) The effort to characterize various systemic economic malfunctions according to this typology of causes. It is hoped that such characterization will be helpful in promoting understanding of socialist centralized physical planning systems, particularly through showing which malfunctions might be stripped away without altering the information system. It is also hoped that this characterization may provide some guidance in predictions as to future potential change in the Soviet economy. (2) The definition and analysis of Soviet-type job rights. Some use of this concept has been made previously in published work [32], but the treatment here is considerably expanded.

Notes

1. I shall ignore a major feature of most such economies, although not of the Chinese, that the distribution both of labor and of final consumer goods is regulated primarily through fiscal rather than through physical means.

2. For different purposes we might, for example, consider the Council of Ministers in the Soviet Union as the Center and the individual ministry as the Periphery. For other purposes, the Council of Ministers together with the individual ministries (or even a single ministry) could be treated as the Center, and the enterprise as the Periphery.

3. This follows from the existence of a large (n) of agents, with the resultant impracticality of collusion among them.

4. Net product is measured in terms of those shadow prices relevant to the maximization of the principal's objective function, and it is defined as net of payments given to the agent which reduce the total product available to the rest of the economy.

5. The word "solely" refers to the absence of incentive criteria in career decisions by the principal, rather than to the absence of political criteria, nepotism, etc.

6. These principles are enunciated on the basis that they are all beliefs that could be held by reasonable men (whether or not they are correct as hypotheses concerning the real world of the Soviet economy), and that together they lead to the bonus policies that can be observed. It is not asserted that Soviet administrators have consciously held these principles in the forms outlined, but only that they have acted as though they did.

7. The distinction between structural demand equation and reduced form equation is significant for inequality 6.10 but is irrelevant to the following two inequalities.

8. The individual may be transferred within enterprise (k) from a job with characteristic (h) to one with characteristic (e), so long as the two jobs have the same skill characteristic and are in the same geographic area. Presumably, the logic is that $(\text{Income}_{k,h} - \text{Income}_{k,e})$ is not considered as a quasi-rent, but rather as payment for the additional work effort required in the job with the characteristic (h).

9. Of course, the observed malfunctions may be part of a larger class of malfunctions than those pertaining exclusively to CPP and to centralized socialist economies. In the case of misinformation and avoidance of substantial plan overfulfillment by enterprises, this is because the relevant aspects of CPP are part of a larger class of information systems. I am indebted to Kwok-Chiu Fung for pointing this out.

10. The efficiency of barter is improved by singling out certain allocated goods as a means of exchange. It would appear that in the Soviet Union there exist at least such partial means of exchange; thus half-inch waterpipe and gaspipe is said to have served "for a long time" as a medium of exchange for the procurement of any other size of pipe. [7]

11. Kletskii and Risina [8] and Khomchenko in Institut Ekonomiki [9] supply 1967 and 1968 data illustrating the ineffectiveness of the reform which provided only 70 percent of the bonuses for above-plan performance that would have been paid if such performance had been included in the plan. Brezhnev [10] asserted that the same ineffectiveness continued into the 1980s. There seems to be no basis for the assumption in such western writing as that of Weitzman [11] that the Soviet reforms of the second half of the 1960s had been successful in reversing this pattern as it had existed pre-1965.

12. This information problem is made still worse by the fact that $(t+i)$, where (i) can take any value from one to about five, can be substituted for $(t+1)$ in the text.

13. By "chaos" is meant the absence of any mechanism — at the disposal of anyone in the system, whether planner or enterprise — for achieving a product mix within a given planned subaggregate that reflects both supply and demand conditions weighted according to any reasonable social welfare function. A welfare function that gives zero weight to demand is considered unreasonable, since each enterprise is a purchaser as well as a producer.

14. Such absence of tautness is indeed found in Soviet industry, at least at the level of the ministry [17].

15. To the degree that markets within a subaggregate are imperfect, there will be the identical violations of Pareto optimality that would occur in a nonplanned economy.

16. This would appear to be one of the two main reasons for the much greater use of castings than of rolled metal in the USSR than in the United States. A metal-fabricating enterprise with its own foundry requires only the supply of a homogeneous material, while if it produces from rolled metal it requires a fairly specific product mix of its rolled metal allocations. [19]

17. On the other hand, this problem of placement in jobs below their skill level does not appear to be serious for graduates of higher educational institutions. In all Soviet industry in the middle to late 1970s, only four percent of such graduates worked in posts intended for *tekhniki* [29]; very few worked as blue-collar personnel.

18. The investment is defined as earnings foregone minus a 70 percent probability of receiving a 45-ruble monthly stipend as a student.

19. This conclusion is drawn on the assumption that the determination of earnings in the Soviet state sector, primarily through the allocation of wage funds to individual enterprises, causes individual earnings to be a reasonable approximation of marginal value of product.

References

1. For a fuller treatment of the Soviet-type incentive system, see Granick, David, "Institutional Innovation and Economic Management: the Soviet Incentive System, 1921 to the Present," in Gregory Guroff and Fred V. Carstensen (eds.), *Entrepreneurship in Russia and the Soviet Union* (Princeton Univ. Press: Princeton, 1983), section 1, pp. 223–257.

2. Montias, J.M., "Planning with Material Balances in Soviet-Type Economies," *American Economic Review,* 49, 5 (Dec. 1959), pp. 963–85.

3. For some evidence that holding of inventories in industry are in any case higher in the Soviet Union than in the United States, see Campbell, Robert W., "A Comparison of Soviet and American Inventory-Output Ratios," *American Economic Review,* 48, 4 (Sept. 1958), pp. 449–65.

4. Although there is a considerable literature discussing this foreign-trade inefficiency, Steven Rosefielde makes an interesting case for the view that, nevertheless, comparative advantage explains the pattern of Soviet foreign trade better than do alternative hypothesis. See Rosefielde, Steven, "Comparative advantage and the evolving pattern of Soviet international commodity specialization 1950–1973," in Steven Rosefielde (ed.), *Economic Welfare and the economics of Soviet socialism: Essays in honor of Abram Bergson* (Cambridge Univ. Press: Cambridge et al., 1981).

5. Krause, L.B. and Sueo Sekiguchi in H. Patrick and H. Rosovsky (eds.), *Asia's New Giant: How the Japanese Economy Works* (Brookings Institution: Washington, 1976), p. 393.

6. Young, A.K., *The Sogo Shosha: Japan's Multinational Trading Companies* (Westview Press: Boulder, Colorado, 1979), p. 6.

7. Dovgalevskii, A. in *Ekonomicheskaia gazeta,* 35 (Aug. 1982), p. 8 as abstracted in *Current Digest of the Soviet Press,* 34, 38 (1982), p. 14.

8. Kletskii, V. and G. Risina in *Planovoe Khoziaistvo,* 1970, 8, pp. 51–58.

9. Institut Ekonomiki AN Latvinskoi SSR. *Ekonomicheskoe stimulirovanie povysheniia effektivnosti proizvodstva* (Zinatne: Riga, 1970).

10. Brezhnev, L. I., Speech of November 16, 1981 in *Pravda,* November 17, 1981, pp. 1–2 as translated in *Current Digest of the Soviet Press,* 33, 46 (1981), p. 6.

11. Weitzman, Martin, "The New Soviet Incentive Model," *Bell Journal of Economics,* 7, 1 (1976), pp. 251–57.

12. Granick, D., "Response to Keren," *Journal of Comparative Economics* (1983: forthcoming).

13. Berliner, J., *The Innovation Decision in Soviet Industry* (MIT Press: Cambridge, Mass. and London, 1976) and Brezhnev, Leonid I., *op. cit.*.
14. Berliner, *op. cit.*
15. Brezhnev, L.I., *op. cit.*
16. Granick, David, "Soviet use of fixed prices: hypothesis of a job-right constraint," in Steven Rosefielde (ed.), *op. cit.*.
17. _____, "The Ministry as the Maximizing Unit in Soviet Industry," *Journal of Comparative Economics*, 4, 3 (Sept. 1980), pp. 255–73.
18. _____, *op. cit.*, (1981).
19. _____, *Soviet Metal-Fabricating and Economic Development* (Wisconsin University Press: Madison et al., 1967), Chapter 5.
20. Weitzman, Martin, "Soviet Postwar Economic Growth," *American Economic Review*, 60, 4 (Sept. 1970), pp. 676–92.
21. Greenslade, R. V., "The Real Gross National Product of the U.S.S.R., 1950–1975," in Congress of the United States, Joint Economic Committee, *Soviet Economy in a New Perspective* (G.P.O.: Washington, 1976), p. 279.
22. *Ibid.,* p. 279.
23. *Economic Report of the President* (U.S. G.P.O.: Washington, 1981), p. 71.
24. Omel'ianenko, B.L., *Tekhnicheskii progress i sovremennye trebovaniia k urovniu kvalifikatsii i podgotovke rabochikh kadrov* (Vyshaia Shkola: Moscow, 1973), p. 27.
25. Korchagin, V. and V. Filippov in *Sotsialisticheskii Trud,* 1974, 8, p. 131.
26. Prokoviev, M.A., *Izvestiia,* April 11, 1982, p. 3 as reported in *Current Digest of the Soviet Press,* 34, 15 (1982), pp. 8–9.
27. Geliuta, A.M. and V.I. Staroverov, *Sotsial'nyi oblik rabochego-intelligenta* (Mysl': Moscow, 1977), p. 75.
28. Bliakhman, L.S., *Proizvodstvennyi kollektiv: v pomoshch' rukovoditeliu* (Politizdat: Moscow, 1978), p. 128.
29. Karpukhin, D.N., in L.A. Kostin (ed.), *Trudovye resursy SSR* (Ekonomika: Moscow, 1979), p. 167.
30. Raiu, O.M., in *Vosproizvodstvo i ratsional'noe ispol'zovanie rabochei sily v narodnom khoziaistve respubliki,* I (Tallin, 1975), p. 78.
31. Neuberger, Egon and Willian Duffy, *Comparative Economic Systems: A Decision-Making Approach* (Allyn and Bacon: Boston et al., 1976).
32. Granick, David, *op. cit.* (1981).

7 INCENTIVES AND ELICITATION SCHEMES: A CRITIQUE AND AN EXTENSION

Sinan Koont and Andrew Zimbalist

Introduction

With the 1965 economic reforms in the Soviet Union came changes in the system of material incentives. The major changes pertaining to the formation of the enterprise bonus fund, however, were not implemented until 1972.[1] The incentive alterations were sufficiently profound as to have spawned a sizeable analytical literature on the performance implications of the new system.

This literature has tended to focus on three issues. One, the coordination-type problem which arises when bonus schemes impel managers to internalize the impact of their performance on other enterprises.[1] Two, the problem of identifying appropriate incentive schemes to induce social maximizing behavior where the agent and the principal hold differing attitudes toward risk. Three, the problem of designing incentives to elicit accurate information on production capacity from enterprises when managers of production units may have different goals than the planners. Although these are related problems,

*The authors wish to thank David Conn for his careful comments on an earlier draft of this piece.

as has been shown by Conn, [2] we shall concentrate primarily on the third issue — elicitation schemes — due to its greater practical significance.

Miller and Murrell have outlined three possible methods for the center to elicit accurate information about the productive capacity of the periphery: [3] one, closely monitoring the operation of enterprises; two, gauging from past performance; and, three, applying incentive schemes like the one introduced in the USSR in 1972, described by Ellman and analyzed initially by Bonin and Weitzman. [4] Well over a dozen articles have since been published elaborating and expanding (e.g., to include managerial risk aversion, multiple performance indicators and managerial effort) the models of decentralized target planning introduced separately by Bonin and Weitzman.

The basic idea of these incentive schemes is to reward the manager for choosing a higher target by offering a larger bonus for fulfilling a higher target than for overfulfilling a lower target. Under certain assumptions, these schemes can be shown to successfully evoke truthful information about uncertain production possibilities of the enterprises as well as to allow the planners to adjust the degree of tautness in an enterprise's plan target to the desired level by manipulating penalty and reward parameters. This result is rather appealing since it suggests the prospect of resolving the insurmountable information problems associated with central planning by permitting the local unit to set its own target. At the same time, it preserves central control by enabling the planners to set the norms which affect the decentralized choice of target output.

A central problem with these treatments, however, is that they depend on a heroic degree of abstraction. Unfortunately, since the original Ellman and Weitzman pieces, the general trend seems to have been away from any grounding in reality. The 1979 article by Bonin and Marcus, which introduced managerial effort as a discretionary variable, in part, to reduce production uncertainty, glibly declared that: "Therefore, Bonin's suggestions would be implementable within the Soviet reform context." [5] Later articles tend to refer to Weitzman's description of the new Soviet incentive system. Weitzman, who didn't describe this system but modeled one important aspect of it, refers readers to Berliner's description.[2] It is not at all clear whether the excellent Berliner source has been consulted by many authors. Furthermore, Berliner described a system put in place in 1972. The system was significantly modified in 1976 and changed several times since then. [6]

It is naturally legitimate to abstract from particular institutional contexts, but, at the very least, the author should be aware of how the abstraction limits the applicability of the study's conclusions. In reviewing the relationship between actual Soviet experience with managerial incentives since 1972 and the theoretical literature, Conn draws the following conclusion. [7]

"In sum, the lesson from this should be that the incentive question is highly sensitive, both analytically and empirically to the institutional context in which it is posed. At a minimum, this means that, in the modeling of incentive structures, great care needs to be given to specifying the associated information and decisionmaking structures being assumed as well as the nature of the underlying environment."

One major abstraction almost universal in this literature[3] is the assumption of a univariate utility function for the manager. The manager is assumed to maximize his or her monetary bonus in a given year. At best, this is highly problematic in the context of any existing centrally planned economy. Given that most CPEs are shortage economies[4] and higher income cannot necessarily be translated into higher utility (e.g., purchase of additional desired goods), it seems more plausible to assume that managers are more concerned with maximizing perquisites, rights to special access, prestige, career paths, power in the local party or government unit, etc. Alternatively, one may assume that managers are altruistic in some sense or that they have similar goals as the center and, therefore, are largely self-motivated. Kontorovich has argued this to be the case for the Soviet Union and Zimbalist has made a similar claim for Cuba where during the first half of the 1970s there were no monetary managerial bonuses but productivity increased at an average yearly rate in excess of ten percent. [8] More eclectically, after reviewing a similar Czech incentive experiment during 1958–1962, Montias concluded: [9] "The choice of the optimal mix of material and moral incentives, threats and blandishments will depend on the environments in which the 'supervision game' is played out."

One of the features of the 1972 Soviet incentive reform is the setting of planned targets and planned bonus funds in advance for every year of a five-year plan. The enterprise manager is given the opportunity to counterplan a higher target in each year relative to the target initially set and, thereby, increase the planned bonus. This feature reduces the impact of the ratchet (higher production one year leading to higher targets the next) for the early years of a five-year plan and helps to explain the modelers' choice to abstract from the dynamic problem. Looking at evidence from the early years of a quinquennium or at the adjusted final targets of each year (enterprise targets are often changed during the year) has led some observers to perceive a diminution or disappearance of the ratchet effect. There is, however, ample evidence of its continued existence (at least its perceived existence by Soviet managers).[5] Hence, the dynamic problem is not obviated and deserves more attention from the modelers.

Yet another grand abstraction is the general assumption of a single objective and/or argument in the bonus fund function, viz., the fulfillment of an output target.[6] In fact, the bonus fund function is extraordinarily complex and even involves an increasingly strong element of discretion on the part of the Ministry. Alec Nove, for instance, has warned readers of his text: [10] "The payments into the incentive funds are calculated in a manner so bewilderingly complex that both author and reader would be reduced to paralytic boredom if the rules were here reproduced."

Indeed, the meeting of the following targets are all relevant to the size of the bonus fund: profitability; absolute profits; sales; share of high, middle and low quality products; labor productivity; product mix and delivery schedule; and, the introduction of new products and processes. Profitability appears to be weighted more heavily than sales in determining the bonus. Given the frequent substantial divergence between accounting costs and prices, meeting the profitability target often entails distorting the product mix rather than cutting costs or increasing output. Additionally, the procedure of managers counterplanning higher sales targets is now constrained by the Ministries' decision that higher output of a particular good is in the society's interest. One recent study by Miller and Murrell [11] relaxed the assumptions of the center maximizing output and the manager maximizing the bonus. They, for instance, modeled behavior under the assumption that the center's objective was to maximize profits net of the managerial bonus. Miller and Murrell conclude that allowing for more complex and realistic goals on the parts of the agent and principal bemuddles the optimization process: [12] "Furthermore, given certain constraints on the information initially available to the center, we prove that there may be no mechanism that encourages honest reporting."

Miller and Murrell, however, do not draw a pessimistic conclusion regarding the payoff to further research. Rather, they urge that future studies (1) recognize material bonus schemes alone cannot yield optimal elicitation behavior and, therefore, (2) combine an analysis of organizational structure with bonus-design questions in order to understand how "hierarchical organizations are to achieve greater efficiency." [13]

In the introduction to this volume, Zimbalist analyzed the role of structure and social relations in affecting information flows and performance within an organization. In the next section, we shall endeavor to modestly improve upon previous formulations of material bonus schemes.

Modification of the Model

Specifically, we make two adjustments to the Bonin-Weitzman type treatment which we feel bring the model a few steps closer to reality. First, we introduce a lower bound on the value of the bonus in order to prevent the possibility of large transfers from the enterprises to the center. This, of course, corresponds to actual practice in the Soviet Union where negative monetary bonuses do not exist. The need for studying such schemes has been noted, for example, by Thomson. [14] It is perhaps fitting in view of our previous discussion, that this modification, while bringing us closer to reality, causes some sacrifice in the precision of the Bonin-Weitzman results.

We include here an analysis of the impact of risk on the enterprise manager's decision by considering the behavior of the variance of the bonus and introducing an expected utility function having both the mean and the variance of the bonus as its arguments. We rederive and explicate in this context the Weitzman result [15] concerning risk averse managerial behavior in a manner which is lengthier but, for expository purposes, less opaque.

Second, we propose to modify the information flow from the enterprise to the center in an attempt to reduce the impact of input supply uncertainties on the target-setting process of enterprises. As Montias [16] has pointed out, this area deserves more analysis and study than it has been hitherto accorded.

We begin by establishing some necessary notation. An enterprise manager has a subjective probability distribution of actual output Q_a expected in the forthcoming planning period. Let $f(Q_a)$ and $F(Q_a)$ be the continuous density and cumulative probability functions of the manager. Let Q_a^1 be the largest value of Q_a for which $F(Q_a) = 0$. Similarly, let Q_a^2 be the smallest value of Q_a for which $F(Q_a) = 1$. Assume $0 < Q_a^1 < Q_a^2 < \infty$.

In decentralized target planning, the enterprise manager makes the decision concerning the level of output targeted by his/her enterprise. Let Q_p stand for planned output and $\bar{Q}_p$ for the actual output target chosen by the manager. Traditional bonus schemes which penalize any plan underfulfillment by the loss of the entire bonus are known to force plant managers to behave extremely conservatively, i.e., by choosing $\bar{Q}_p \leq Q_a$. Hence arises the need for the elicitation of bonus schemes previously discussed. Our first modification to the Bonin-Weitzman type scheme is that, following actual practice in the Soviet Union, we do not permit negative values for the bonus $B(Q_p,Q_a)$:

$$B(Q_p,Q_a) = \begin{cases} (a - b)Q_p + bQ_a & \text{if } 0 < Q_p \leq Q_a \\ \frac{a}{1-c} Q_p - \frac{ca}{1-c} Q_a & \text{if } Q_a < Q_p \leq cQ_a \quad (7.1) \\ 0 & \text{if } Q_p > cQ_a \end{cases}$$

where $a > b > 0$ and $c > 1$ are parameters determined by the center. Figures 7-1 and 7-2 depict the behavior of the bonus as a function of each one of its variables in turn, the other one being held constant. Thomson [17] calls such schemes individually-rational.

The enterprise manager is assumed to act in such a way as to maximize the expected bonus $[E(B)](Q_p)$:

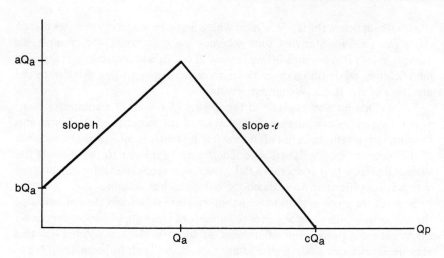

Figure 7–1.   The bonus as a function of planned output, actual output being held
              constant

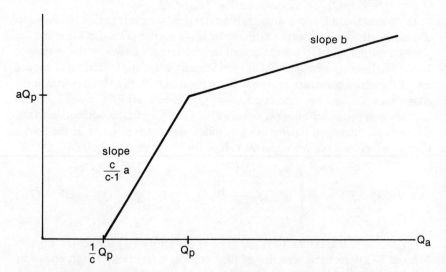

Figure 7–2.   The bonus as a function of actual output, planned output being held
              constant

$$[E(B)](Q_p) = \int_{Q_a^1}^{Q_a^2} B(Q_p, Q_a)f(Q_a) \, dQ_a \tag{7.2}$$

Thus $\bar{Q}_p$ is that value of Q_p which will yield a maximum value for $E(B)$. Let us look for a critical value of $E(B)$ in the interval $Q_a^1 < Q_p < Q_a^2$ by differentiating and setting the derivative equal to zero. In this interval we can rewrite the expected bonus as:

$$[E(B)](Q_p) = \int_{M(Q_p)}^{Q_p} B(Q_p, Q_a)f(Q_a)dQ_a$$

$$+ \int_{Q_p}^{Q_a^2} B(Q_p, Q_a)f(Q_a)dQ_a \tag{7.3}$$

where $M(Q_p) = \max{(Q_a^1, Q_p/c)}$. Then, with B_p standing for the partial derivative of the bonus function with respect to planned output,

$$[E(B)]'(Q_p) = \int_{M(Q_p)}^{Q_p} B_p(Q_p, Q_a)f(Q_a)dQ_a + B(Q_p, Q_p)f(Q_p)$$

$$- \frac{dM(Q_p)}{dQ_p} B(M(Q_p), Q_p)f(M(Q_p))$$

$$+ \int_{Q_p}^{Q_a^2} B_p(Q_p, Q_a)f(Q_a)dQ_a - B(Q_p, Q_p)f(Q_p) \tag{7.4}$$

Two of the nonintegral terms cancel (obviously) and the third is always 0 since either $M(Q_p) = Q_a^1$ and $\frac{dM(Q_p)}{dQ_p} = 0$ or $M(Q_p) = Q_p/c$ and $B(Q_p/c, Q_p) = 0$. Now, letting $h = a - b$ and $\ell = a/(c - 1)$, we obtain

$$[E(B)]'(Q_p) = -\ell \int_{M(Q_p)}^{Q_p} f(Q_a)dQ_a$$

$$+ h \int_{Q_p}^{Q_a^2} f(Q_a)d(Q_a).$$

If we define

$$L(Q_p) = \ell \int_{M(Q_p)}^{Q_p} f(Q_a)dQ_a \text{ and } H(Q_p) = h \int_{Q_p}^{Q_a^2} f(Q_a)dQ_a, \tag{7.5}$$

the critical point $\bar{Q}_p$ for which $[E(B)]'(Q_p) = 0$ can be found by setting $L(Q_p) = H(Q_p)$. Now $H(Q_p) = h(1 - F(Q_p))$ and if c is such that $Q_a^2/c \leq Q_a^1$, $L(Q_p) = \ell F(Q_p)$. Then we have the Bonin-Weitzman result: Q_p is determined by

$$h(1 - F(\bar{Q}_p)) = \ell F(\bar{Q}_p)$$

$$\text{or } F(\bar{Q}_p) = h/(h + \ell). \tag{7.6}$$

But if c is such that $Q_a^2/c > Q_a^1$, then for all $cQ_a^1 < Q_p < Q_a^2$

$$L(Q_p) = \ell \int_{Q_p/c}^{Q_p} f(Q_a)dQ_a < \ell F(Q_p) \quad \text{(See figure 7-3).} \quad (7.7)$$

The critical point $\bar{Q}_p$ will then lie strictly to the right of the Bonin-Weitz-man point $\bar{\bar{Q}}_p$, whenever $cQ_a^1 < \bar{Q}_p$ (which is certainly not ruled out). It is now a straightforward computation to show that $E(B)' > 0$ for all $Q_p < \bar{Q}_p$ and $E(B)' < 0$ for all $\bar{Q}_p < Q_p < Q_o$ for some Q_o at which point $E(B)$ becomes and stays zero. We can conclude that the critical point $\bar{Q}_p$ is in fact a global maximum for the expected bonus.

Thus, with a truncated piecewise linear bonus which rules out negative values, and for sufficiently small values of the parameter c (i.e., sufficiently stiff penalties for plan underfulfillment), the expected bonus maximization may well lead to somewhat tauter results than those obtained in the Bonin-Weitz-

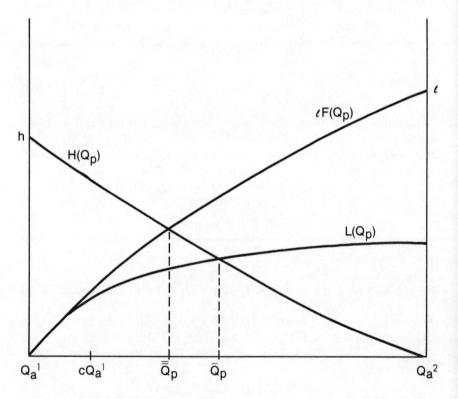

Figure 7-3. The determination of $\bar{Q}p$

man formulation. This result is to be expected since the penalty for underfulfill-ment is considerably reduced by the truncation of the bonus function. We note here the inevitable loss of precision in the results. Although we know that tauter targets are chosen, in the absence of prior and exact knowledge of the probability density function f, we, and the center, cannot determine the precise value of the probability that Q_a will exceed $\bar{Q}_p$ or, as a bit of computation will show, the signs of $\frac{\partial Q_p}{\partial a}$, $\frac{\partial Q_p}{\partial b}$ and $\frac{\partial Q_p}{\partial c}$.

We now turn to the question of taking into account the variance as well as the mean of the random variable $B(Q_p,Q_a)$: let $[V(B)]$ (Q_p) stand for the variance of $B(Q_p,Q_a)$ for a given fixed Q_p. Then,

$$V(B)(Q)_p = [E(B^2)]\,(Q_p) - [E(B)]^2\,(Q_p)$$

$$= \int_{Q_a^1}^{Q_a^2} B(Q_p,Q_a)^2 f(Q_a)dQ_a$$

$$- \left[\int_{Q_a^1}^{Q_a^2} B(Q_p,Q_a)f(Q_a)dQ_a \right]^2 \qquad (7.8)$$

We prove the following two propositions:

Proposition. On the interval $[0,Q_a^1]$, $V(B)$ is a constant.

Proof. If we differentiate $V(B)$ with respect to Q_p, we obtain (suppressing variables in an obvious way)

$$[V(B)]' = \int_{Q_a^1}^{Q_a^2} 2BB_p f\, dQ_a$$

$$- 2 \int_{Q_a^1}^{Q_a^2} Bf\, dQ_a \cdot \int_{Q_a^1}^{Q_a^2} B_p f\, dQ_a \qquad (7.9)$$

But, since $Q_p \le Q_a^1$, $B_p \equiv h$ throughout the interval of integration. Therefore, $[V(B)] = 2hE(B) - 2hE(B) \equiv 0$ and $V(B)$ is a constant for values of Q_p between zero and Q_a^1. By a similar reasoning we also have:

Corollary. If $Q_a^2/c < Q_a^1$, then, on the interval $[Q_a^2,cQ_a^1]$, $V(B)$ is constant.

Proposition. There exists a $Q\epsilon(\bar{Q}_p,Q_a^2]$ such that $V(B)$ is strictly increasing in the interval (Q_a^1,Q).

Proof. Let $Q_p\epsilon[Q_a^1,\bar{Q}_p]$ and note that

$$[V(B)]\,(Q_p) = \int_{M(Q_p)}^{Q_a^2} B^2 f\, dQ_a - \left[\int_{M(Q_p)}^{Q_a^2} Bf\, dQ_a \right]^2 \qquad (7.10)$$

The piecewise continuity of B_p and the fact that $B(Q_p/c,Q_p) = 0$ allow us, as we saw before, to differentiate under the integral sign

$$[V(B)]' = 2 \int_{M(Q_p)}^{Q_a^2} BB_p f \, dQ_a - 2 \int_{M(Q_p)}^{Q_a^2} Bf \, dQ_a \cdot \int_{M(Q_p)}^{Q_a^2} B_p f \, dQ_a \quad (7.11)$$

As before, let $F = F(Q_p)$ stand for $\int_{Q_a^1}^{Q_p} f \, dQ_a$ and set $G = G(Q_p)$ $= \int_{M(Q_p)}^{Q_p} f dQ_a$. We assume, for the time being, that $G > 0$, and define three new probability density functions:

$$f_1 = \begin{cases} f/(1-F+G) & \text{for} & Q_a \epsilon \, [M(Q_p),Q_a^2] \\ 0 & \text{elsewhere} \end{cases}$$

$$f_2 = \begin{cases} f/G & \text{for} & Q_a \epsilon \, [M(Q_p),Q_p] \\ 0 & \text{elsewhere} \end{cases}$$

$$f_3 = \begin{cases} f/(1-F) & \text{for} & Q_a \epsilon \, [Q_p,Q_a^2] \\ 0 & \text{elsewhere.} \end{cases} \quad (7.12)$$

If we let $E_i = \int_{-\infty}^{\infty} Bf_i \, dQ_a$, it follows from the definitions above that $E_2 < E_1 < E_3$. We can now rewrite $V(B)'$ in the following form: $V(B)' = -\ell GE_2 + h(1 - F)E_3 - (1 - F + G)E_1[-\ell G + h(1 - F)]$.

Since $Q_p < \bar{Q}_p$, we have $-\ell G + h(1 - F) > 0$. Therefore, $1 - F + G$ can be replaced by 1 to obtain:

$$V(B)' \geq - \ell GE_2 + h(1 - F)E_3 - E_1[- \ell G + h(1 - F)]$$

$$V(B)' \geq - \ell G(E_2 - E_1) + h(1 - F) (E_3 - E_1) > 0 \quad (7.13)$$

for all $Q_p \epsilon (Q_a^1,\bar{Q}_p)$.* By continuity of $V(B)'$ the assertion of the proposition is established.

It is easy to verify that if $Q_a^2/c < Q_a^1$, Q can be picked to be Q_a^2, and that variance starts decreasing once Q_p passes beyond cQ_a^1.

Now that we have analyzed the behavior of both $E(B)$ and $V(B)$ we can plot them together in a coordinate system. Figure 7–4 gives a typical situation with $Q_a^2 < cQ_a^1$, the arrows indicating increasing Q_p (A,B,C,D corresponding, respectively, to 0, Q_a^1, $\bar{Q}_p$, Q_a^2.) We now assume that the enterprise manager acts so as to maximize an expected utility function $Z(E(B),V(B))$. I, II, and III are representative iso-expected utility curves indicating the risk averse enterprise manager's trade-off between mean and variance. The target output level chosen by the manager will then be the one associated with point E rather than the risk neutral Bonin-Weitzman point C.

---

*If $G = 0$ (as, on occasion, it might), f_2 can't be defined. However, $V(B)' > 0$ still holds since the only effect on equation 7.13 is to make the $- \ell G(E_2 - E_1)$ term disappear.

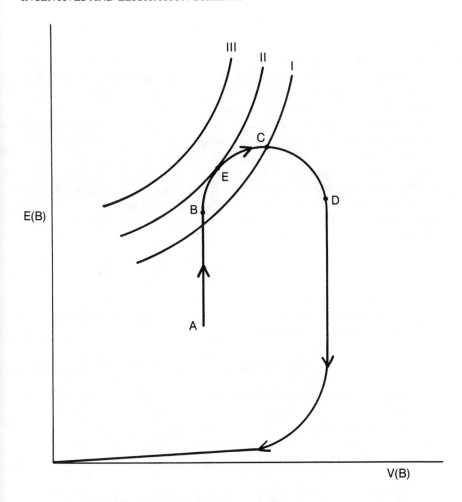

Figure 7–4.   The trade-off between the mean and variance of the bonus

Thus, it can be expected that any set of the parameters a, b, and c chosen by the center will yield a lower or equal level of tautness than would follow from a pure expected bonus maximization model.

Our second modification concerns the condition of environmental uncertainty and a method to adjust for it which coaxes less cautious targets out of the enterprise manager. Input supply uncertainties (concerning centrally allocated inputs) that firm managers face will seriously impair the workings of an elicitation scheme (such as discussed above) designed to reveal the productive capacity of the firm at a predetermined level of tautness. If the center simply sends a message of the type: "You will be allocated I_0 units of input. Tell us your target output," it is highly unlikely that the peripheral firm will reveal its true capacity for production (i.e., with the desired and planned level of tautness) with I_0 units of input. For, the firm's subjective expectations about possible outcomes can best be described by a bivariate probability density function $f(Q_a, I) = g(Q_a | I) h(I)$ where $h(I)$ is the subjective probability density function associated with the distribution of expected actual deliveries from the center (possibly historically formed), after the center has allocated I_0 units of input to the firm, and $g(Q_a | I)$ is the conditional density function associated with the expected distribution of output levels given a level of inputs. Assuming that $f(Q_a, I) \equiv 0$ outside of the rectangle determined by $0 \leq Q_a \leq \bar{Q}_a$ (for some $\bar{Q}_a$) and $0 \leq I \leq I_0$, the marginal density function for the actual output Q_a will be

$$\bar{g}(Q_a) = \int_0^{I_0} g(Q_a | I) h(I) \, dI. \tag{7.14}$$

We can further impose the following reasonable condition, assuring that lower input levels will make higher levels of output less likely: for all $0 < I < I_0$, and for all $A > 0$ we have

$$\int_0^A g(Q_a | I) \, dQ_a \geq \int_0^A g(Q_a | I_0) \, dQ_a \tag{7.15}$$

with strict inequality whenever the left hand side is not 0 and the right hand side is not 1.

It then follows that

$$\int_0^A \bar{g}(Q_a) \, dQ_a = \int_0^A \left[\int_0^{I_0} g(Q_a | I) h(I) \, dI \right] dQ_a$$

$$= \int_0^{I_0} \left[\int_0^A g(Q_a | I) \, dQ_a \right] h(I) \, dI$$

$$\geq \int_0^A g(Q_a | I_0) \, dQ_a \tag{7.16}$$

with strict inequality whenever the first term is not zero and the last term is not one. Thus, the two probability distributions $\bar{g}(Q_a)$ and $g(Q_a | I_0)$ will be as pictured in figure 7–5.

The problem is obvious. When the center tries to get the firm to reveal, say with a Bonin type elicitation scheme, its median capacity T_2 with the allocated level of inputs I_0, the firm will react by planning a much slacker T_1 taking account of the possibility that something less than I_0 will in fact be delivered as input.

One way out of this problem may be to ask the firm to set target levels of

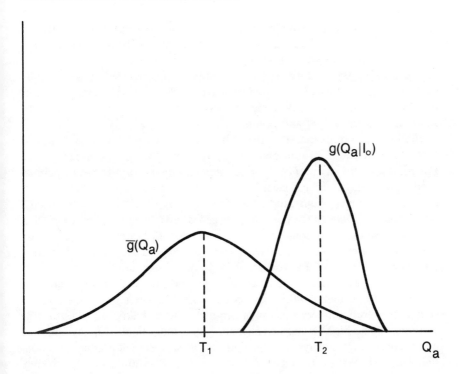

Figure 7–5.   The marginal density function $g(Q_a)$ and the conditional density function $g(Q_a|I_o)$

production not only for the promised level of inputs, but for all (or some reasonable number of) lesser levels: $\bar{Q}_p(I)$, $0 \leq I \leq I_0$. The bonus would then be computed on the basis of $\bar{Q}_p(\bar{I})$ where $\bar{I}$ is the level of inputs actually delivered. That is to say, the firm would receive $B(\bar{Q}_p(\bar{I}),Q_a)$ as its bonus. Of course, one drawback here would be the extra effort the firm must put into computing a whole schedule $\bar{Q}_p(I)$ of target outputs, rather than just one. Nonetheless, with this procedure we gain a more accurate revelation of productive capacity (at the desired level of tautness) by eliminating an important source of uncertainty.

A Direction for Extension of the Model

In this last section, we briefly suggest an extension to previous bonus/elicitation modeling, but we leave its elaboration and formalization to future research. We can identify three sources of uncertainty which confront the enterprise manager at the time of plan negotiations: one, environmental uncertainty (i.e., the timeliness, quantity, quality and mix of inputs delivery); two, random shocks; and, three, productive and creative efforts of the entire work force. The first source of uncertainty and its possible attenuation we have partially analyzed above. The second source we leave for theologians. The third source is a logical extension of the conception of managerial effort introduced by Bonin and Marcus, [18] and others.

Bonin and Marcus maintain that when discretionary managerial behavior (effort) is introduced into the analysis production uncertainty can be reduced. For instance, they write: [19] "To counter unforeseen supply bottlenecks or production delays, the manager may monitor subordinates' activities more closely, work longer hours and expend more energy himself on production." Apocryphal *xiafang* to the contrary, we can dismiss the implausible vision of an enterprise manager doing manual labor. Notwithstanding, managers can, of course, tighten supervision. Perhaps a better method to reduce uncertainty, however, is to involve the workers directly in the elicitation process.

In any factory in the capitalist or socialist world there is a distinction to be made between potential work and actual work. Managers introduce supervision and incentives to coax as much productive and creative effort out of the workers as possible. Yet, as Leibenstein, Vanek and others [20] have pointed out, there is almost always an enormous untapped reserve of productive potential. This reserve takes the form of, *inter alia,* absenteeism, turnover, shirking, fewer worker suggestions[7] as well as more aggressive behavior in the form of striking and sabotage. If the agent-principal relationship between the planners and the enterprise manager were applied to the relationship between the enterprise manager and the workers, a substantial amount of additional information (and effort) could be obtained about production potentialities and probabilities.

Modeling this relationship presents some analytical and empirical problems. Analytically, it would seem desirable to postulate homogeniety, common information or uniform utility functions among the work force. Empirically, we need more information about actual practices in the Soviet Union and elsewhere. Of course, it is claimed that workers in the Soviet Union are involved in discussing yearly and five-year plans for their enterprises. The work of Yanowitch [21] leads one to be skeptical about how effective these production meetings are in eliciting accurate information. It would seem that a more genuine worker involvement in the enterprise decision-making process and in plan generation would be necessary to evoke more reliable information (and greater worker effort).

Although it is universally ignored in the formal incentive literature, workers in the Soviet Union receive a share of the enterprise bonus fund. This is the same fund from which come bonuses for top management and engineering and technical staff. Of course, on a per capita basis the production worker bonus is much smaller than the bonus of top executive personnel. Nonetheless, the production worker's share in the enterprise bonus fund has grown significantly since 1965: from 34.8 percent in 1967, to 46.5 percent in 1970, to 49.4 percent in 1975 (the share itself being purportedly subject to negotiations with the trade union). [22]

Thus, the Soviet incentive system has in place the structural forms (production meetings and bonus sharing) needed to elicit accurate information and greater effort from the workers. The realization of the structural potentials, however, is another matter and depends upon the extent of real worker participation and influence. The latter, in turn, seems to run up against the standard Soviet political constraint.

This brings us full circle. Attention to and analysis of the institutional or political contexts is desirable to elucidate the potentialities and limitations of incentive systems.

Notes

1. This is commonly referred to as the Groves problem. Theodore Groves, "Incentives in Teams," *Econometrica* 41, July 1973, pp. 617–633.

2. J. Berliner, *op. cit.* A fascinating elaboration of Berliner's study can be found in R. Amann and J. Cooper (eds.), *Industrial Innovation in the Soviet Union.* New Haven: Yale University Press, 1982.

3. Granick, in this volume, is an exception.

4. The term and implied analysis are, of course, from Kornai, *Economics of Shortage.* Amsterdam: North Holland, 1980.

5. An interesting debate on this issue is in process, see: David Granick, "The Ministry as the Maximizing Unit in Soviet Industry," *Journal of Comparative Economics* 4, September 1980, pp. 255–273; Michael Keren, *Journal of Comparative Economics* 7, 1983, forthcoming.

6. One early, but flawed, exception is Snowberger who introduced multiple targets into his analysis. Vernon Snowberger, "The New Soviet Incentive Model: Comment," *Bell Journal of Economics* 8, Autumn 1977, pp. 591–600.

7. David Granick points out that in 1956 in the Soviet Union 1.3 million workers presented one or more suggestions, of which 1.4 million were implemented. D. Granick, *El hombre de la empresa soviético (The Red Executive).* Madrid: Ediciones de la Revista de Occidente, 1966, p. 201. Evidence from Khitrov, if reliable, indicates that workers' suggestions are increasingly important. L. Khitrov, "The Role of Management and Workers in Raising the Efficiency of Soviet Industry," *International Labor Review* 3, June 1975, pp. 507–526.

References

1. Berliner, J., *The Innovation Decision in Soviet Industry.* Cambridge: MIT Press, 1976, p. 432.

2. Conn, D., "A Comparison of Alternative Incentive Structures for Centrally Planned Economic Systems," *Journal of Comparative Economics* 3, Sept. 1979, pp. 261–276.

3. Miller, J. and P. Murrell, "Limitations on the Use of Information-Revealing Incentive Schemes in Economic Organizations," *Journal of Comparative Economics* 5, Sept. 1981, pp. 251–271.

4. Ellman, M., *Soviet Planning Today.* Cambridge: Cambridge University Press, 1971, pp. 115–117. M. Ellman, "Bonus Formulae and Soviet Managerial Performance: A Further Comment," *Southern Economic Journal* 39, April 1973, pp. 652–653. John Bonin, "On the Design of Managerial Incentive Structures in a Decentralized Planning Environment," *American Economic Review* 66, Sept. 1976, pp. 682–687. Martin Weitzman, "The New Soviet Incentive Model," *Bell Journal of Economics* 7, Spring 1976, pp. 251–257.

5. Bonin, J. and A. Marcus, "Information, Motivation, and Control in Decentralized Planning: The Case of Discretionary Managerial Behavior," *Journal of Comparative Economics* 3, Sept. 1979, p. 238F.

6. Adam, J., "The Present Soviet Incentive System," *Soviet Studies* 32, July 1980, pp. 349–365. Also see Kushnirsky, F., *Soviet Economic Planning, 1965–80.* Boulder, Co.: Westview Press, 1982, pp. 21–48.

7. Conn, D., *op. cit.,* p. 275.

8. Kontorovich, V., "What Do Managers in the Centrally Planned Economy Do?" Xerox, University of Pennsylvania, 1982. A. Zimbalist, "On the Role of Management in Socialist Development," *World Development* 9, Sept./Oct. 1981, p. 973. For glimmers of a similar view, see also: A. Bergson, "Market Socialism Revisited," *Journal of Political Economy,* October 1967, p. 658.

9. Montias, M., "Incentives: A Comparative Perspective," *Journal of Comparative Economics* 3, Sept. 1979, p. 323.

10. Nove, A., *The Soviet Economic System.* London: George Allen & Unwin, 1977, p. 88.

11. Miller and Murrell, *op. cit.*

12. Ibid., p. 253.

13. Ibid., p. 270.

14. Thomson, W., "Eliciting Production Possibilities from a Well-Informed Manager," *Journal of Economic Theory* 20, Fall 1979, p. 374.

15. Weitzman, M., *op. cit.,* p. 255.

16. Montias, M., *op. cit.,* p. 322.

17. Thomson, W., *op. cit.,* p. 376.

18. Bonin and Marcus, *op. cit.*

19. Ibid., p. 242.

20. Leibenstein, H., "Allocative Efficiency vs X-Efficiency," *American Economic Review* 56, June 1966, pp. 392–415. Jaroslav Vanek, *The General Theory of Labor-Managed Economics.* Ithaca: Cornell University Press, 1970, pp. 402–403. Also see, Juan Espinosa and A. Zimbalist, *Economic Democracy.* New York: Academic Press, 1981, ch. 7.

21. Yanowitch, M., *Social and Economic Inequality in the Soviet Union.* New York: Sharpe, 1977, ch. 5. M. Yanowitch (ed.), *Soviet Work Attitudes: The Issue of Participation in Management.* New York: Sharpe, 1979.

22. Jan Adam, *op. cit.,* p. 360.

Contributing Authors

David Conn, Department of Economics, University of Arizona, Tucson

David Granick, Department of Economics, University of Wisconsin, Madison

Ruud Knaack, Department of Economics, University of Amsterdam, Amsterdam

Sinan Koont, Department of Economics, Smith College, Northampton, MA

Deborah Duff Milenkovitch, Department of Economics, Barnard College, Columbia University, New York City

Alec Nove, Department of Economics, Institute of Soviet and East European Studies, University of Glasgow, U.K.

Andrew Zimbalist, Department of Economics, Smith College, Northampton, MA

About the Editor

Andrew Zimbalist is Associate Professor of Economics and Chairperson, Department of Economics at Smith College, Northampton, Massachusetts. His other books include: *Comparative Economic Systems: A Political Economic Approach.* New York: Academic Press, 1984, forthcoming (with H. Sherman); *Economic Democracy: Worker Participation in Chilean Industry, 1970–1973.* New York: Academic Press, 1978 (with J. Espinosa): and *Case Studies on the Labor Process.* New York: Monthly Review Press, 1979 (editor).